TRUMP
Tribalism and the God Module

James A. Lahde

DORRANCE
PUBLISHING CO
EST. 1920
PITTSBURGH, PENNSYLVANIA 15238

Dorrance Publishing Co
585 Alpha Drive
Suite 103
Pittsburgh, PA 15238
Visit our website at *www.dorrancebookstore.com*

ISBN: 978-1-6491-3381-6
eISBN: 978-1-6491-3518-6

Other Books by the Author

- Planning For Change
- Urban Wildlife Management
- Dumbing Down Deer Hunting
- The Venison Cook Book
- Divine Right of Politicians

To all the brave men and women who fought
so heroically helping those suffering
from ravages of the coronavirus

CONTENTS

Forest Tribalism

Young forests are like democratic states
Where, given freedom, equity, and space
Countless tribes of grass and fern,
Daisy and fairy,
Plus, aspen and cherry,
Spruce budworm, beetle and tern ...
Compete for dominance ... but discover, late,
That elites of lesser number than their own
Take root in shade beneath their dome.
And soon stout hemlock, birch, and maple of size
Devise a plan for their demise.
They compete with equal rights decrees
Suppressing all rights of lesser trees
Including relative budworm, beetle, and tern.
-Author

PREFACE

When I hear the word evolution, the theory "survival of the fittest" comes to mind. This simplified definition of evolution details not only the ravenous manner in which social vertebrates like chimpanzees, lions, wolves, killer whales and dolphins track down and devour their prey but gets the most exposure in television documentaries and movies. While the focus on the brutal titillates and provides a small insight into how evolution works, it reveals little or nothing about the subtle biology that goes into the complex dynamics of humans living within a social context. Indeed, it's within the social context where the dynamics by which humans became the dominant species on Earth were spawned, and the biology that could spawn our extinction for failure to recognize the bad and ugly of that heritage.

When discussing tribalism, it's important to realize that while socialization offered better protection from large predators as well as better hunting and foraging opportunities, it does not explain the success of humans in dominating all other life forms. After all, primates like chimps and gorillas share alliances. Although predation of other species is a hallmark of the human condition, the current view among scientists is that humans dominate because they are social animals and, like all social organisms must follow nature's ultimatum they *compete for survival between members of their own species.*

For humans, Darwinian competition between tribes of humans took on a cerebral context by (1) utilizing ideologies and their defined moral ideals as distinct tribal signatures, and (2) by spiritualizing membership energies to devotionally protect that ideology at all cost. As a result, those portions of the human brain that deal with cognition—understanding and manipulating complex relationships within the social context—increased dramatically, giving man the upper hand over less intelligent creatures.

Today, tribalism has a pejorative connotation implying those expressing such behavior as being somewhat uncultured. Sometimes nationalism, populism or ethno-culturalism are used in discussing tribalism. Regardless, tribalism is here to stay, and its tenets expressed daily by presidents, popes, imams, news editors, senators, congressional leaders, and a vast awry of city folk.

To understand the behavior defined as 'Trump Derangement Syndrome' that Americans are exposed to each and every day in the press and on public television since the 2016 election, it's helpful to have some understanding of just WHY tribalism evolved as a biological necessity for humans; HOW it evolved over a period of a million-and-some years; and, most importantly, just how spiritually addictive and destructive the process can be during times of tribal infighting.

Our basic problem with tribalism is we recognize ourselves as highly cognitive, willful creatures. We assume our intellect is capable of weathering the stresses and strains that comes with being social animals. But the intellect is struggling at this time in America. And, examining much of the elite behavior driving the Derangement Syndrome, it's evident most all the aggrieved have little or no freewill either. They are zealot tribalists of the most fundamental order.

The problem is we find it difficult to grasp how tribal bias and conflict evolved and why it is so important to the human species. Christian and Muslim tribes have wage war against each other for

centuries, with hair-raising violence and no regret after each successful slaughter, only to return home and worship the same god? This is
classical tribalism, where members of each tribe are spiritually addicted to their brand of secular or religious governing and are willing
to die to maintain that brand. For rational humans, such hatred, violence and mind-numbing adherence to secular and religious dogma
simply does not make sense, its irrational behavior taken to extremes.

The internecine tribalism we are witnessing today with the
Trump Derangement Syndrome evolved much later during the Historic Period among advanced tribes along the Mediterranean Sea and
Far East. Although initially less deadly, it often is much more destructive to a tribe when liberals and conservatives cannot agree on a unifying ideology to channel their emotion.

Tribes simply do not survive without physical and psychological
boundaries. The great Roman Republic quickly collapsed with tribal
infighting, as did some of the Western medieval nations like France.
The two great religions, Christianity and Islam, were also dominant
tribes throughout that period but have both—especially Christianity—suffered greatly from modern liberal factions challenging long-
established conservative factions.

The strategies needed to survive when confronted by ice storms,
swollen rivers and dangerous animals are relatively easy to comprehend and, to a large degree, humans have been successful in combating these forces of nature. Yet, in social environments where the
relevant elements are other humans with divergent values, the existence of survival strategies is not so obvious. Consequently, we have
not been successful in reducing bias and conflict.

The purpose here is distinguish between "Classic Tribalism"
which goes on between different tribes, and "Internecine Tribalism"
which goes on within tribes. The inhouse hysteria over President
Trump is internecine tribalism at its best and the main focus of this
narrative. It's an attempt to explain how this enigma shaped the
human mind and by extension cultural intellect with sufficient bias to

destabilize all forms of government, especially democracies that eventually slide into some form of authoritarian rule. Fortunately, a number of new disciplines like cognitive psychology, neuroscience, evolutionary biology and behavioral genetics have emerged to provide insight and offer some resolution to the nature-versus-nurture stalemate that has consumed science discourse in the past.

I propose no solution to the readiness with which humans adopt ideologies. Perhaps recognition of that fact is the first step to change. Nor is there any solution offered to our willingness to assist in the amoral consequences of some ideologies or the bewildering lack of remorse for moral transgressions. The goal is to show that things turn out one way instead of another because people make decisions and act on them in a tribal manner with little to no regard for those harmed in the process or for generational sustainability on a global scale.

The attempt here is not to promote tribalism as much as illustrate tribalism for what it is, explain its evolutionary roots, and the reason for them. I argue that bias and conflict so necessary for human domination is a manifestation of man's desire for freedom and equity within the tribe. And I argue this fundamental drive for freedom and equity is not an intellectual process, but rather an inherent mandate shared by all humans: a mandate all large governing bodies attempt to satisfy; an endless struggle no mega culture is able to achieve; a tribal virus in which all efforts to intellectualize with psalm and verse, scripture and testaments, with constitutions and bills of rights have done little to throttle down the bias and conflict that result. It's been a philosopher's nightmare designed by God (Mother Nature, if you prefer) to keep cognitive-supreme humans ever vigilant and resourceful.

It's an attempt to explain our biased behaviors and the mysteries behind man's selfish, shortsighted nature, as well as the effect that shortsightedness has on governing, including the democratic process we all treasure. Simply put, by understanding the process Mother Nature uses to motivate humans, we will realize what the human mind is designed to do and how culture influences and is influenced by that process.

Overview

Until retirement, my main business was teaching biology, environmental science and consulting to community planning commissions threatened by urbanization. If I claim expertise at all, it's an understanding of how natural ecosystems operate, the biological rules that govern that process, and how developers and average homeowners can build in an ecological sensible fashion. Too that end, several textbooks were written as high school and college references.

During that period, I had several years of political experience on a city planning commission and as major pro tem, experiences that got me thinking—in retirement—that humans are not much different from other social animals, and governed by many of the same natural laws, but … they don't seem to know it. Therefore, rather than work within the tribal framework, we simply reject those parameters and continue to destroy the planet and each other.

By 2019, politics became a deplorable situation with the American public divided to the point of becoming a non-functional democracy by-way of Postmodernism, a movement to fundamentally change America. It's within that context I felt a book on the biology of tribalism might be useful. Part 1: History of Classical Tribalism – The Paleolithic Period – The Basic Democratic Model details the many altruistic and aggressive behaviors tribes genetically evolved to defend themselves from other tribes; how the human desire for freedom and equality, became subservient to community demands for solidarity; an overview of the million-plus paleolithic years when our ancestors evolved the classic Small Tribal Model (STM) as the competing-ideology structure; the neurological modules (clusters of nerves like the God Module) that genetically hard-wired human minds to spiritually accept, facilitate and energize these behaviors; and several examples of these paleolithic tribes that survive to this day.

Part 2: History of Autocratic Tribalism – Historical Period is also a trip down memory lane when a few small paleolithic cults grew large, with populations in the hundreds of thousands; their hierarchal, genetic evolution; several examples of autocratic cultures that evolved beyond the STM during the Historic Period; and the role Manifest Destiny and Colonialism played in the destruction of hundreds of less evolved tribes while promoting autocratic rule as the world-wide model.

Part 3: Birth of a Postmodern Cult – The Enlightenment details, in 5 Phases, the receptive democratic philosophy Enlightenment philosophers provided for the young Postmodern cult; the receptive environment colonial romantics provided for the cult in America; its democratic implementation strategy via Freudian Psychoanalysis; the evolving battle strategy the fields of psychology used to compete against the empirical sciences; and energizing and verifying the young Postmodern cult via eminent and not-so eminent scientists.

Part 4: History of Postmodernism – Modern Period covers the enormously successful Postmodern movement from its juvenile stage in the mid-1960 in America when the Gang of 5 (Income Elite, academia, social sciences, Democrat Party, and media) was formed; the Gang's successful use of identity politics to institutionalize and weaponize the young cult into Postmodernism that elect President Obama, then Trump; and the immediate hysterical inhouse fighting that followed.

Part 5: Post-Modernism Pathology (aka - PMP) **starts** out with the "Tribal Virus," a history of internecine tribalism that evolved years ago resulting in the destructive Trump infighting; details of the hysterical *viral pathology* that evolved to rid the world of President Trump; the role rationalized, linguistic warfare played throughout the hysteria and during impeachment; the role Muslims play in dividing America into factions; the benefits of a return to small community lifestyles; and the role the empirical sciences should play in our drift back to nationalism around the world.

An Author's Note

The problem for anyone writing about tribalism like the Trump Derangement Syndrome is being accused of having a conservative bias against liberals. The reality is, all successful secular or religious cultures are conservatives in protecting their beliefs and values from rebel upstarts, who by definitions have a *liberal orientation to that of the existing conservatism.* In the case of Trump, the very fact he was elected revealed half of the US felt liberal Postmodernism not only lacked the ideological ability to bond the country together, but was intent on dividing the nation and eradicating the ideology that made America the great nation it was.

A biological understanding of classic and internecine tribalism shows the human brain wasn't designed to function as "a house divided." Our brains were designed to put community interest above individual interest. That's the whole purpose of being social animals. God is not stupid. The prophetic phrase, "a house divided against itself cannot stand" is a quote taken from the New Testament written thousands of years ago; a quote the great Roman politician Cicero should have taken to heart before he was killed by Caesar and his severed hands nailed to the senate door for leading a revolt; a quote made famous by senator Abraham Lincoln on his way to the presidency, where he united the divided states into the great nation they became.

Plus, from the standpoint of this narrative, it doesn't matter whether President Trump is re-elected or not. What's important for humanity to realize is the winner will always be the tribe—driven by a cluster of nerves all humans carry (the God Module)—willing and able to destroy the opposition at all cost. Until we learn to control tribalism, civil or international wars will be our children's future.

PART 1

CLASSICAL TRIBALISM
– Paleolithic Period-
The Basic Democratic Model

Tribes have distinctive moral commitments whereby moral authority is vested in constitutions, rights, traditions, deities, and local individuals, that other groups don't recognize as authoritative.
-Author

Chapter 1

CLASSIC TRIBALISM

Tribalism is the most powerful force in the world

-Patrick Dixon

As social animals, humans evolved a full spectrum of altruistic behaviors used to promote community solidarity, ranging from love to tolerance of individual differences, and a full spectrum of aggressive behaviors, ranging from suspicion to hate to total intolerance for opposing tribes. Only recently has science been able to show this competition a tribal process in which different related groups intellectualize discrete tribal ideologies designed specifically to emotionally bind tribal members to their moral beliefs and values, while vigorously blinding them to moral beliefs and values of competing tribal ideologies.

With tribal ideologies came biased thinking and partisanship. In short, human are pack animals who live in ideological bubbles. It's from these biased and blind bubbles that our ancestors came out of the Paleolithic Period as winners in the struggle between a number of protohumans because of their creative use of all their evolved altruistic and aggressive tribal behaviors.

To be a successful, competitive social animal requires several basic skills: (1) How to physically and psychologically attach oneself to a tribe, and (2) How to protect oneself and tribe from other social tribes trying to steal your territory and resources. What makes tribalism tolerable are the many behaviors like compassion, empathy, love, solidarity and kindness that go into the process of making tribal life enjoyable. The sense of pleasure our mind fabricates for us when tending the sick or performing neighborly deeds are pleasant feelings, we want repeated, like wanting one more potato chip or one more tiny chocolate éclair.

The pleasures we get when caring for a child, working toward a common goal, holding hands or simply sharing a cup of coffee with a friend should remind us of those billions of caring incidents that had to occur before these traits became indelibly etched into our genetic code as survival traits. That beautiful cooing baby has enormous powers of persuasion. So do mothers and lovers, young puppies, beggars and amputees. Each generates a degree of emotional discharge that can be as moving as a bully's threat. While aggression works because it threatens life and limb, compassion works because it preserves life and limb.

Much of any tribal success has to do with a social norm called reciprocal altruism, a response mechanism that constantly revitalizes itself by animating those involved to appreciate and cooperate. The more often a friendly activity occurs, the more bonding occurs; more bonding results in more prosperity and cooperation; the more prosperity and cooperation, the more impervious the love bubble. It's the familiar give-and-take we see in business and personal relationships. A process in which old platitudes like "I'll help you, if you help me," and "You scratch my back and I'll scratch yours" come into play.

For our ancestors, community alliances were as vital as eating. Those who refused to compromise and share, were in danger of being marginalized by those who did. Reciprocal altruism is the glue holding tribes together, the emotional vapors that keeps the ideological bubble inflated, the spiritual bonds binding dictators to their police force, presidents to their political coalitions and bishops to their parishioners. These are the sensibilities our Paleolithic ancestors evolved and honed to perfection while roasting mammoth steak over the fire, sensibilities that relegated aggression to a second-rate behavior in communal relationships.

Although altruism is the flip side of aggression and the backbone of maintaining tribal order, it takes a backseat to aggression when other tribes threaten with border crossing, resources stolen, or members carted off as slaves. Aggression critics like to insinuate that hunting and warring are prehistoric behaviors with no relevance to the present, but such opinions deny their long history and the ubiquitous roles they played in the past and play today.

Aggression was needed to subdue large animals, to question neighbors' motives, to rebuff any attack and extract any retribution. Hunting and warfare left a deep and permanent yearning in the human condition. Religious and secular leaders killed with no remorse in the past and continue killing with little or no remorse today. Wars and terrorism, gulags and concentration camps, mob rule and police states, blood sports and athletic events also continue receiving the most press today.

Not only do aggressive behaviors receive the most press but their long and venomous tentacles can reach across continents. Individuals involved in violent behavior often suffer psychologically so that fear, anxiety and confusion replace compassion, empathy and trust. In the clash of emotions and, especially when survival is threatened, humans will express a virtual endless repertoire of morally questionable and ethical behaviors.

Nazi atrocities before and after World War II provide a mind-numbing example of the length, width and depth to which fear, jealousy, hatred, anger, denial, suppression and self-deception joined forces in a nation smitten by reprisal and humiliation after World War II. In their fascinating book, *What They Knew: Terror, Mass Murder, and Everyday Life in Nazi Germany: An Oral History*, Eric Johnson and Karl-Heinz Reuband surveyed and interviewed more than three thousand Jews and non-Jew Germans about their experiences during the Hitler years. One of the questions they attempted to answer was how much the German population knew about the mass murder of European Jews while the Holocaust was being perpetrated. In their final paragraph they conclude:

Most Jews lived in perpetual or nearly perpetual fear of arrest during the Third Reich. Those who survived usually did so by emigrating abroad well before the Holocaust began. Nearly all of those who remained in Germany after the war started were eventually murdered. Most non-Jews, however, experienced a very different Third Reich. Few harbored any fear of arrest, even though they often broke the law in minor ways. Most knew instinctively that the terror apparatus was not intent on punishing them so long as they broadly accepted and went along with National Socialism, which most did. Difficult as it is to fathom, given most people's conception of dictatorship, most Germans appear to have led happy, productive, even normal lives in the Third Reich. This indicates that a dictatorship can enjoy widespread popularity among the majority even while committing unspeakable crimes against minorities and others.

Inherent tribal aggressions are powerful thought regulators and, by extension, controller of the collective self. Under the right circumstances, they can move the mind to unthinkable acts of kindness, or delusion, or numbness, or madness. Under the Third Reich, people redirected their passions to National Socialism where, once firmly imbued with a cult personality, the populace in lockstep marched to Hitler's fascist tunes while most Jews, shackled and encased by the repressive ideology, suppressed their creative and rebellious spirit.

In a 1951 poll conducted in West Germany, only five percent of those surveyed admitted they felt any guilt over what happened. The population had lived in a state of moral tension so long it became hard to distinguish fascist from enablers, to separate collusion from coercion. After years of violence, fear and uncertainty, almost everyone began to mimic the perverse values to the point that they eventually internalized these values psychologically and denied their depravity.

The ever-present fact that whole nations can commit the most heinous of crimes and suffer no remorse the very definition of psychopathic behavior supports the idea that there's an absolving quality that comes with tribalism. A quality illustrated by the lack of remorse for moral transgressions that covered the whole continent during and after World War II. During the war, Austria supplied half of all concentration camp guards; France, with a population of more than forty million, offered little resistance to the six thousand Nazi policemen; a smaller, near skeleton team was sufficient to quell resistance in the Netherlands; except for Denmark, local officials in every occupied country—including the US—shut their eyes to the deportation and extermination of millions of Jews while hundreds of thousands of non-Jews appropriated the businesses and occupied the houses of their exiled neighbors.

After the war, reprisals and trials touched only a small fraction of the people who perpetrated the atrocities. Many countries, including Argentina whose President, Juan Peron and his government, encouraged and helped resettle elite Nazi criminals including the infamous Adolf Eichmann—so-called "Mastermind of the Holocaust" and doctor Josef Mengele—notorious for his selection of victims to be killed in the gas chambers at Auschwitz, as well as performing unscientific and deadly experiment on prisoners. (Eichmann was captured in 1961 by Israeli commandos and hanged while Mengele lived out his life in relative security until his death by drowning in 1979.) Most German officers convicted of war crimes accepted leadership roles in the new Germany after being pardoned by the Allies during the de-Nazification program. Many of the new Communist bosses who went on to control half of the continent, were old fascist bosses in different uniforms.

Obviously, the list of psychopathic behaviors throughout history could go on to fill endless volumes but there's enough here to make the point that Machiavellian tribal politics is the rule and not the exception in tribal affairs. We are tribally Machiavellian to the core and blind to the situational ethics we practice as rule rather than exception. Blind, situational ethics is fundamental for a culture to have any staying power; and, for humans to function effectively, rationalization, denial and duplicity are essential at all levels.

The theme of British philosopher Jeremy Campbell's book, *The Liar's Tale: A History of Falsehood*, claims the impulse to transcend mere literal fact occurs throughout nature and lying and denying are indispensable facts of life: "We have come full circle from the ancient thesis that truth and goodness are inseparable twins. The notion embedded in our cultural attitudes is that humanity would never have stayed the grueling course to its present high place on the evolutionary ladder on a diet as thin and meager as the truth."

Denial and repression are common in childhood; rationalization and sublimation prevail in adolescence and adulthood; self-deception is evident at all ages. There is even a cogent argument that self-deception, cognitive bias and blindness become more pronounced and sophisticated with increasing age. From the time a person's worldview is fully developed, the individual will attend to incoming information that supports his or her values and ignore contrary information, in some cases expelling contrary views from memory. And, in each and every case, emotions play a major role. The greater a person's emotional commitment, the stronger his or her tendency to reject contrary evidence and distort the objective world to reduce anxiety. If we envision self-deception as but one more function of a neural, reasoning mandate to protect self-esteem from cognitive dissonance, then it's not difficult to understand its prevalence.

Chapter 2

TRIBAL BEHAVIOR MODULES

*I am a brain, my dear Watson, and the rest of me
a mere appendage.*

- Sherlock Holmes

The reality is no tribal activity can occur without the appropriate mental architecture. Without a brain, we would not see, hear, feel, smell, talk, move, eat or sleep. Nor would there be any of the strategic behaviors we apply to competition, cooperation, idol worship, division-of-labor, trade, sharing, lying, loving, cheating, bombing, burning, rationalizing and denying. All normal behaviors used by our creative ancestors—for good and evil—to survive.

As an organ, the brain functions as part of the whole, for the survival of the individual as well the tribe. Brain mission, though, has not been so easy to decipher as, say that of the heart or liver. Some early studies showing neural pathways from the eye, ear or nose to related portions of the brain were relatively easy to follow and understand. As medical technology improved, other areas of brain were identified as playing significant roles in behavior, such as one's ability to speak a language, one's tendencies toward addictions, as well as one's aptitude to music, mathematics and other more abstract functions and feelings.

What remained puzzling, were the mysteries that percolated in the brains of philosophers regarding how the brain has a sense of a "self," a "self" that harbors a conscience as well as a freewill. Over time, they collectivized these mental understandings as the "mind," a state of mental awareness. Simply put, the mind is how the brain works to experience the world around us. The heart works to pump blood, the liver works to cleanse the blood, and the mind works to experience the world, including nurturing and protecting love relationships or political relationships like one's tribal feelings toward democracy or communism.

Suggesting the mind has an innate ability to focus on a political belief like communism or democracy as well as the ability to energize that belief to divine status in the mind of its beholder is controversial to say the least. Yet, how else do we explain the devotional beliefs of Presidents Trump, Bush, Clinton and Obama? Likewise, who would dare question the ideological zeal of representative Nancy Pelosi or Pope Francis or the countless billions of partisans living today and in the past?

Since no one really knows, reality models are construed here to be pretty much a 50/50 proposition—fifty percent genetic and fifty percent social. Cultural capital like inherited wealth, family habits and values, schooling, playmates, and other environmental connections provide the accent and intonation to a hard-wired genetic framework. Traits like the language we speak, our tenure as educators, the religion or political ideology we practice are also culturally dependent. The mental architecture for language proficiency, intelligence, religious tendency as well as left- and right-brain thinking giving us a liberal or conservative slant on life are heritable traits.

The brain structures of particular tribal interest that act on emphasizing and systemizing incoming data are the thalamus, amygdala and the prefrontal lobes of the neocortex. We've known for some time that sensory information from the environment goes first to the thalamus at the very core of our brain. That information is then passed on in milliseconds to the amygdala (a nut-sized structure just below the thalamus). The amygdala is part of our limbic system—our older so-called reptilian brain—that screens sensory data for threats or opportunity and applies an appropriate amount of emotional energy to the information. Several milliseconds later, the data goes to both sides of the large, convoluted outer neocortex, which injects moral value to the data to act appropriately.

This neocortex is part of the outer layer of the brain called the cerebral cortex that developed much later in our evolution and is often referred to as our new "reasoning brain." Thus, a gap exists between quick amygdala response and the slower, more thoughtful, neocortex response. As a result, we are wired to respond in two ways: first, with our quick-response reptilian brain that screens and applies emotional values to incoming data—the old fight-or-flight reaction—and next by our newer brain in a slower more thoughtful fashion.

The neocortex is the place where high-level thinking modules (clusters of nerve cells acting as behavior templates) accept incoming information, sort the new data into strips of related information, compare it to other strips and then process and weave it into a more current rendition of a worldview from that which existed just moments before.

Science tells us these modules, these clusters of neural circuitries, relate to distinct behaviors like language, abstract thinking, music, suspicion, fear, sex, etc. Scientists call each distinct pattern of behavior a "cognitive schema" or "neural module." Psychologists Toby and Cosmides argue that these patterns of thinking are each content-sensitive to interact with regularities from the environment and that they evolved through natural selection. These patterns of thinking we recognize as language, abstract thinking, music or sex, exist alongside modules for sociality, religion, imitation, cooperation, conformity and politics. The renowned cognitive psychologist Steven Pinker writes in *The Blank Slate* that we are:

> .... equipped with different kinds of intuitions and logics, each appropriate to one department of reality.... They emerge early in life, are present in every normal person, and appear to be computed in partly

distinct sets of networks in the brain. They may be installed by different combinations of genes, or they may emerge when brain tissue self-organizes in response to different problems to be solved and different patterns in the sensory input. Most likely they develop by some combination of these forces.

Can anyone deny the existence of a girl module or boy module that drives the sexes into never-ending mating rituals? Surely there must be a baby module specifically designed to elicit that warm, fuzzy feeling on seeing a newborn baby or puppy. And what about the adoration one has toward those tribal iconic figures or symbols such as god, flag and country, president, imam and pope. Plus, can anyone deny a love module actively at work between parents, siblings, biological kin, and ideological kin.

Who of us as parent or teacher does not recognize the ability of children to understand the notions of dominance, conformity and imitation? Assuredly there must be a hierarchy module that accurately assigns relative status to peers and associates because we all learn early in life to work the system, whether that system be made up of parents or teachers, government officials or gang members. If there are behavior modules by which we so readily learn to suck and cry, walk and talk, sway to music and participate in sex, why not modules for empathy and hate or cooperation and conformity to ideologies like communism and democracy?

The Music Module

It's important to remember all these behaviors have a tribal context. Even an innocent subject like music exhibits an imprinting process with modules sensitive to repetition, rhyme and rhythm. By 2008, enough research existed to suggest modules for music helped humans remember phrases or stories while bringing members together by way of community-styled music and dance. How else to explain the ability of young children to respond to music as quick as they do; or the thousands of fans swaying and arm waving to their favorite band; or millions finding weekly joy in listening to fiery sermons enhanced by inspirational hymns; or the marching of soldier to a measured cadence. Even though we are not certain of music's evolutionary connection, we know ice-age ancestors (35,000 years ago) played flutes made from swan bones and that early Greeks, guided by mnemonics, sang in meter.

It doesn't take much of an imagination to see how rhythm and rhyme evolved along with storytelling as young, creative individuals competed for the cherished position as tribal historian and/or poet. After all, for thousands of years before writing, storytellers became revered members of society who passed valued traditions on from generation to generation. The *Iliad* was long chanted before being set down in writing by Homer. The druids employed bards to record their chronologies and treatises on geography, the sea and the techniques of farming in mnemonic rhyme.

As late as 1510, bards to Henry III rhymed chronicles, epitaphs and the like. Not only do we remember words, phrases and ideas better when put to music, but once firmly etched into our mental makeup, individuals soon become partial to specific genres of music. Some become partial to the poetic morals embedded in fairy tales (think *Cat in the Hat* by Dr. Zuess) or the ideology nurtured by repeating a catchy mantra or slogan. Even in 2019, millions of Americans pay millions of dollars to sway to loud, repetitious drumming in much the same fashion early movie footage of native tribes were shown doing.

What music, religious mantras, chanting, poetry, schools, think tanks, bedtime stories, old wives' tales, prayer meetings, and uniforms have in common is that they provide positive incentives as well as repetition to mold tribal beliefs structurally. Living is but a series of rituals with countless religious and civic activities shaping ideological worldviews.

The Freedom/Equity Mandate

I think it's safe to say the scientific consensus today is that humans evolved with unique sets of physical attributes like brown hair, shaded skin, a compassionate temperament and so forth, that provide a countenance expressed as a "self," an individual. To this end, I like to think there exists within our mental framework a 'self-module', expressed as a spirited, psychic imp that chauffeurs us through life and constantly feeds us tidbits of self-enhancement or, perhaps, self-deception.

For evidence of the imp's energetic skills, we need look no further than the inner self we all possess. Don't we all cherish our self-awareness, the mental picture we have of ourselves? Don't most people search for self-esteem, the sense of worth, respect and confidence we have of ourselves? And, above all, don't we all cherish the *freedom* and autonomy we practice when setting and achieving goals we perceive as *equitable*, moral structures defining right and wrong, normal and abnormal?

Recognizing that freedom/equity drive, suggests the source of such energy presides with a *Freedom and Equity Module* embedded in our mental architecture that becomes an active, motivational force whenever we feel our security is threatened, or our need for self-actualization goes unmet. It's a behavior module   a greedy, self-interest module   that can easily take the form of a *Freedom/Equity Mandate* demanding bias and blindness toward others who do not have the moral values or worldview we have. Without a biased, willful self, there would be no desire to realize dreams and, without an intolerance mandate, the drive to achieve equity would bog us down in a quagmire of confused social compliance. This *Freedom/Equity Mandate* will come to cause humans great joy and severe problems later in this narrative.

Chapter 3

THE GOD MODULE -BINDS & BLINDS-

The force of any passion or emotion can so surpass the rest of the action or the power of a man that the emotions adhere obstinately to him. For a man who is submissive to his emotions does not have power over himself but is in the hands of fortune to such an extent that he is often constrained, although he may see what is better for him, to follow what is worse.

-Baruch Spinoza

The Freedom/Equity Module is a major motivational force in our story on tribalism because, as social animals predestine to compete against other tribes of intelligent humans, this module had to be subservient to a larger community force: a "tribal ideology." A force strong enough to relegate not only one person's self-interest to community interest, but a force strong enough to package and elevate all tribal self-interest into one dynamic, competitive force. For this extremely important tribal force to mature, a neural module in our brain called *"The God Module"* evolved in all humans, a module that deserves its own chapter.

And who better to start the chapter off than Sigmund Freud, who once argued that sexual desire is the primary motivating force in human life. In light of our knowledge of the God Module, perhaps Freud was wrong. Perhaps man's first passion is to a tribal ideology and its moral authority, a base instinct ensuring tribal members live to participate in sex. After all, we are here today because our ancestors survived the swarms of diseases, disabilities and tribal fighting they had to endure for over a million years. Survived, had sex, and here we are.

For all the complex emotions that go into procreation, one can also assume an equal amount of love and hatred, lust and revenge go into our political ideologies. Like sex or heroin, once you get hooked on a political narrative, you become a true believer. And, like all human trait, humans will show a wild range of devotion to their adopted religious and/or secular ideology.

True believers are defined here as that ten to twenty percent of any population who believe whole heartedly in their political ideology as a religion, a grounding spiritual faith that shapes their daily activities, an emotional core sufficiently strong to override inhibitions. As such they are considered zealots, fanatics, radicles or ideologues. Just consider the blinding emotional commitment necessary for suicide bombers to ignite explosives in the midst of mothers and children, or the hard, cold, zealotry Timothy McVeigh possessed to bomb the Alfred P. Murrah Federal Building in Oklahoma City, killing 167 people including nineteen children.

Given such psychopathic deeds, one is left to question why and how the human mind evolved such extreme behaviors? Why the 'fire-in-the-belly'? To answer this question a number of scientists have identified a spiritual center in the brain that is highly sensitive to ideologies with the ability to override social constraints. The research describes such emotional sites as emotional markers or modules that define a myth as emotionally real, although the experience might have no substance whatsoever in physical reality. It's only real in the mind.

In 2002, Italian neurologist Joseph Giovannoli dubbed one such neural cluster as the "God Module." This amazing research is notable because it suggests the human mind is hardwired not only to apply strong emotions to feelings that have substance in reality, but also strong moral attachments to a beliefs that have no substance in physical reality, yet, are considered inspirational and rational simply because they work to solidify community energy to a spiritual, community cause, like Christianity, or communism, or democracy.

> Here, the God Module is defined as a cluster of nerves that spiritualize the human brain to a secular or religious ideology to ensure tribal solidarity that, in turn, promotes survival for the tribe.
>
> The role of the God Module is to addict tribal members to an ideology; provide the emotional biased energy in promoting the ideology; provide the emotional biased energy in blinding members to contrary ideologies; and finally, act as a damper on member's Freedom/Equity Module by limiting those energies to facilitate community solidarity.

It's in this twilight zone of abstract reasoning that the God Module allows the cognitive portion of our mind to *emotionally inspire* humans to accept inspirational ideas and ideals as concrete *truths* worth fighting and dying for. God Module emotions are sensations we seldom give much thought to, but they are the glue that locks us unto tribal ideals; bonds us to the tribe; and provides the emotions to make moral statements for or against, gets us moving in one direction or another. As moral gate keepers, they make us belief addicts. As such, all political tribal activities take on a moral or ethical dependency subject to whether a person is inside or outside an ideology bubble.

Given their intimate nature, morals need not be taught so much as observed and imitated. Habituation will occur when a child simply observes others, learning what works and what doesn't. Street urchins will learn what it means to be loyal and show street-gang courage and integrity. That being the case, there must be clusters of sympathetic neurons that register good and bad, and offers appropriate emotional responses to environmental clues. Clusters of sympathetic neurons that are either part of or related to God Module influence.

Only lately have scientists begun to recognize the God Module's addiction qualities with TV talking-heads using such phrases as *"cognitive capture"* to describe a practice in which liberal or conservative elites *"capture"* followers' God Modules to believe in their ideology or their brand of art, poetry, economics, science, global warming, etc. Within the captured framework, God Modules then practice *"unconscious or cognitive bias,"* a binding type of thinking where a person remembers information selective to their ideology, interprets it personally and acts on it in a bias manner. An additional bias is also practiced once cognitive capture occurs, *"cognitive blindness,"* an unwitting type of thinking in which people are "incapable" of recognizing and accepting a political ideology contrary to their ideology.

One research example. A Yale study, *Fixing the Communication Failure*, showed that individual beliefs were more powerful than any other individual characteristic in explaining global warming. The study suggests that people with strong liberal values toward collective action and social justice overwhelmingly accept the climate change charges, whereas those with strong conservative values labeled 'hierarchical' and 'individualistic' against big government, strongly reject climate-change charges. Mr. Kahan, the lead researcher in the study, attributes the disparity in worldviews to "cultural cognition," (another term for cognitive capture and bias) the process by which our brains filter information to protect our worldviews.

Given their habit-forming and casing qualities, ideologies can generate an intense moralized energy that colors behaviors black or white, shades of gray or explosions of red, moving some to commit the most inhumane acts against humanity and nature. This moral intensity is the "fire-in-the-belly" that drives true believers to succeed at all costs and free of remorse. All highly evolved social organisms including ants, mound-building termites and honeybees, exhibit devotional tribal behaviors, but none, not even social elephants, display the range of moral intensity—that range of love and hate—on the scale humans do.

While we are just beginning to appreciate the relationship between small shifts in brain chemistry and our various appetites, we little appreciate the intimate, endearing chemistry between beliefs we hold dear and the high-level thinking modules that promote the devotional zeal needed to protect those beliefs. Of interest then are the addictive mechanics that tie us to secular and religious beliefs, behaviors we define as spirituality, passion, devotion, loyalty, fidelity, nationalism, populism, patriotism.

More important in the discussion of politics is the fact that God Modules function as natural opiates providing feelings of pleasure or apathy which, over time, addict us to or against idols and their ideologies. Political action serves no purpose unless it becomes habit forming and that requires emotion, lots of emotion to bind to a cause and act in an altruistic or aggressive fashion to protect the valued cause. It follows then, that, given the wide range of human diversity, some individuals are born with God Modules more vulnerable to religious and secular ideologies and others less vulnerable. If true, these highly charged modules drive some individuals and groups to satisfying their utopian quest in any fashion they deem necessary. No imagination is needed to envision a cluster of neurons sensitive to an ideology that, on the one hand, provides people with the wherewithal to live in relative harmony and yet blinds them to the beliefs of others to the point of terrorism: ergo, the Timothy McVeigh's of this world.

Chapter 4

PALEOLITHIC TRIBALISM
THE SMALL TRIBAL MODEL

To run an effective political party You need a degree of tribalism, It' the glue that holds everyone together.

-Charles Kennedy

The number one natural law all life forms must obey to survive as a species is to 'compete' for life-giving resources. For our ancestors that competition began its slow evolution during the tediously long Paleolithic Period which extended over a time span of some 1.5 million years. In the beginning, civil society consisted of small family units (clans) living in caves, that mastered the art of fire building and a simple language by which they communicated, cooperated and coordinated their efforts at raising children, gathering plants, capturing and sharing animal protein. As social organisms, these clans that were bonded genetically by birth, would over this long period of time, evolve into larger, highly successful tribes of perhaps several hundred individuals.

To understand tribalism, it's necessary to understand how the minds of our ancestors were genetically hard-wired to be devotionally bonded to a politically democratic ideology; how such bondage allowed them to function as a single unit; and, how they used their collective physical, technological, and social skills to protect their territory and ideology at all cost from intrusion by neighboring tribes.

This process is defined here as an inherent *"Community Mandate"* demanding the individual set aside his/her desire for freedom and equity *(the Freedom/Equity Mandate)* and focus their God Module energy on community interests to ensure the community functions as a single organism to maximize survival in a competitive world.

Scientists tell us there's evidence to suggest that all the small tribes coming out of the Paleolithic Period believed in a beneficial, religious-life force of some kind offering hope and salvation. Such devotion probably started with our ancestors' attempt to understand some powerful natural force effecting their lives. Eventually such an intangible and elusive force was incorporated into tribal tradition as a communal totem—a force to fear or cherish as good fortune. Over time a recognized good force might be looked upon in a spiritual, divine fashion to be worshiped as a supreme being.

There is some traceable evidence all the major religions show a similarity in terminology and fundamental values rooted in Animism, our ancestor's close relationship with what they perceived as spirits of their prey. Joseph Giovannoli, in *"The biology of beliefs: How our biology biases our beliefs and perceptions"* describes how such a belief may have evolved among our ancestors:

> Imagine you are one of your ancestors. … You believe that plants, trees, animals, and natural events have human-like consciousness and spirituality…. You treat the animals you kill and the trees you cut with respect because you believe the spirits of all things are interconnected…. You may eat the bodies of slain enemies to obtain the power of their spirit…. Your shaman discovered the trance-inducing effects of certain plants and thought it a gift from one of your animal spirit….As time passes, your mythological spirits (bodiless animal analogs) evolve into var-

ious omnipotent, immortal gods with animal forms, possessing supernatural power that can relieve your suffering, ensure fertility, and steel you against the forces of nature.

Trouble is, except for their fossilized remains and numerous examples of the Acheulean hand axe, few fossils or artifacts exist to show any cultural advancement reflective of those spiritual thought pattern. Consequently, there's confusion among evolutionary scientists regarding how such complex tribal behaviors evolved during this period. What's so remarkable about this knowledge gap is that around 40,000 years ago there appeared evidence of massive cultural change, with widespread advances in tools, cave art, dwellings, religious thinking, clothes and music, a time period scientist describe as "The Great Leap Forward." The obvious question is, Why?

More interesting, fossil skulls from the long period preceding The Great Leap Forward show the cognitive portion of the human brain being little different from those who perpetrated The Great Leap Forward. Again, Why? What were our Paleolithic ancestors doing with their thinking, planning and creative minds if not making life more comfortable for themselves? What threshold was needed to cross before technology picked up to make The Great Leap Forward possible?

The philosophical argument here is that brain growth was driven not by technology intelligence but rather social intelligence, learning how to get along with tribal friends and relatives, all exhibiting self-serving interest. Not an easy task even today. We must always remember the selfish human element (the *Freedom/Equity Mandate*), that can easily take the form of intolerance demanding aggression against someone you don't like.

Apparently, that was not an issue during this period mainly because community values and solidarity were essential survival tools in the existing harsh social and physical environments during this long period. Such complex, demanding environments make great demands on memory and application of memory. If true, then the human mind was being flooded during this period with neural modules concerned primarily with interactive, touchy-feely behaviors that forged personal feelings into communal relationships but, left no hard evidence behind. The threshold crossed was the discovery of how to manage fire mankind's greatest discovery.

The drawing power of fire brought people together at gathering sites like caves and similar shelters, paleoanthropologist call "nesting sites." Socializing around fires helped transform guttural sounds into language; language into communal feelings and knowledge; communal feelings and knowledge into communal memories and political ideologies; and, eventually into better technology and The Great Leap Forward, a process that took a vast amount of time.

When discussing evolutionary time, it is important to understand that biologists use the word evolution to mean a carefully defined process of systematic shifts in *gene frequencies* within populations, together with the resulting changes in how animals and plants actually look and function as the generations go by, with no way of improving on their survival advantage except through sexual reproduction. Consequently, DNA change—characterized by the random expression and survival of genetic traits like a gentle touch or smile—was tediously slow.

Plus, given the number of individuals in a clan (twenty to eighty) and a tribe (eighty to two hundred), communal relationships evolved even slower due to the diversity of needs and talents as well as the elusive, delicate and subtle nature of emotions in play. Countless generations lived and died with ever-so-slight modifications to the voice box, tongue and facial muscles—the basis for modern language on which cultural creativity depends. Endless generations were needed to progress from grunts, head nods, a primitive language and new facial muscles capable of expressing feelings like a smirk and a smile.

Finally, an endless period of time was needed for brain architecture to refine, smooth and polish these social interactions not only on a personal level, but on a complex cultural level as well. Virtues like tolerance and respect for others and their opinions; consideration for the weak, old and infirm; a belief in good intentions and respect for privacy; a sense of humor and kindliness; a dislike of oppressive power; and, the ability to rationalize a tribal ideology as the one-and-only belief in how the world works. Snakes, bed bugs, and golden eagle can't duplicate those behaviors. But such things happened, and they happened when efficient, adaptive, creative minds found themselves sitting around a hot fire roasting chestnuts and mammoth steaks. But...... it took time!

Hunting and scavenging wild game also added to communal solidarity. In studies of hunting-gathering societies, scientists found that one-third of the average diet consisted of meat containing fat and protein essential to brain development. Here, again, fire played an important role as recent experiments show cooked meat has a much higher nutritional value and is more digestible than raw meat. Numerous studies also demonstrate that it would have been biologically implausible for humans to evolve large, complex brains without fire and an omnivorous diet.

Hunting often resembled the tactics of other pack animals. Matching the cunning and cooperation exhibited by wolves, for example, man's hunting skills became more effective at killing game much larger than himself. Likewise, humans learned to store surplus kill at cool cache sites and fed solid food to their young. Hunting, as it might have progressed with Homo erectus, a Stone Age ancestor that lived from about 1.8 million to 50,000 years ago, also illustrates how early thought processes evolved along tribal lines.

At first, these early hunters were opportunists, savaging carcasses left by more efficient predators and killing as luck would provide. As hard cognitive knowledge about an animal's habitat and travel patterns increased, guidelines and instructions were formulated to harvest them with consistency. Studies of campsites made by Homo erectus during his long stay on Earth show remnants of chopping tools and chop marks left on bones of butchered mammoths and large deer.

The fact such large animals were hunted, killed and butchered at shelter spots indicates not only an extensive hunting knowledge, but also an evolving knowledge of tool making and complex thinking modules like the social powers of careful observation, coordination and cooperation, all essential to the hunt. The cooperative nature of the hunt practiced by these pre-moderns also contributed much later in human evolution to the production of various forms of shelters, clothing from hides, a wide range of implements and weapons, and several methods of transporting heavy objects that eventually led to The Great Leap Forward.

For eons as communal relationships evolved, authority, power and resource distribution were fairly equal. It was a communal, democratic system where needs were balanced with social responsibility. Somewhere along the Middle to Late Pleistocene Period (100,000 to 40,000 years ago), as a result of hunting big game, cooperation during the hunt and meat sharing became two of the most essential tribal endeavors to have evolved.

Men hunted, trapped, fished and made tools. Since killing was carried out with clubs and spears, individuals born aggressive, strong, courageous, agile and clever were destined to lead the hunt. Over time, good leaders learned to balance hunting with more altruistic skills that made them attractive to females, good with children, thoughtful and cooperative with related clan members and skillful negotiators. Others, because of their physical, psychological, and emotional makeup, drifted toward harvesting wild foods, healing the sick, making tools or interpreting the unknown each a valued, definable communal niche.

Women collected, cooked and cared for children. Since children require years of tutelage and near constant care, women advanced strong nurturing, communicating and bonding behaviors conducive to maintaining family continuity and cohesiveness. Children learned tribal discipline and responsibility through play and participation. When old enough, they helped the women capture game by setting snares and spring traps, or participating in net drives, cliff drives, and surrounds. Resources and feelings were shared. The old were respected for their wisdom; the weak and sick cared for and comforted. This fairly equitable division of labor and power provided clans and tribes with a personalized social reality created through trial and error.

Important to our story on tribalism is the fact that communal reality during this period became a physical reality, involving story lines related by sequence of thought that, with further experience over time, might prove to be reliable knowledge and behavior reflecting the sound logic of physical reality. For example, having little empirical knowledge to draw upon, early man's intuitive response to yearly cycles was justifiably subjective. Stories about the role the moon, the sun and the stars played in serving man's many needs were like dream narratives: personal theories on how these features related to earthly events. By integrating a number of events into time frames with causal relationships, early man projected general principles and thematic subject matter into story form, giving events a logical sequence. As more knowledge became available, thematic patterns became discernible so that a reliable calendar comparing celestial events to plant growth and animal movement was realized.

More important to communal reality during this period was the spiritual forces that came with devotion to gods that proved to be a reliable psychic reality, the classic Small Tribal Model (STM): a community model where patriotic feelings were expressed as a way of valuing the present, preserving the past, protecting the future, and most important, a way of codifying codes and creeds of right and wrong, to ensure community solidarity. Community qualities that distinguish humans from other animals: reasoned dialogue, freedom, equity, trust, cooperation and empathy.

Within this social matrix composed of reality and idealism, the God Module evolved a casing quality shielding a belief in a bubble-like envelope. As with the unique love between a couple, the bubble grows larger and more impervious as additional bits and bytes of devotion are stored in the ideology bubble, until it eventually becomes a unique, one-of-a-kind ideology, unique to the Fearsome Tribe near Dead Swan Lake, or the Avengers living at the mouth of the Clear Water River a million years ago.

The French utopian Henri de Sait-Simon once observed that political ideals are like musk, one need not actually touch them to undergo their influence. It's this addictive quality that allows individual God Modules to elevate ideologies to devotional status while acting as a damper on the Freedom/Equity Mandate.

Chapter 5

MODERN EXAMPLES OF PALEOLITHIC TRIBES

Nothing is more noble, nothing more venerable than fidelity. Faithfulness and truth are the most sacred excellences and endowments of the human mind.
                                        -Marcus Tullius Cicero

The essence of tribalism started with pair bonding when a male and female found quality of life better by staying together and extending the female's emotional demands for raising offspring to the male, a powerful bond that eventually became genetically solidified, and advanced to the extended family, clan and tribe. Because the demanding desire for sex between male and female was always a powerful force, it's easy to understand how the same demanding emotions were genetically applied to family and eventually to a small community. Over eons of time, the process proved eminently successful for a large number of tribes with God Modules designed to capture, bind and blind member minds to a unifying, spiritual ideology.

Twenty-first century humans seem not to appreciate just how tribal they are and believe our cave-man past was left behind, in the caves, thousands of year ago. Plus, we believe our thinking has become highly sophisticated and intellectualized to warrant no psychological connection with past Neanderthals. But such thinking is wrong. Scientists prior to World War I estimated the number of small, tribal-like villages throughout Russia were in the hundreds; 155,000 secular/religious tribes world-wide in 1945; 78,000 in 1972; and, 43,000 tribes in 2015.

In 2013, it was estimated that there were more than 100 uncontacted tribes around the world, mostly in the densely forested areas of South America and New Guinea. One such tribe, the Sentinelese, are an indigenous people who inhabit North Sentinel Island in the Bay of Bengal, India. The tribe, estimated to be 30,000-year old, is one of five reclusive, native tribes in the chain of islands and considered one of the most protective by actively threatening and killing, if necessary, anyone attempting to visit them. It received national attention in November 2018 when a missionary, John Allen Chau—breaching local law strictly prohibiting contact with the isolated people—travelled to North Sentinel island where he was apparently killed with bow and arrow and buried on the beach.

It is illogical to assume that cultures so disconnected by time, space and environment could develop similar lifestyles without a shared biology driven by common, inherent, tribal-motivated God Modules. As Matt Ridley, the prolific writer and Chair of the International Center for Life in Newcastle, England so aptly points out about Inuit lifestyle: "Equipped with only snow, dogs, and dead seals, human beings will gradually invent a lifestyle complete with songs and gods as well as sleds and igloos." The same can be said for the Incas, Iroquois, Bushmen, and the thousands of past and present cultures. Ridley goes on to point out that as early as 1920, "... the precocious Russian anthropologist Lev Semenovich Vygotsky described how more than those of any other species, they [human minds] swim in a sea called culture." *In Origin of the Modern Mind*, Merlin Donald writes:

> .... even the most isolated modern human groups, some of whom were still living in the Stone Age when first discovered by Europeans, possessed highly elaborate systems of religion, myth, and kin-

ship relations at the time of their discovery. For instance, the original Tasmanian, who were driven into extinction in 1876 and whose cultural artifacts had not changed in 35,000 years, had produced at least five distinct linguistic dialects, a rigid tribal structure with clearly defined territories, religious ritual, and various decorative arts, including elaborate body decoration, and rock engraving. The Tasaday of the Philippines, the pygmies of the African rain forest, and the Bushmen of southern Africa when first contacted by Europeans, still had the same type of tool culture associated with the very earliest modern human remains. But they all possessed elaborate spoken languages and highly developed tribal structures, rituals, myths, and religions.

Our earliest on-the-spot knowledge of such universal tribal behavior comes to us from the Greek Herodotus, who wrote about the Scythians and Thracians in 424 BC. He was followed by a host of writers describing the exploits of the Goths, Huns, Vandals, Vikings and finally about the Mongols and Tartars in the 13th century. In the book, *Caesar and Christ* by Will Durant, Caesar describes the "noble German savage" of 55 BC:

They do not pay much attention to agriculture, and a large portion of their food consists in milk, cheese, and flesh, or has any one a fixed quantity of land or his own individual limits; but the magistrates and the leading men each year apportion to the tribes and families, who have united together, as much land as, and in the place in which, they think proper, and the year after compel them to move elsewhere. For this enactment they advance many reasons—lest seduced by long-continued custom, they may exchange their ardor in the waging of war for agricultures; lest they may be anxious to acquire extensive estates, and the more powerful drive the weaker from their possessions; lest they construct their houses with too great a desire to avoid cold and heat; lest the desire of wealth spring up, from which cause divisions and discords arise; and that they may keep the common people in a contented state of mind, *when each sees his own means placed on an equality with those of the most powerful.* (Emphasis added.)

What we have here is the meeting of the democratic old and autocratic new. Goths, Huns, Vandals and Mongols representing a tribal system that offered relative equity for all, up against Greeks and Romans who, with their powerful war machines and desire to conquer, offered freedom and equity for only a select few. If more resources and slaves were needed, you simply took over heathen lands. Anyone complains, nail him to a cross. Yet, both Greece and Rome with their powerful Gods, beautiful architecture, impressive engineering, frightening war machines, battle tactics, and limited democracy, died out and were replaced by a tribe of Christian theocrats who stamped out all attempts at equity.

Charles Mann in his book, *1461: New Revelations of the Americas Before Columbus* describes in some detail the lifestyles of several thousand-year-old cultures indigenous to South America and Meso-America before natural disasters, climate change and, later, disease and predation by colonial powers brought their extinction. They managed complex trade routes with remote tribes; had a tortuous religion that focused on human sacrifice; a dozen different writing systems; a 365-

day calendar; and recorded their history in books of folded paper made from fig-tree bark. Since many of these skills were more advanced than those of their contemporaries in Europe at the time, it's thought the cultures were older as well.

In the US, history usually starts with Greece and Rome, then quickly moves to America, its discovery, settling the wilderness, the growth of our republic, then on to our representative form of governing. Children are led to believe the road from Rome to Washington D.C. was relatively smooth with the exception of the Dark Ages when everything shut down for a thousand years or more, and battles were fought only to mark the passage of time.

This period was, in fact, turbulent as nomadic barbarians swept down time and again from the steppes of Eurasia to plunder and pillage Western Europe, the Middle East, India and China. There are still a few of these amazing people around in the 21st century to provide us with eye-witness evidence of their Mongol lifestyle. Known as the Buryat and Kalmyk clans living in northern Mongolia, China and Russia, their ancestors go back thousands of years.

These nomads exist today in the same area their ancestors lived and exhibit much of the same lifestyle. We know they were horse and sheep herders who lived across the vast expansive steppes of central Asia. More important for our tribalism story is that, while their membership was large, it was dispersed across the vast steppe grasslands into small clans that were constantly on the move to provide grazing for their animals. Thus scattered, they had no central government, were illiterate and expressed no formalized religion except for Animism.

Their longevity as a paleolithic-like culture is the result of remaining a loose-knit confederation of nomadic clans, dependent on a lifestyle that offered several survival advantages. First, the inherent need for freedom and equity that is so disruptive in large, complex cultures was lacking in these small clans. Instead, at work was the STM offering relative comfort and security, thereby eliminating the need for an oppressive central government. Second, since their belief in the supernatural never progressed beyond Animism, no strong, central religion evolved to harness or restrict their behavior. Consequently, their uncluttered God Modules, Freedom/Equity Mandates were directed at perfecting their hunting and warring skills giving them an enormous advantage when the "Mongol horde" swarmed in mass to prey on larger, sedentary cultures.

We know something of their warring tactics from histories written by men of the cultures they subdued, like Rome, Persia, India and China, but only such events that affected the writers. Consequently, most of the stories are murderous and brutal. Even Marco Polo's 13th century description of his travels through the Mongol Empire and life in Kublai Khan's court , is more an account of a life-style influenced by the culture conquered, than a reflection of the steppe lifestyle.

The mounted Mongol warrior reigned not only over the Eurasian steppes but, for some thirteen centuries, over the entire European continent. He was a dominant force because he, like the wild animals he hunted, were creations of the environment itself; offspring of a want-and-need habitat he challenged with horse and bow to eventually became its master. When Genghis Khan succeeded in conquering his world, he was able to do so because, as teens, he and his brother Jochi the Tiger, were experts at stalking, harassing and bringing down game much larger than themselves. By that age they were also expert horsemen and took great pride remaining on horseback during the brutal buzkashi games of getting a sheep's head or calf's carcass into a net, or enduring the days and nights on horseback to harass and vanquish an enemy.

While considered uncivilized for their murderous ways, whether Turk, Mongol, or Hun, they belonged to an intelligent, thoughtful, practical people who were driven by periodic droughts from their northern grasslands to raid and plunder neighbors. Though illiterate and backward in material wealth, they were unequaled in battle. Applying wolf-pack tactics they seldom confronted their enemy directly.

Rather, scholars at stealth, they would launch surprise attacks upon him, then vanish, reappear, pursue, harry, and weary him until, at last, bring him down, exhausted. It was a tactic, many 20th century military tacticians, as well as American politician in the late 20th and early 21st century would modernize to subdue the opposition. Much more on this warfare strategy, later.

They were also totally uncharacteristic in their post-conquering style. Lacking a devotional ideology, they were only interested in booty, not converts, so their invasions repeatedly followed the same cycle. When a sedentary, urbanized community yielded under their onslaught, many of the indigenous population were massacred, and the nomad seated on the defeated ruler's throne, as Khan of China, King of Persia or Emperor of India. Soon, though, the nomads left behind to govern became assimilated into the conquered culture, grew soft and were just as quickly plundered and pillaged by the next hungry horde reappearing off the frontier.

On horseback, with bow and arrow, none was their equal. They were the epitome of the pastoral-hunter lifestyle. They gave the world the chariot, the wheel, the covered wagon, the re-curved bow and an unparalleled array of equestrian paraphernalia including saddle, bridle, mouth bit and stirrup. Each item, at its time, an unparalleled achievement. Their reign came to an end in the fifteenth century with the invention of gunpowder and the rise of a feudal system when cannon, cavalry, armor, the long bow, siege engines and moats became fashionable with the hunter-warrior class in Europe.

These magnificent people are a wonderful example of a lifestyle our paleolithic ancestors produced. Proud people, married to a STM. A practical pattern of thinking that offered a relative degree of freedom and equality, with an equal amount of responsibilities so that trust, cooperation, dialogue and solidarity governed; an inner tribal contract that did not extend to neighboring tribes; a Darwinian contract where competition is the intermediary between who wins and who loses; a simple ethos that left cognitive artifacts in the brains of all succeeding generations, far more significant than all the physical artifacts that came with The Great Leap Forward. In short, the brain and tribal culture defined the individual, and the mental anatomy that makes up individual's personality, temperament, moral standards and worldview.

Tribal Duplicity

Just as moderns believe they no longer are tribal like their ancestor, they also assume the average man and woman raising a family in a magnificent nation like America, would never stoop so low as to participate in killing other humans, like the Mongols who slaughtered with no remorse. And, yet, we are all guilty to some degree. Thus, it might be revealing early on to point out a study illustrating just how adept the human mind is at ignoring any responsibility for the deaths and destruction that comes with their partisan devotions.

The revealing study was carried out over a period of eighteen months prior to the first Nuremberg trials in 1946 by American psychiatrist, Dr. Douglas Kelly, who interviewed and gave Rorschach personality tests to twenty-three top Nazi prisoners present for the trial. It was a study designed to show these men to be psychotic or at least, severely neurotic for the crimes they committed or fostered during the war.

Jack El-Hai in his 2013 book, *The Nazis and the Psychiatrist: Hermann Goring, Dr. Douglas M. Kelly and a Fatal Meeting of the Minds*, showed Kelly could find no evidence of psychosis or even severe neurosis among the prisoners. El-Hai went on to show Kelly's close eighteen-months proximity to the prisoners—some he talked to daily—convinced him they shared several qualities: ".... unbridled ambition, weak ethics and excessive patriotism to justify nearly any action of questionable rightness" and, therefore, "could only reluctantly conclude that an enormous number of people had the potential to act as the war criminals had."

El-Hai goes on to note that, later in 1946, Kelly told an American audience: "I am quite certain that there are even people in America who would willing climb over the corpses of half of the America public if they could gain control of the other half, and these are the people today who are just talking who are utilizing the rights of democracy, in anti-democratic fashion."

Recognizing the conduct of Hitler's henchmen as normal came as a shock then, and remains a shock today. At the time such behavior was considered abnormal, evil, and anyone perpetrating such atrocities were exhibiting psychopathic behavior, a personality disorder characterized by persistent antisocial behavior, impaired empathy and remorse, with confident, egotistical traits.

What the Kelly study did was remind people that World War II was brutal classic tribalism, fought between numerous tribes made up of *normal* people, exhibiting *normal* behaviors *typical of their tribe's ethical and moral standards at that time and place.* Trouble was, the study had little or no impact on the scientific community or public at the time, nor in 1946 with Kelly's American audience, nor with people struggling with Trump Hysteria in 2019.

People simply do not view themselves as social animal who willing indulge in brutal, destructive behaviors or, giving nodding approval to the behavior while safely sitting on the sidelines. They see themselves as being social but, God forbid, not social *animals* who go around killing and beating each other up. The very implied addiction to such tribal behaviors people find repulsive. This problem of refusing to recognize our tribal nature is a very sad commentary because until we do, humanity will continue on its brutal, bloody way into the future.

Summary Part 1

****

The Paleolithic Period provided humanity with a distinct survival format (STM) of how to live and survive in a competitive world with other human animals. The reasoned thinking used to justify this normal, tribal behavior in prehistoric times, is what psychologists today call, *"objective relativity," a conservative process* in which all tribal members focus their devotional energy on a single community ideology. It was biased, blind, and irrational behaviors considered *normal* behaviors for every tribe or clan. It's what social humans did to survive. They used the spiritualized devotion to their beneficial "Gods" as bonding agent to operate as a single powerful organism.

They justified the objective, mystical logic as moralized truth that worked for them and their lifestyle. A way of thinking psychologists call "rationalization:" Whatever works for the tribe. Normal behavior was tribal behavior. Truth was tribal truth. Their ideology, a devotional ideology. All actions carried out within the STM format controlled by **one motivational forces, the God Module**, with the job of: addicting tribal members to an ideology; providing the emotional biased energy in promoting the ideology; providing the emotional biased energy in blinding members to contrary ideologies; and finally, act as a damper on member's Freedom/Equity Module by limiting those energies to facilitate community solidarity.

PART 2

AUTOCRATIC TRIBALISM
-Historic Period-

It is a strange fact that freedom and equality, the two basic ideas of democracy, are to some extent contradictory. Logically considered, freedom and equality are mutually exclusive, just as society and the individual are mutually exclusive.

-Thomas Mann

Chapter 6
CULTS TO CULTURES

A cult is a religion with no political power.

-Tom Wolfe

Today, in 2020, the STM would be considered a cult because of its size. Like the STM, none of the religious and secular governing bodies that exist today are scientific creations with absolutes, satisfactory to all humanity. Those STM existing today as well as mega cultures, all started out as small struggling cults. All were cut from whimsical, sometime quirky, always creative cloth. All starting with a leader, several disciples along with a small group of followers that either blossomed into a large, mature culture or died out as failed entities, and exists only as historical relics. Of the few cults that succeed, hundreds, if not thousands, have disappeared because they simply lacked, what Thomas Wolfe called the political power to compete.

In the process of spiritualizing a cultish ideology, the human brain is forced to accept spiritualized dogma as psychic reality, something on the order of Jesus rising from the dead. Ideology addiction during paleolithic times was not difficult to understand given the evolving brain didn't recognize the difference between psychic and natural reality. Nor did our ancestors care. Whatever worked was reality. Given the historic trend toward ever-evolving cultures, it might be helpful to examine just how individuals and the masses are so easily addicted to ideologies by skilled individuals who start cults and manage their growth.

Actually, the root word for culture is cult, and to understand how tribes grow into mega tribes, it's helpful to think of cultures as independent organisms that exhibit embryonic, juvenile, and adult stages. The embryonic stage might be considered the cult nursery where a young culture learns to get around and communicate; the juvenile stage a time when the idealized organism sets out on its own to find its niche in a competitive world; and the adult stage those few cultures with clearly defined ideologies and millions of followers.

This analogy is not new. Numerous individuals have expounded on it, the most famous being the English philosopher and political theorist Thomas Hobbes (1588-1679). In 1651, Hobbes wrote a book titled *Leviathan*, in which he describes society as constituting a new form of life composed of exceedingly complicated humans. He compares society's heart to a spring, its nerves to so many strings; its joints to wheels; society's soul to the sovereign; and society's wealth to society's strength.

Stuck with this evolutionary reality, the typical small paleolithic tribes would, by modern standards, be considered an embryonic cult, a gang-like, or Mafia-like group of a hundred-or-so individuals, seeking political power, who survive in some nefarious fashion within the confines of a host tribe that, as a rule does not tolerate foreign ideologies muscling in on its territory. If so, the host culture might charge the group as some crazed, primitive occult only weirdos like James Jones or Charles Manson practiced.

If the cult persists, perhaps a siege is necessary to make a point, like the eleven-day Ruby Ridge incident involving Randy Weaver and his wife Vicki. Suspecting Weaver of belonging to the Aryan Nation, a White Supremacist group, the government in a complicated plan to force Weaver to infiltrate and gather information for them from the Aryans, charged him with possessing illegal weapons. Weaver refused to cooperate, and after his failure to appear on a weapons charge in Idaho, an eleven-day siege on his home by the US Marshal Service and FBI resulted in the death of a marshal, Weavers' wife, a son and their dog. The courts awarded Randy Weaver $100,000 and his three daughters one million each.

Later, a siege by the Bureau of Alcohol, Tobacco, Firearms and Explosives was initiated on the Branch Davidians, an offshoot of the Seventh Day Adventist Church run by David Koresh. The branch resisted the Bureau's attempt to raid their ranch. A gun battle ensued with four government personnel killed along with six cult members. The failed raid eventually ended in a 51-day standoff, ending with an unexplained explosion, a fire, and 80 dead Davidians. All for want of failing to respond to a weapons charge. The courts found the government not guilty of any criminal behavior.

But not all cults fail. The tactics use by cult prophets of old to manipulate the God Modules of their flocks are as old as history itself, tactics that bombard us in endless 24-hour news cycles, today. A major power player in these news cycles is one of the most successful of all cults, Islam, with a typical cult-like beginning proffered by Muhammad, born around 570 AD in the city of Mecca. Raised by a foster mother and uncle, little is known about his life until the age of 40 when he reported being visited by the angel Gabriel in a cave where he often secluded himself and where he received his first revelation.

Three years later he started preaching to enslaved women and men whom he felt needed justice, apparently a rare commodity at that time. Eventually, after many bloody battles with opposing tribes, he was successful in turning Arabia into a single Muslim polity, ensuring his teachings, practices and the Quran he wrote would form the basis of an Islamic religion that would survive for centuries to come, and, he was right.

There is little or no difference between what psychologists define as cult psychology today and that used by Muhammad or that used by Joseph Smith in his thought-reform strategies to establish the rightful, one-and-true brand of Christianity: Mormonism. There are thousands of thought-reform examples carried out by thousands of charismatic politicians and religious idols who charm and, in many cases, literally magnetize people to the point of achieving physical and psychological control of their minds, but few, if any in modern times, rival Smith's speed in merging a small cult into a great ideological tribe.

Smith was capable in the short span of some 14 years (1830-1844) to launch a spiritual revival that resulted in some 20,000 followers at the time of his death, and some 5.9 million in 2016. Mormonism is especially informative because times were different then. There was no national media to ferment daily dissension between existing government entities and youthful ideologies challenging their power as with Ruby Ridge and Waco. What newsprint that did exist, was often remote and of little use to the many who were illiterate.

Pretty much home schooled, Smith worked early at asking God for guidance as to which church he should join and, at the age of 16, he reported a visit by God the Father and Jesus Christ telling him to start his own church. A year later he had a visit by angel Moroni who guided him to ancient records—buried in a stone box and written in a reformed Egyptian language—inscribed on thin gold plates he translated into the *Book of Mormon*. The translation was accomplished by using seer stones he placed in a hat, which allowed him to see the translated words, after which he returned the plates to the angel Moroni, who, like the gold plates were never to be seen again. The only persons to verify the plate's existence were eleven members of a special group of Mormon reviewers.

Smith ended up in prison for smashing all the equipment of an opponent's newspaper, and was shot there along with his brother by a mob in 1844. The church carried on under Brigham Young with membership eventually scatter around the world, including a dozen or so break-away branches, primarily moved by differences with polygamy practiced by Smith who is claimed to have had some 20-plus wives. The *Book of Mormons*, published in 1830, the same year he organized The Church of Jesus Christ of Latter Day Saints, was eventually translated into 108 languages with over 150 million copies sold by 2016.

Joseph Smith's thought control was quite easy to follow because he was dealing with individuals with God Modules highly sympathetic to religious causes before they met him. Since many of his followers were raised in households where books consist primarily of bibles, God Modules were stimulated from early to late formative years by family during the week and preachers on Sunday. Smith need only capture their God Modules with a simple emotional, repetitious narrative that involved both hate, love, hope and salvation—a narrative that Smith controlled; a narrative that stressed insiders as enlightened, saved and elevated, while those outside the bubble, pitied as lost and depraved.

Another reason for Smith's success has to do with the fact ideology addiction is a natural, addictive hold-over from paleolithic times when, apparently, Mother Nature could not resist the temptation to divide tribal populations into roughly 50 percent liberals and 50 percent conservatives, with polarizing tendencies that can fluctuate depending on time and place. For example, Smith was born with liberal tendencies into a conservative culture, rebelled, was killed for his liberal behavior, but succeeded in forming a Mormon culture considered conservative, today.

Given the fact a 50/50 percentage is fairly consistent whether discussing church policy among a thousand Catholics or art among a thousand artist, the percentage is assumed an inherent process like the God Module. As a result, a sympathetic liberal audience of Haveless is available in most any large conservative tribe once a new movement is started. A Haveless membership quickly available if the appeal is made to satisfy individual needs for all the benefits a new, strong, devoted ideology will promise.

One of Smith's elders, James Strang was not as successful in growing his branch. Strang became a member of The Church of Jesus Christ and the Latter Day Saints in February 1844, and was quickly recognized as an Elder and sent by Smith to create a Mormon settlement in Wisconsin. There, Strang devised a number of Smith-copy-cat schemes to ensure his ascendance in the church by claiming he was guided by an angel to buried gold plates that only he could translate revealing God's plan for him and his Mormon branch.

After Brigham Young was chosen head of the Mormon Church upon Smith's death, Strang breaks away from the sect and moves his followers to Beaver Island, Michigan in 1849. There he decrees himself "King of the Kingdom of God on Earth" and sets about taking over commerce on the island resulting in skirmishes breaking out when he demands the locals pay a tithe to the church.

When word reaches the White House, President Fillmore sends the USS Missouri to bring Strang to trial for tax evasion, counterfeiting and mail delay, charges which Strang, acting as his own lawyer, beats in open court. Shortly after, King Strang orders David Bedford lashed for sleeping with his business partner's wife. So chastised, Bedford and friends ambush Strang who is shot three times, after which the two men charged with the shooting are taken on the USS Michigan to Mackinac Island, where a mock trial takes place, and the two men are fined $1.25 and released. Strang, who survives the shooting, is taken back to Wisconsin where, with his five wives, four pregnant at the time, dies some three weeks later from his injuries.

We must remember the brains of all social animals were designed for such pack competition and all, whether social ants, elephants or wolves, start out in a cult-like fashion. A social ant colony starts out with a single female, who, if she survives bird attacks or the marauding soldier ants of a competing colony, may live to raise her own colony. In a wolf pack of 10 different animals (Sierra Wolf Pack), the strongest and most healthy male and female will become the pack's Alpha leaders and breeders. One or two aggressive, but less dominant males, may decide to leave the pack and establish their packs. In human terms we can think of these lone wolves as Smith and Strang, cult-like figures in temperament, personality and ability to sway young females away from other packs, not an easy task given the stability and strength of established packs. But the lone wolves will try and sometimes, not often, one will succeed, and you have a new pack called the South Sierra Pack.

Diaspora Tribes

One thing the Sierra Wolf Pack nor the South Sierra Pack would tolerate is adopting a fringe pack into their tribe like large human cultures do by adopting smaller diaspora tribes that enjoy a symbiotic relationship with their larger host culture. Diaspora may be a new term for many since it usually refers to the dispersion of peoples from Africa during the Transatlantic Slave Trades, the expulsion of Jews from Jerusalem by the Romans, or the scattering of South American tribes by the Spaniards. Today the term applies to groups like the Mormons and Jews who are able to provide their followers with their own unique religious ideology, while happily immersed and benefiting a much large culture's ideology. In both cases, the diaspora tribes are good examples of sincere efforts to balance rights and responsibilities between two disparate ideologies.

Jewish communities are the oldest of diaspora cultures which, for several millennia, struggled to become a respectable nation with borders of their own, but for lack of enough gun powder and militia, they have become one of the most respected diaspora cultures. Their relatively small bourgeois, materialistic settlements scattered around the world started as small groups of farming Jews, who—sometime between 750 AD and 900 AD—left their fields in the Middle East, moved to settlements in big cities throughout the Byzantine Empire and began specializing in education-based professions.

Their historic practice of staying small and promoting reading, writing, and mathematical skills did them well so that, by the 12th and 13th centuries, Jews were the accepted money lenders in Spain, Portugal, England, France, Italy and Germany. Much of this success had to do with the Muslim takeover of the Iberian Peninsula (now Spain) in 711 AD. With the Muslims came their bankers the Jews with their religion and economic skills—a period known as the Golden Age of Jewish culture, lasting roughly from 800 to 1100 AD.

Over the centuries other diaspora cultures followed. Once firmly grounded in the wilderness of Utah in the mid-19th century, Joseph Smith's Mormons went on to challenge the Jewish people as 21st century leaders in the fields of academia, marketing and finance. Other small religious cultures like the hundreds of Amish and Mennonite horse-and-buggy settlements—made up of some 20-/30 families—reside, comfortably throughout the US and Canada. With more rigid religious standards and lifestyles controlling their movements, they are neither as economically or academically accomplished as the Mormons and Jews, yet, given the number of children who marry and remain within their cloistered habitat, they apparently are quite content with their STM lifestyles.

What the long, successful histories of these diaspora cultures offer America is a reminder that all successful cultures need not be mega monsters. Diaspora cultures show how small decentralized communities succeed. First, their members are all indoctrinated early and late and remain devoted to a common folklore and a devotional ideology. Next, devout followers are brought up among devout friends and relatives they respect and, together, promote strong educational and community service. More important, members respect the opportunities their host cultures offer and work hard to meet the rights and responsibilities of that culture.

Gang Cults

Marauding big-city gangs are a different story. For years, Mafia-like cults operated as organic parasites sucking up the life blood of Western democracies where, in some cultures like Mexico they operate with impunity and take on cultural status for their size, organizational skills and wealth.

The reason few if any politician care to address the gang problem is because roots of the problem are indigenous to cultural drift away from devotional community values in large cities. Many gang problems stems from the decay of traditional family life, where mothers and fathers are lost to long hours of tiring work, separation, or where 7 out of 10 black babies are born without fathers; the role indifferent corporate marketplaces play as soulless communities where everyone's a stranger; and schools and religions fail to channel student energy and interest in promoting family and community solidarity. It also doesn't help when industrialization destabilize decades-old, living standards by shipping production overseas.

Unmoored and their spiritual integrity lacking in any form, young men look for ways to assert a manly definition. Left to their own wits, they waste their energies on gaming, bars, escort services, motels, tattoo parlors, gyms or gangs. Gangs are a tribal leftover from paleolithic and historic times when men forged strong hunting and warring relationships, bonding's many men still find necessary. For those isolated, energetic and demanding of male bonding or a sense of chivalry, they find camaraderie in gangs.

The chivalry aspect is a leftover when strong, young men were groomed as warriors, went into battle and fought bravely for king and queen. Men who now become professional gang members. Unlike their knightly ancestors who came home with booty and honor, nearly all gang members end up with a history of drugs and alcohol abuse, along with long criminal records. Many leave behind children who, lacking father figures, follow in their father's footsteps.

Where larger communities become too impersonal, gangs become vigilante in nature and, like the Mafia, make their living and reputations by providing the community with illegal services and protection. In US cities like Chicago, Los Angeles, St. Louis and Baltimore, gangs can rack up thousands of murders each year. South of the border, Mexican cartels from 2007 through 2014 killed over 164,000 people, 22,600 in 2016, 23,000 in 2017 and over 30,000 in 2018.

Since the purpose of tribalism is competition, aggressive behaviors were essential for tribal survival. Hence, one of the essentials all social species evolved was a percentage of the male population as a warrior class for defensive and offensive purposes. One need not search too far to note social ants, elephants, lions, monkeys and killer whales all have their warriors. As a rule, these individuals are born aggressive, strong, adventurous and more willing to risk life and limb to protect the tribe and vanquish the enemy. Trouble is, unlike the hundreds of Amish and Mennonite diaspora tribes living in harmony in North America, these inhouse tribal gangs create only discord for host tribes.

Chapter 7

ADVANCED CITY STATES
-FRACTAL BIOLOGY-

*To form groups, drawing visceral comfort and
pride from familiar fellowship, and to defend the
group enthusiastically from rival groups, these
are the absolute universals of human nature and
of culture.*

-Edward Wilson

The STM was a social contract, a set pattern of thinking that took over a million years to perfect, illustrating those tribal qualities that distinguish humans from other animals: freedom, equity, trust, cooperation, community, reasoned dialogue and solidarity; a *Community Mandate* that did not extend to neighboring tribes and limited individual rights; a Darwinian contract where competition is the mediator between who wins and who loses. Since it was a successful process, we can assume, under today's standards, it was both stable and tribally moral.

For hunter-gatherers, the problem of individuals achieving freedom and equity within such a context was not a serious one to overcome. On the whole, personal equity in terms of freedom, status and resource was desirable but not altogether necessary. More important was the comfort and security that consensus between friends and relatives provided, for it was through strong alliances that security and survival lay.

As a result, tribal prosperity was spectacular to the point where success became the downfall of the STM, its democratic dominance subjugated to various forms of governing hierarchies that germinated and matured roughly ten thousand years ago with the rise of mega-cultures in China, the Middle East and North African. Throughout this period, the God Module became more sophisticated as kinship and friendship bonding became less community driven and more power driven, giving rise to a hierarchy of needs and wants, the Haves and the Haveless.

Roughly 30,000 years ago our ancestors began leaving behind records of their activities in religious practices, art, writing, clothing, tools, and advanced shelters. As time went by and technology improved, a few settlements around the Mediterranean grew larger as they learned to tame wild animals and grow wild plants, allowing for more sedentary lifestyles. Simultaneously, the whole cultural complexion changed when labor and alliance became more diversified, unstable, and impersonal as ancestral linkages were lost.

Examples of these governing hierarchies are everywhere. The Egyptian civilization prospered for some six thousand years under autocratic rule. Even though the vast majority of its population remained illiterate for centuries, countless millions lived relatively stable lives governed by echelons of rulers and priests. Today, Egypt is still under military rule, having survived the 2012 Arab Spring effort for democratic rule.

Several thousand years of secular and theocratic tribalism by the Incas, Mayans and Aztecs came to a halt with the conquest of their states by Spain in the late 15th and early 16th centuries. In contrast, theocratic rule with a Christian flavor continued in Europe until well into the 17th century and continues today throughout Asia, Indonesia and the Middle East with an Islamic twist to Christianity by Muhammad in the 7th century.

Although autocratic tribalism is far from democratic, the cultural standards instituted were considered ethical, moral and normal behaviors at the time, otherwise the cultures could not have survived for as long as they did. Essentially, absolutism is the best example of addictive minds and God Modules working to suppress contrary views via compassion, fear, intimidation, rationalization, and obfuscation. No one group or individual in our remote past masterminded such a top-down model, it merely evolved as the most efficient pecking-order process for handling large numbers of humans with active Freedom/Equity Mandates. In simple terms, police-states standards, generated by secular and/or religious codes and creeds, became the governing models in complex cultures until the Enlightenment. In like manner, these different historic tribes, cobbled together language and law, science, technology and sociology into ever-larger cultures.

Although each tribe had its own unique qualities, all followed an assembly-line process describe as 'fractal biology' to grow both physically and psychologically. Fractals are complex patterns made up entirely of copies of successful genes from past generations. Once a genetic process has shown itself successful, more complex creatures or cultures expand the process and develop more efficient patterns of growth with the same base components. Such revisions can be seen with the eye, ear and nose as they evolved from lower species of vertebrates to more complex vertebrates. In each case, long established neural-related modules become genetically expanded upon as individuals with those traits leave behind more offspring. The same is true with cultural features as well, including the God Module.

Urban/Regional Design

Urbanization was a radical shift from the STM, not only in lifestyle, but also in social organization. Food production was organized to generate stored surpluses, permitting economic specialization and social stratification. Surpluses were used to feed tiers of chiefs, bureaucrats and other elites. No longer were all able-bodied individuals needed to hunt and forage. Some used their non-food-producing skills and knowledge as scribes, soldiers, artisans, engineers, architects or teachers. Those of a more contemplative nature became the philosophers, shamans and priests of their age. Over time cultural traits like cooperation, compliance and planning—forged to perfection at clan and tribe level—were used in forming powerful alliances between individuals sharing similar interests in education, politics, engineering, architecture, medicine, religion, warring and the like.

On a cultural level, fractal biology is most evident in urban and regional design where cities developed along hierarchical lines with markets and businesses flourishing near city centers. Radiating out from the central core were rings of buildings housing bureaucratic work centers, homes of the elite and other functionaries. Farther out were the homes of commoners and farmers. With minor differences, each of the more advanced cultures had a ruling class and priests; bureaucrats and merchants; rich and poor; thinkers and doers; slackers and sinners; monuments and markets; warriors and hunters; master builders and architects; those who grew crops and those who raised animals; carvers of wood, stone and minerals; potters and metal workers; astronomers and calendar keepers.

To the detriment of many, oppression and inquisitions of one sort or another imposed on the poor, slaves and heathens were considered normal. In most cultures, slavery was an institution with slaves always in demand, since one could hardly expect 'the chosen' to shovel, rake or carry heavy stone to build monuments, roads, water canals, and sewer systems. In addition, no thinking person among the chosen would consider immolating him or herself before their Gods if slaves or infidels were readily available.

Urbanization provided for a vibrant geopolitical interaction as well. Access to unique resources—knowledge, metals, timber, shells and so forth—permitted community specialization resulting in trade with neighboring communities rich in other resources. Haim Ofek, in *Economic Origins of Human Behavior,* suggests that market trading was a key factor in human evolution since the Stone Age, important enough to be a key factor in man's increased brain size.

Exchange played the same role in cultural evolution that sex played in biological evolution. Where sex brings together and filters out genetic innovations in different organisms, trade brings together and filters out cultural innovations produced by different groups. Ofek believes the ability to calculate the relative value of "distinct commodities" like fire, Stone Age tools and beads, helped expansion of the human neocortex. He also believes that trade in herded animals permitted cultivation of crops to extend geographically. "This specialization allowed new kinds of resources to be exploited, thereby increasing the number of individuals that can be supported in an area while extending our species' geographic range."

Once tribes get too large and neighborly ties fail to override the Freedom/Equity Mandate, elites quickly learned to use the supernatural powers of religion as a divinity mantle to quell envy, resentment and revolt between the Haves and the Haveless. For example, there are numerous accounts by Romans describing Druids (members of an ancient pre-Christian order) as the only ones in Celtic cultures to judge, punish and reward. Should someone fail to respect their decision, they had the power to exclude that individual from all public and religious services an early form of excommunication. In short, humanities' inherent desire for freedom and equity would now be defined and administered by a hierarchy of elite bureaucrats.

Tribal Idols

This transfer of power to recognized secular leaders and priests was a crucial tribal advancement because it led to social order where elites, in return for status, offered protection, helped distribute resources, and act as reservoirs of cultural knowledge. More important, they established and enforced a moral framework with a governing ideology and, in the process, became the iconic reflection of that ideology.

Idol Addiction

An interesting side-note to idol addiction is the *staying power* it can have on the human mind once a leader reaches idol status. Interesting because, whether president, monarch or high priest, these icons became the embodiment of tribal pride and the focus of God Module energy, with the ability to channel that energy into codes and creeds that moved the population in mass during times of real or perceived crisis. In the highly emotional process, the iconic leader can have an indelible impact on the human mind that may endure for generation regardless of negative impact of his/her policies.

For example, in the early 20th century, Vadimir Lenin and the Bolsheviks (The people's Communist Party) replaced the three-century-old-decaying Romanovs dynasty and set in motion democratic governing by the proletariat working class. The Bolsheviks were not the largest political sect in Russia at the time, but they were the most passionate and aggressive. After Lenin's death in 1926, Stalin took over the reins and refocused Lenin's vision of world transformation to a national resettlement program (Russian Korenizaya Resettlement) in which the hundreds of small, paleolithic-like tribes scattered throughout the vast expanses of the Russian Empire, would be assigned national status.

Within these nation states, each ethnic minority, however small, was granted its own national territory where it enjoyed a certain degree of autonomy, with recognized leaders. If lacking in national standards, each sect was then compelled to develop a written national language; establish national schools, train native teachers, and print books written in the native language that defined ethnic values and standards, within the context of the ideology of Mother Russia. The goal: a unified, stable form of government, defined by rapid urbanization, industrialization, and commerce, an older rendition of modern globalization, Russian style.

When the rapid re-organization showed signs of failure, Stalin set out looking for scapegoats to blame. An amoral psychopath and paranoid, Stalin found scapegoats for his failures everywhere, and, over a period of 30 years carried out purges, manufactured famines, forced displacement of thousands of villages, imprisoned in labor camps, tortured, mass murdered and massacred. It was a death toll estimated to be somewhere around 20-30 million. The Russian literary giant, Aleksandr Solzhenitsyn, estimates the number could have been 62 million.

The point here is to show there's no better example of just how susceptible the human mind is to idol worship than the poling in Russia over the last 80 years showing Stalin still ranking number 1, or at worse number 2, as the greatest of all Russian leaders. The logic for such an irony must lie somewhere with God Modules that permit irrational pathology to register in the tribal mind as righteous logic and blinds the mind to contrary, sane behavior. Time and time again, we see the duplicity humans must deal with when forced to examine behavior from the inside or outside the ideological bubble.

Fractal Codes–Creeds-Rights & Responsibilities

There is no better example of the God Module as equal-opportunity employer than its ability—century after century, millennium after millennium—to capture, bind and blind young children born into large tribes with prescribed rights and responsibilities. Whatever rights accrued are entitlements bestowed by the culture, whatever responsibilities expected are culturally defined duties enforced by codes and creeds. These defined rights and responsibilities, codes and creeds what the German philosopher Immanuel Kant called 'regulative principles' become the accepted ethical standards for individuals in their search for status and recognition within the tribe. They are birthrights, an inheritance sanctioned by secular or religious beliefs that program citizens into conforming to agreed-upon norms of conduct.

Compare, for example, the self-image and reality model of a Taliban girl in Afghanistan who is trained from childhood (cognitive capture) to be good and moral within the ethical constraints (regulative principles) of her culture. To this end, she will probably be a pious, illiterate childbearing homemaker, subservient to men in all respects. On the other hand, consider an American girl who is trained from childhood (cognitive capture) to be good and moral within the ethical constraints (regulative principles) of her culture. To that end she will probably be less pious, literate, independent and subservient to no one. In both cases, the child is born with a cluster of neural modules designed around language, sex and other behaviors programmed around traditional values her culture considers equitable and moral social norms. In both cases, the emerging young woman will find self-esteem, freedom and autonomy along with a satisfying self-image among the moral dictates of her culture. And both will look upon the other as living within a reality model that is rather strange and distorted by her cognitive bias and blindness.

Nepotism-Cronyism-10/20% Rule–Groupthink

Throughout these cultural advances, leaders learned how to deal with freedom and equity mandate's that remained embedded in our neural circuitry since Paleolithic times. Although science has little direct molecular knowledge of just how God Modules are energized within the brain itself, the universal role nepotism, cronyism, patronage and groupthink play in controlling all ideologies, is evidence of the module's presence and tenacity to balance rights and responsibilities. Simply put, these behaviors reflect fractal biology at work as leaders around the world use blood bonds between family and relatives as well as tribal belief bonds between friends who share similar values, folklore, religious or secular ideologies.

The most dependable source of help and devotion usually comes from blood relatives. For centuries, Egyptian dynasties were controlled by incestuous inbreeding until that practice was found to be biologically dangerous. Throughout the Middle Ages, social counterparts in Europe consolidated their power by inbreeding between royal families and, thereby, extending their divine bloodline between dynasties. Nepotism of a record scale in modern times, must be held by the House of Saud of Saudi Arabia. According to *Wikipedia*, Abdulaziz Ibn Saud united nearly all of central Arabia in 1932 into the Kingdom of Saudi Arabia. As King he had 22 wives, many daughters and 45 sons. The king died in 1953 but, by 2015, his direct bloodline was composed of some 15,000 family members with the majority of power and wealth controlled by some 2,000 family members. That is patronage and nepotism on a really grand scale. Abdulaziz Ibn Saud was, obviously, a very busy man.

Another essential pecking-order tool in a leader's arsenal is cronyism, the role radicalized friends and belief brothers play in controlling a political agenda. Given that a degree of freewill and social responsibility is lost when addictive minds attach themselves to ideologies, core crony radicals can be depended upon to do the 'heavy lifting,' the 'dirty work' of controlling and marginalizing the opposition where the less devote will not. Cronyism is usually achieved by simply identifying those zealots and activists who share the same liberal or conservative beliefs and rewarding the affection in any number of appealing ways. One need only study the increased pattern of family wealth of many elected to congress in Washington DC to appreciate the value of nepotism and cronyism.

There is evidence to suggest this range of devotional zeal that manifests itself in any large political group is an inherent process with roughly 50 percent displaying a liberal bent, and 50 percent with a conservative bent. Within those two populations, some ten percent of membership will show zealous (radical) behavior; an additional ten percent function as dependable activists; leaving a moderate 30 percent "base" membership. The result is a core 20-percent of dependable workers in each party such as in the Democrat and Republican parties in the US, today. That leaves some sixty percent of the population as liberal/conservative moderates who could sway left or right depending on which side is able to control their interests over time.

Given the lopsided ratio of moderates to activists, one would think moderates rule the day, but they do not. What's so fascinating about the 10/20 percent rate of zealots and dependable activists is that, in most all cases, they are spiritually devoted and aggressive enough to dominate the majority and, in the process, make the views and values of the majority often irrelevant. Such minority rule is so pervasive to warrant its own designation as the "10/20 Percent Rule." Germany and Italy during and before World War II were governed by some seven-percent zealot fascist. At the same time, two percent of zealot communists controlled Russia's massive population. Modern Islamic Egypt is governed by a small militia, and Syria and Iraq by Muslim minorities. Prior to the 2013 revolt, Ukraine was governed by an oligarchy of elite businessmen. Much of the power in the US lies with a collection of 10/20 percenters: the politicians in Washington, national media outlets and CEOs representing industries, unions and corporations that, together, drive the whole asymmetrical system.

Although nepotism and cronyism play dominant roles in societies no matter how small the unit, they were not enough to maintain stability in very large groups facing powerful adversaries. Given the distorted ratio of leadership of some 20 percent to a wayward population of some 60 percent, "groupthink" became organic in mobilizing and focusing God Module energy. Over time, leaders learned to use classic biased indoctrination strategies—public education and media—to culturally capture and induce cognitive bias and blindness into their populations.

With indoctrination carried out consistently, from birth to late adolescence and enforced by fear of death from a despotic regime, a population can be programmed to act as radical drones as is the case with North Korea. With indoctrination carried out consistently, from birth to late teens and enforced by emotional religious reverence, a large percentage of a population can be programmed to act like modest acolytes as with most great religions and democracies. With indoctrination carried out daily from birth to death and enforced daily by religious zealots who believe non-believers should be beheaded fellow Muslims included should they question the zealot's interpretation of the Quran a murderous percentage of a population can be programmed to act as executioners as with numerous radical Muslim factions, today.

Such organically programmed tribes can operate more efficiently by allowing the cognitively smart and aggressive 10/20 percenters to produce a cult fidelity from supporters who will swarm by the thousands with mob brutality, if needed, to ensure their demands are carried out. Such devotion comes with powerful emotional adhesives binding core beliefs to God Modules that permit believers to operate on a higher moral plane than nonbelievers. It means some values are considered not just worthy but sacrosanct. It means pleasure and reward in toeing the tribal line or guilt, fear and pain with their abdication. It means total rejection of logic, freewill and objectivity. It means blind faith to the point of self-sacrifice. Think of the eight-hundred thousand union and confederate soldiers who died in the Civil War, many tramping, stoically headlong, side by side, into deadly cross-fire from barricaded enemy a mere hundred yards away. That is flocking, herding, groupthink on a grand, spiritualized scale any leader would be content to witness.

This flocking/herding instinct is so fundamental to social order that all social species exhibit it in one form or another. Therefore, it's not surprising to hear secular and religious leaders refer to their constituency as flocks. A related vestigial behavior called 'unconscious synchrony' is where humans are easily moved to dance, yawn, laugh, sway to music, or cry because they see friends dance, yawn, laugh, sway, or cry. There is even a body of evidence showing such behavior exists in large stock markets as irrational emotions drive the buying bubble ever larger. At some point, the bubble starts to disintegrate, and the herd begins frantic selling.

Today we consider such behaviors leftovers from a time when quick herd response was essential for individuals to function as a unit. The odds of survival for those choosing not to run when others ran or not to eat and sleep when others ate and slept were slim. Though we dare not admit it, herding, groupthink, idol worship and unconscious synchrony continue to play major political roles as survival tools. One need only attend a political convention to see how laughing, dancing, crying, yawning and winking at a possible bed mate helps provide the emotional fabric in keeping the political bubble fresh and durable.

Only in the last decade or so has the media found it helpful to reference such infectious behavior as cultural bubbles, with some bursting as quickly as they form. In June of 2003, noted journalist Thomas L. Friedman wrote an article in *The New York Times* suggesting that the main reason for the Iraq War was to burst the terrorism bubble that the world had come to accept as appropriate behavior in partisan warfare. In a 2004 book titled *The Bubble of American Supremacy*, George Soros attacks President George W. Bush's actions after 9/11 as abusive and symptomatic of a foreign policy designed to run roughshod over other nations.

Like stock market behavior, bubble behavior in politics begins and ends with frenzied periods of politicking as the bubble grows, followed by a frenzied period of fear when the bubble is threatened. Part 5 will go into great detail describing the political panic that occurred after the Trump presidency; the deceptive tactics attempting to destroy his presidency; and, the extreme hatred and resolve to have him impeached as a last resort.

Obviously cognitive capture via nepotism, cronyism, patronage and groupthink are two-edged swords, asset or debit, moral or amoral, depending on whether one is standing inside or outside the ideology bubble. As bonding agents, they keep organizations sharp, focused and to a degree, comfortable, yet, outside the bubble, the prospects for conflict exist, especially when the aggrieved energize their God Modules to find ways of bridging the gap between the Have and the Haveless.

Chapter 8

NUMBER of GOVERNING MODELS

Tribes have distinctive moral commitments, typically religious ones, whereby moral authority is vested in local individuals, texts, traditions, and deities that other groups don't recognize as authoritative.

- Christopher Hitchens

To better understand the prevailing effect of autocratic and democratic tribes struggling to define themselves, it's useful to look back in history and examine just how many governing formats have proven successful in the last 30,000 years since humanity left the STM behind as an extremely successful form of governing. To get there it's necessary to examine the biology of how good ideas live or die.

If science tells us human success is due to the political dynamics within and between tribes, then it's reasonable to assume that humans matter only in groups, and groups matter only if they act or don't act by internalizing and using their cognitive skills to aggressively generate new ideas to ensure their success, a process known as "cognitive fluidity," the motivating mechanism in cultural evolution.

A major argument against cultural evolution by way of natural selection is the view there was insufficient time for natural selection to work out the many differences between modern and Stone Age cultures with genetic diversity alone. Early man was believed to be too isolated and mobile to build efficient cultures. An emerging theory dispelling this charge, claims cultural evolution is driven less by genes and more by the interaction of good ideas, the multiplication of which increased dramatically with the discovery of agriculture and animal husbandry approximately 11,000 years ago.

The first record of categorizing ideas was carried out by the Greek Aristotle, who in 350 BC claimed humans exhibit three basic methods of thinking: episteme (scientific), techne (technological) and a practical, political process labeled "phronesis." Both science and technological thinking he characterized as being based on universal invariables, context-dependent knowledge. In other words, variables that are changeless and consistent throughout time, like gravity or the rotation of the planets around the sun.

Once settled around farming communities, humans used these-two styles in a dynamic, diversified fashion and thereby speeded up the process of cultural evolution. Depending primarily on variations in geography, different cultures acquired food production at different times. Some, such as aboriginal Australians, never acquired it at all. Out of this urbane mix came an endless supply of ideas, many of which proved exceedingly advantageous as trade in different products gave rise to a burgeoning middle class of clever tradesmen meeting ever-changing demands.

Writing came into existence about 4,000 BC but did not reach its present methodical and analytical form until around 700 BC with the Greeks. Although people in South America, Mesopotamia, China, and Egypt recorded events in graphic form, none linked the events with details of the process or theory involved. Moreover, the Greeks recorded their thoughts in written form that could be stored, studied, easily duplicated and improved upon. From that time onward there was a progressive stream of technological and theoretical developments in the various fields of science, and metaphysics, including religion.

Approximately 15,000 years ago the wolf was domesticated in East Asia. By 9,000 BC, wheat and barley were being cultivated in the Middle East; flax in Mexico around 7,000 BC, with lentils, citrus fruits, peaches, avocado, date palms, cotton, millet and squash grown a few thousand years later. By 5,000 BC, Sumerians in the Fertile Crescent perfected the art of writing, made jewelry and cosmetics, built libraries to house their books and institutionalized slavery, law, banking and complex clerical systems. At the same time, the first horse was domesticated in the Ukraine as irrigation and the use of mortar for casting cement were discovered in Mesopotamia, along with mummification techniques. Somewhere around 4,000 BC, the plow and high-temperature kilns for firing bricks, pottery, smelting copper, silver and gold were in use.

Aristotle argued the third thinking style, "Phronesis," is a thoughtful, reflective, emotional process that allowed for individuals to debate and solve polarizing issues dealing with flexible variables that have a moral, ethical, metaphysical context. Essentially political variables like tribal ideologies composed of *spiritualized variables* that only make sense from inside the ideological bubble. Variables that tribes outside the bubble finds amoral and spiritual nonsense.

Therefore, while Aristotle found truth in logic devoid of emotion, myth, and the arbitrary linkage to cause and effect, he nonetheless, realized that since ethics have a moral context, they need not reflect universal behaviors. The moralized behavior can be whatever a person wants it to be. That's the beauty of phronetic reasoning, it brings the practical, reasoning brain and the more intuitive, emotional reptilian brain together at solving everyday problems. If it's practical and works, do it!

Neurologists went on to define such reasoning memes as 'psychogenes' having inheritance value and the ability to replicate themselves with individuals taking an *emotionally active role* in the process. God Modules fall in here. We can think of a God Module as a tribal manifestation of a psychogene, a cluster of nerves organized to help humans promote an ideology. It's this active role that's of interest here because it adds substance to the argument that addictive minds with emotionally charged God Modules are necessary for ideologies to take on lives of their own, a driving predatory force to insure their own survivals.

Without the ability to accumulate and hybridize ideas, people would never have had settled communities or invented kilns and libraries to hold their books, ideas that set the stage for the great cosmopolitan cities to come. Only about 2,000 generations stand between our relatives back then and us today. From an evolutionary standpoint that may not sound like much time for cultural evolution to occur, but if the selective pressure is strong enough, and non-adaptive ideas are weeded out fast enough, cultural evolution can proceed rapidly, and it did.

Recently, a number of scientists picked up on this evolving idea dynamic and proposed the theory that ideas function in a fashion somewhat parallel to genes. This relatively new science of interactive ideas called "Memetics" is defined as the ideas, knowledge, beliefs, values and ideologies held by individuals and cultures. Memes acts as a unit for carrying cultural ideas, symbols, or practices that can be transmitted from one mind to another through writing, speech, gestures, rituals. Supporters of the concept regard memes as cultural analogues to genes in that they self-replicate, mutate, and respond to selective environmental pressures.

What makes the evolution of God Module memes so compelling a tribal-interest is the fact that, while millions of SciTeck ideas are with us today, *only two (2) basic governing models evolved,* autocratic and democratic. It's compelling also to realize that, for the first million years or so, democracy prevailed with the STM and, for most of the next 30,000-historic years, autocratic rule was most successful. Only in the last few hundred years has there been a drift toward the Marxist democratic model and capitalist democratic model with these years marked by extreme colonial destruction, wars, terrorism and tribal infighting.

Chapter 9

HINDUISM

My precious brain Sees, Hears, Promotes self-interest; While.......My tribal brain Pools self-interest into many Threads of compassion, bias and conflict; Within and Without.

-Author

Just how tied social organism are to tribal behaviors is best illustrated by comparing the hierarchy of an ant colony to that of India's caste system. One species of social ants, the *Attini*, show a variety of body-style starting with the large egg-laying Queen who, in tribal parlance is the colonies heart and soul. Next powerful are the large Majors, the soldiers, followed by the most abundant Mediae, infertile females of medium size that forage and harvest plant materials. The all-purpose Minors come next. Their jobs are to masticate plants for larvae, construct tunnels, and clean. Finally come the small Males who only exist for a short period of time for reproduction purposes. Since the concepts of morality and diversity do not exist in ant culture, only one male will get to mate, and that will be with the queen, and them die. Unlike King Abdulaziz Ibn Saud of Saudi Arabia, who was a very happy man, I don't believe these males are very happy males.

Similar cast systems are evident among Eastern nations that practice Hinduism and Buddhism placing man in harmony with nature that have flourished for thousands of years. A major reason for India's longevity is tied to the Hindu religion. While its admirers in the West view Hindu rejection of materialism, its oneness with nature and its striving for nirvana in a selfish world commendable, one of its basic tenets states that all men are created unequal.

For more than 1500 years, this core precept has succeeded in separating Indian culture into five groups. At the top are the Brahmans, elite intellectuals, priests and teachers. Next are the Kshatriyas, rulers and soldiers. A third group, the Vaisyas, include merchants and traders, while the Sudras encompass the laboring class. At the very bottom of the social heap are the millions of Dalits, the "Untouchables" who do the cleaning.

While Hinduism is a classic example of tribalism it's also a classic example of the spiritualized rationalization needed to justify India devotion to cattle, peacocks, mice, monkeys, tigers, and elephants over Untouchables. Or, the logic that Hinduism is a convenience to the poor because it tells them to shun their earthly desires, work hard to please, build up a positive karma, and be content with their humiliating state in life so that, in the end, each might be reincarnated as a Brahman or a Kshatriya or, perhaps, a Sudra.

So successful has the spiritualized segregation been that studies show India's ruling class to be more genetically related to light-skinned Aryans from Iran—who are theorized to have settled India thousands of years ago—than to any class below. As such, Hinduism is just as effective in gaming conformity as fear generated by more tyrannical states. After World War II, Mahatma Gandhi, the leader of India's independence movement from British rule, introduced democracy and attempted to eradicate the unjust social aspects of the caste system. Himself a member of the Vaisya caste, Gandhi was influential in having India's constitution ban the category of Untouchables. Yet the age-old practice remains especially in the countryside.

A tribal historian looking in with an impartial eye might conclude: "Amazing! Spiritual rationalization at it best." Not only is the Indian government not recognized as repressive, but such amoral, repression is considered normal, spiritually sanctioned and, for the most part, beyond reproach. In addition, India has been recognized as progressive and politically democratic. Yet, given its longevity, it's very difficult to argue for the efficiency of a divinity module elevating cattle and elite while curbing the civil rights of millions of humans. Like its sacred cow, Hinduism provides a certain legitimacy—a something of value—to the Indian culture that is itself, untouchable.

The reality is all large modern cultures operate on the caste system with a small number of leaders at the top, followed by military, business elite, workers, and garbage men. The only difference is their secular or religious ideologies do not, like India's, provide absolution, and rewards for the less fortunate in an afterlife. That is unless your tribe believes in a heaven.

Obviously, the key to understanding this rather bizarre state of affairs, is recognizing the enigmatic nature of the God-module to not only trump man's need for freedom and equity, but its incredible ability to sustain our inherent need for duplicity. How else do we explain people who are intolerant of Christianity yet tolerant of Islam; intolerant of liberals yet tolerant of conservatives; intolerant of untouchables yet tolerant of cows, peacocks, mice, monkeys, tigers, and elephants?

One need not pick on Christians or Muslims or Hindus to find autocrats using religious dogma to stifle freedom and equity. No one can dispute the stabilizing effect that codes and commandments have on civilization. Without them we would be back living in caves roasting only chestnuts, given mammoth with their steaks, were killed off long ago. Nonetheless, religion could not exist if it did not support the existing needs of the state by casting a blind eye toward human-right infractions.

You need only watch the nightly news for daily examples in the US of widespread hypocrisy, denial and duplicity gussied up as situational ethics that soothes the ever-present demands of cognitive dissonance. Take, for example, comments made during a single October 14, 2005, news cycle when Louis Farrakhan, leader of The Nation of

Islam, told Fox News he received inspiration for many of his activities from deceased black leaders he met when beamed up to a spaceship. Or when Pat Robertson, a Southern Baptist minister and founder of the Christian Broadcasting Network, suggested Hurricane Katrina, the devastating earthquake that killed some 87,000 in Pakistan and Afghanistan, and the tsunami that ravaged Indonesia killing some 200,000, might indicate the biblical Judgment Day was near. Or, on directions from Pope Benedict XVI, Cardinal Andrea Gemma re-instituted a program to train priests in the ancient practice of exorcism.

If I were to spout such unfounded proclamations, any doctor would consider me psychotic or at the least delusional. Yet, Mr. Farrakhan, Mr. Robertson, Pope Benedict, and Cardinal Gemma are held in high esteem, and, because these major players help hold our social fabric together, their beliefs are considered rational because, like India's sacred cows, their clairvoyant views offer something of value and are therefore beyond reproach. These behaviors are wonderful examples of society subscribing to the cognitive fluidity rule claiming rationalization and denial are essential in keeping the social fabric from unraveling.

The general theory behind the excessive devotion religion demands is that complex cultures could not survive unless there were some mechanisms guiding their moral authority to override humanity's base behaviors. While research into this neural makeup is fairly new, evidence of mythical gods and goddesses restraining individual interests predates written history. The main concept people should take away from any study of tribalism is that rationalization and its partner obfuscation became the fundamental mind tools around which social intelligence revolves.

Our ability to ignore or accept mendacity and duplicity provides the stimulus and resolve so necessary for political systems to work. If our ancestors had to stop and moralize over every injustice, they would never have survived. The healthy solution to such a conundrum was to ignore or justify the problem in some fashion and move on.

Ignoring and suppressing unwanted information allowed our ancestors to operate unencumbered by moral constraints, a valuable trait
for individuals who found it necessary to safeguard their emotional
energy to ensure survival in an amoral world. Much more on this biology, later.

Chapter 10
CHRISTIANITY

*Faith is to believe in what we cannot see, and the
reward of this faith is to see what we believe*
                                                    - St. Augustine

Although Greece and Rome flirted with democratic rule, their lack of a unifying, devotional ideology generated serious infighting and wars that destabilized, and in the case of Rome, returned rule by emperors. With the birth and death of Jesus Christ, social values shifted to one-god religions throughout the continent and north Africa. The two most fascinating one-god models that gained deep spiritual roots, and mature cult status during medieval times, are known today as Christianity and Islam, two religions believing in the same God.

Like their paleolithic ancestors who used a One-for-All philosophy to drive their small democratic ideologies, Christianity and Islam also used the One-for-All philosophy to capture, bias and blind. But there was one exception, vengeful gods were added to codes and creeds to certify devotion as governing became more autocratic. Their autocratic models are especially fascinating because, although Christians and Muslims have been at odds for centuries, their shared heritage provided each with an extremely powerful, emotional foundation on which their inherent God Modules were super-energized by an early Christian meme, the "Image of God thesis" that proposed humans were made in the very image of God! It was a God Module "Big Bang."

There probably is no better example of God Module power and its addictive ability to capture human minds than the marriage of paleolithic God Modules with the Image of God Thesis. As described by early Christian theologians, the thesis defines humans as rational beings made in the Image of God and, therefore, spiritually elevated above the rest of creation.

This marriage of two established memes working harmoniously to facilitate their own survival resulted in a remarkable twist of human destiny. Remarkable because the union permitted the already ingrained, highly energized and highly successful God Module of tribal man to be super-charged by an appealing belief claiming tribal man was made in the image of an omniscient being. More important, this being was no larger-than-life Zeus or Buddha.

No!

No!

No!

This was a *supreme being, divinely human* in his ability to feel pain, get angry, show empathy and compassion, fight for the underdog and suffer the consequences. He was essentially tribal man, yet super-human; a man, yet the one and only God. As a result, the knowledge of being made in the image of such an almighty deity placed tribal members of both religions on a much higher moral plane than non-believers. Thereby making possible an acceptable indifference to the exploitation of nonbelievers and nature. So blessed, it sanctioned, by divine decree, those tribal mandates that generate the moral authority to exploit at all costs and with no regret. For better or worse, the two religious ideologies that emerged from this union dominate the world's political landscape to this very day.

Speaking in evolutionary terms, the union was one of those Great Leaps Forward, one of those Big Bangs that scientists use to describe extraordinary transformations in the human condition. And, like all Great Leaps Forward, it had support in a long-held science narrative fostered by early Greek philosophers, like Plato, who believed man had an evil nature and a rational divine nature that governed all aspects of his behavior. It must be understood that, given the scientific process was not yet discovered, the only rational reasoning at this time came from philosophers like Plato, who's logic was considered reliable fact, truth beyond contradiction in accordance with all known evidence.

While Plato and other early philosophers believed in supreme beings, they at first felt gods had no place in civics and attempted to discredit myth-based governance by creating ethical secular systems. In the end, however, they came to realize that the mass of society was *controlled more by spiritualized reasoning* than by informed, deductive reasoning. Consequently, these philosophers acknowledged the emotional power of myth and granted *any form of governance to be a dual secular, religious effort.*

Plato's student, Aristotle preached an altogether different viewpoint. The son of a physician, Aristotle was more scientific and claimed reasoned ideas arrived in our minds through the senses. He believed that the only way to perceive reality was through accurate observation and inductive reasoning, therefore, rational thought should govern. His top-down philosophy a man-centered philosophy less the deity became known as "Naturalism" where metaphysical values and design, while not necessarily invalid, are excluded from consideration. Nonetheless, he realized that since ethics have a social context, they need not reflect universal norms, rather thoughtful reflections of tribal standards.

Saint Augustine, who developed the Christian doctrines of original sin and divine grace, divine sovereignty and predestination was another influential intellectual to provide 'scientific' momentum to the thesis. He used the writings of Plato, Plotinus and Origen to show that the core elements of Christianity were actually supported by a "Reasoned Scripture," a view that continued into the seventh century with the teaching of Muhammad and well into the fourteenth century with the writings of St. Thomas Aquinas.

All of these profound thinkers felt humans were rational beings having intrinsic value, with a dignity that set them apart and above all other life forms along with a free-willed soul capable of an intellectual reality above and beyond physical reality. At a time when sound reasoning was religion based, their spiritual logic lent enormous credence to the man-over-nature view by declaring cause and effect the rightful domain of their God. After all, He created the world and everything in it, including Adam and Eve and Satan.

Over time, this 'reasoned' logic was woven into two slightly different narratives that would form the foundations of two formidable tribal civilizations, one with some 2.1 billion Christians as of 2017 and the other with some 2.2 billion Muslims. It was the beginning of religious tribalism on a truly grand scale.

As the Roman Empire declined and the Christian meme infected more people, so too did the predatory power of its God Modules to control competing ideologies, a power relying mainly on keeping all thought primarily mythical. Since myth, by definition, has no basis in reality and therefore not subject to attrition by objective logic, its existence can only be maintained by suppressing objective study and debate. Such was the case under the Catholic Church's commanding reach. Never was the power of rationalization more evident than in the period from approximately 350 to 1400 AD in Western Europe. It was then, that the Catholic Church enjoyed a monopoly in education, protected by a virtual wall of compliance in which all men of learning (the media of their day) were priests and all learning and intellectual activities in Western Europe were pursued within a firmly established religious context.

For centuries after Roman legions marched across Europe the roads and harbors, they built were still the best to be found throughout the continent and British Isles. Except for the design and construction of magnificent cathedrals and the introduction of the waterwheel and windmill, there was no invention of significance. Basic farming tools remained scythes, sickles, pitch forks, and rakes. The great library of Alexandria was burned three times by the Romans and Muslims, a library that once held up to 500,000 volumes covering all aspects of life in the ancient world were lost.

Pertinent knowledge, like Aristotle's spherical theory of the Earth, was lost to medieval scholars who believed the world to be flat. Elementary understandings of the scientific process that started with the Greeks, like Herodotus and Thucydides, were forgotten as were Socrates's and Aristotle's writings on the scientific approach to knowledge stressing eyewitness evidence and the logic of multiple causes of events. Also forgotten was knowledge by the Greek architects Ictinus and Callicrates, who designed the beautifully powerful Parthenon in the Acropolis of Athens; writings by Epicurus, who taught the Universe was material and composed of indestructible matter called atoms; work by Herophilus, who performed the first recorded public dissection of the human body; and writings by the great physiologist Erasistratus describing brain anatomy. Also lost was Egyptian astronomer Ptolemy's calculations of the Earth's surface being twenty-five thousand miles in circumference, his partitioning of the globe into 360 degrees of latitude and longitude, as well as numerous Egyptian inventions to measure latitude and longitude. For all practical purposes, deductive and inductive reasoning was at a standstill in Europe. It was memetic predation on a massive scale.

The darkest of these times, roughly 400 to 1000 AD. were widely known as the Dark Ages. Because of its politically incorrect connotation, modern historians discarded the phrase Dark Ages and replaced it with the Age of Faith, although that era's effect on scientific thought was indeed, dark and dim. Literacy was scorned, so ignorance manifested itself in all forms of mythical obsessions. Witchcraft, sorcery, exorcism, lawlessness, corruption, inquisitions, and warfare were rampant. Famine and plague were recurring events, culminating in the Black Death that ravaged Europe during the 14th and 15th centuries. Although Christianity played a major role in Europe's cultural decline, it was the only common thread that offered some degree of earthly and eternal peace.

A wonderful, mild case of God Module predation occurred with a book written around 200 BC by the great intellectual Archimedes. Born in the city of Siracusa, Sicily, and educated in Egypt, Archimedes wrote extensively on geometry and anticipated much of what was to be described as calculus several thousand years later. In the field of mechanics, he defined the principle behind the level and invented the compound pulley as well as the hydraulic screw for raising water. He is best known for what is called Archimedes' principle, which he deduced one day while bathing. The story goes that, while in the tub, he noticed the water overflowing and surmised there might be a direct relationship between a body submerged and the volume of water displaced. After further experiments, he discovered that a body immersed in water loses weight equal to the volume weight of water displaced.

The essence of his work was explained in *The Method*. For a time, the book was meticulously copied by scribes, but was gradually lost to Western civilization during the Age of Faith. Sometime in the twelfth century, the last copy of *The Method* known to exist was washed and recycled by a Mideast scribe into a book of prayers. Then it lay hidden until an Englishman discovered it in a Constantinople library in 1912. Since then, slow and meticulous work has been carried out to decipher the written-over, painted-over, glued-over and otherwise washed-out words to their original meaning. For several thousand years, scientific principles of incredible value to mankind were lost to a ravenous religious meme.

While survival of the fittest among political ideologies may be an amoral process, the system works. For an ideology to work, it must be selfish. It must want to live for no other reason than to live and be sustained as an entity, just like its genetic counterparts. Mother Nature, in Her effort to bind-and-blind does not care if a leader's attempt at Christianity results in success or failure. If Archimedes' mathematical formulas are buried by a theocracy that burns heretics and their books, that's okay too. A lag time of two thousand years in understanding Archimedes' principle is meaningless to Mother Nature. Calculus and Christianity have meaning only if they succeed as ideas; if not, they are forgotten.

Chapter 11

ISLAM

Every religion is true one way or another. It is true when understood metaphorically. But when it gets stuck in its own interpreting them as facts, then you are in trouble.

— Joseph Campbell

Although arriving on the political scene much later in history, Islam has shown itself not only just as predatory, but more disciplined than Christianity. Given the fact that governing in Europe at the time was shared between popes and nobles, restraints among Christians were far from rigid, even for the clergy, and demands except during the Inquisition less enforceable. Not so with Islam. With Islam, the prophet Muhammad was able to convince Muslims that their scripture, the Quran—which he divined from periodic interventions with heavenly beings—was the reasoned, timeless word of Allah devoid of human interpretation and, therefore, invulnerable and demanding.

The single most important truth all leaders learn in cementing a relationship between themselves and the masses is to *condition, condition, condition* the human mind by repeated demands to express their devotion to the cause as often as leaders deem physically possible. From the beginning, then, Islam has been a more exacting religion with indoctrination starting early and prevailing throughout Muslim society, with Muslim men prostrating five times a day for prayer, along with all Muslims adhering to strict rules regarding education, drinking, eating, dressing, socializing, marriage and child rearing. Given the recurring indoctrination, zealot leaders were able to maintain a relatively aggressive, highly successful secular/religious culture well into the 21st century.

As the dominant force in the Middle East throughout the Middle Ages, Muslims also had control of the Holy Land, a controversial heritage they shared with the Christians and Jews that resulted in the Crusades. The Crusades are a good example of two great ideologies using their God Module addictions to ward off cognitive dissonance by killing and mutilating each other on an astonishing scale, a scale evident when malice to neighbors and devotion to deities were carried out in unison. In *The First Crusade*, Thomas Asbridge writes in great detail about the length to which crusaders (mainly French and Italian) went to sate their covetous impulses during the sack of Jerusalem in 1099.

> The plundering of Jerusalem proves one thing beyond contestation. In the minds of the crusaders, religious fervor, barbaric warfare and self-serving desire for material gain were not mutually exclusive experiences; they could all exist, entwined in the same time and space. So it was that, fresh from bloodthirsty slaughter (about 10,000 Saracens) and rapacious plundering, the French suddenly turned their hands to acts of worship and devotion.

Looking back, one is left wondering how the flame of religious devotion could continue to burn amid such a storm of violence. The answer is the addictive mind's ability to ignore gross hypocrisy and its steadfast ability for intolerance. With both sides advancing unrelenting propaganda over the centuries, memory of the Crusades was rehashed and refreshed to solidify the aversion between Europe and the Middle East, between Christian and Muslim. By the 13th century, the memory of the Crusades as a brutal and fanatical religious war had become embedded in the Muslim collective consciousness. In like manner, it became a unifying, triumphant social cause for Western society.

Hindus and Muslims fought for decades until India and Pakistan became separate states in 1947. Some seventy years later, the two countries are still bitter enemies. Recently, a compulsory goodwill was forced upon old ethnic factions in Bosnia, where unrest broke out in a civil war after the downfall of the Soviet Union. The essence of the conflict was longstanding hatred between Christians (Croats and Serbs) and Muslims.

Talk about God Module staying power. A thousand years after the first crusade, that long and bitter hatred is with us today, as evidenced by the 9/11 attacks on the Twin Towers; the never-ending Israeli-Palestinian conflict; the wars in Pakistan, Afghanistan, Syria, Yemen, Iraq and dozens of smaller Islamic wars around the world. And let us not forget the extreme radical groups like Al-Qaeda, Taliband, ISIL/ISIS, Al-Shabaab, Hamas, the Houthi in Yemem and Boko Haram in northern Africa that emerged in the late 20th century to challenge the old Sunni and Shiite guard. So rapid has been the turmoil in and around the Middle East that by 2013 it became difficult to keep track of who is killing who, with what and why.

Surely someone in this scenario should receive a "Distorted Reality Award," if for no other reason than to highlight the fact the three major religions Judaism, Christianity and Islam practice a rigorous monotheistic, man-over-nature philosophy presided over by the same deity. Islam teaches that Muhammad was the last in a series of prophets and messengers who was commissioned to preach the essential and eternal message of Islam. Where Islam differs from Christianity and Judaism is in the Christian belief that Jesus was not just a prophet like Muhammad, but also the Son of God. Consequently, the perceived mission of Islam is and has been to re-educate the ignorant Christians, Jews and other non-believers.

In static and traditional Muslim society, beliefs are more settled than not, leaving little room for debate. Diversity, relativism and equity do not exist as social moral precepts. It's a world in which most believers view the West as self-possessed, ungodly, debauched, arrogant, bigoted cultures in the process of destroying themselves. Much of the negative image comes from an unabridged and unbridled mobile Western media that supplies the globe with movies, rap music and television shows that offer hedonistic views of the West. On the other hand, Westerners view Muslims as stuck in a fundamentalist time warp where a small percentage of uncompromising fanatics, the 10/20 percenters, threatened by modernity opt to fight back.

Chapter 12

FEUDALISM THE DIVINE RIGHT OF KINGS

The metaphor of the king as the shepherd of his people goes back to anc2ent Egypt. Perhaps the use of this particular convention is due to the fact that, being stupid, affectionate, gregarious, and easily stampeded, the societies formed by sheep are most like human ones.

- Northrop Frye

Unlike the Mongols who were free of religious constraints, settled Mediterranean tribes like the Greeks and Romans appreciated the communal benefits deities offered in their attempt to restore democracy as a governing model after thousands of years of rule by monarchs and chiefs. Since the Greeks believed pure equity impossible, they tried a representative form of city-state democracy with the goal of preventing central authority. Sometimes their idea of shared rule resulted in governance by a limited group (oligarchy) and sometimes by the entire male population. In much the same way Romans flirted with representative democracy, and for a time with republicanism with senators providing leadership and Citizen Assemblies passing laws.

At one point in the 6th century BC, Rome's Citizen Assembly consisted of 193 representatives. Like the Greeks, Rome paid homage to the rights of the common man, but rarely lived up to these ideals. There was equity before the law, but the law was always skewed in favor of tribal elites, with lower classes and slaves left struggling as best they could for scraps of equity dribbling down from above, snippets of hope that eventually ignited into revolutionary change.

Later, under Feudalism, an elitist form of absolutism emerged where God Modules of monarchs took on deity status high above that of countless serfs and lesser nobles. During the 11th century, the feudal order throughout the region was composed of leaders, the monarchy; those who did the fighting, the nobles; those who prayed, the clergy; and those who worked, the peasantry. In theory, the common ideology binding the four together was Christianity, with balance of power shared between clergy and kings.

Although the Magna Carta of 1215, placed limits on royal authority and defined representative government, the Christian-Feudal system remained, though not as a strong union. There were numerous systemic cracks primarily due to weak devotional linkages throughout. The main problem was with monarchs who came to believe their rights were as divine as any pope's. Division also prevailed with kings claiming all the land in their realm as Crown Land, to be portioned off in bits and pieces, here and there, to lesser nobles as protective nodes or for peasants to harvest food and other resources for the Crown.

During the period, freedom and equity were in short supply. Serfs found themselves without protection from knights and nobles who often ventured off to dozens of wars in France, England, Scotland, Germany and Spain as well as crusades in the Middle East. Such indifference moved the peasants to establish walled communes for their protection, some of which, over time, became city states. Often centered around a rising middle class made up of tradesmen, these communes became powerful entities in their own right, with many, as those in Italy, lasting well into the nineteenth century.

Royal indifference to peasant plight is epitomized best by the monarch's and noble's leisurely pursuit of hunting. Like the Mongols, feudal aristocrats put an emphasis on hunting and combat skills. Such skills were in the Crown's interest because they provided strong leaders unaffected by bad weather and scarce rations, men able to cope with physical exertion at a time when combat was still a hand-to-hand affair.

During the High Middle Ages (1001 to 1300 AD), the feudal lords of Europe imposed extensive restrictions on hunting, effectively placing vacant woodland and common land under the jurisdiction of the monarch, thereby limiting the taking of game. For example, in 1066, after the Battle of Hastings, William of Normandy converted most of the countryside of eastern England into private hunting land by evicting peasants and landholders. During this period, the poor and middle class raised poaching to a fine art with the perfection of traps, nets, snares and other illegal devices a dangerous sport that cost many brave fellows their heads.

Across the English Channel, kleptocrats followed suit in limiting the harvesting of game by taking the sport of hunting to extremes, a practice exemplified by Gaston Phoebus who wrote of his exploits in *Le Livre de la Chasse* or *The Book of the Hunt*. Phoebus proved an expert authority on French hunting and his text left its mark on hunting literature for generations. Phoebus was truly a man of the times. In his book, he describes his three life passions: les armes, l'amour, et la chasse. According to historians, Phoebus maintained some 600 horses and 1,600 hounds for his hunting pleasure. He died at the age of sixty in 1391, while carousing after an arduous bear hunt. Today, some forty copies of a translated version titled *The Master of Game*, written some twenty years later by Edward of York survive.

Phoebus was not alone in his passion. The Elector of Saxony spent most of his time hunting red deer during the disastrous Thirty Years War. Louis XV is credited with killing 10,000 red deer over a fifty-year period. James I of England was similarly afflicted. After his ascendancy to the throne in 1603, he defended spending the better part of his time hunting with claims it was the only way of maintaining his health and, therefore, the health of England. Louis XVI was so abstracted by hunting that when the Paris mob swarmed to take possession of his estate, he was found shooting at driven game. It is understandable, then, that while nobles frittered away their time hunting, peasants and a rising middle class were whittling away at their ethical moorings.

Lasting change came to Europe with the printing press heralding the moral decay of feudal lords and ladies along with gunpowder that challenged Mongol terrorism and leveled the playing field between feudal lords and peasants. Consequently, the fourteenth through eighteenth centuries saw Western Europe in a state of social upheaval. In 1640, proud Charles I, King of England, made a mistake that compromised medieval monarchy in England forever. He went in person to arrest four members of the House of Commons who only recently demanded the impeachment of his most trusted counselors. It was the final provocation. Parliament rose in revolt, Charles was forced to flee, and civil war erupted. It was a war pitting the poor and a rising middle class both committed to representative rule against the King and his terrible doctrine of divine right terrible in its elitism and oppressive taxes and, for many, terrible in its suppression of religious freedom.

Although the Magna Carta placed limits on royal authority and defined representative government, Kingship was still considered sacrosanct. In the minds of poor peasants tied to the King's land, kingship was simply a natural order. For knights and barons, viscounts and earls, kingship was the apex on the nobility ladder from where the view of the less fortunate was most clear. Yet, no matter how well-heeled in pomp and ceremony, Charles lost the war as well right of future English monarchs to serve as sovereign representatives of God on English soil. He was tried, convicted and executed for high treason in January 1649.

Such was classic medieval tribalism. Classic in that the spiritualized component holding the Christian and Islamic cultures together proved stronger than the Divine Right of Kings in holding society together. Even, today, the two religions remain highly successful and one is left with the questions of how and why such social transformations occur? Aside from the God Module/Image of God Thesis marriage presented here, one could argue there must have been genetic mutations resulting in corresponding changes in brain chemistry and behavior to account for this religious surge affecting billions of followers and the energetic tenacity of that devotion.

The fact is, such transformations occur yearly, around the globe, albeit with less of a Big Bang. Freudian psychology was one such occurrence, as were Einstein's theory of relativity, the invention of the computer, the Internet and cell phone. On a Christianity and Islam Big Bang scale are the old religions like Hinduism and Buddhism in the Far East and a very old South American religion we know little about except for 4,000-year-old gourds bearing engraved images of the "Staff God" worshiped by ancient South American cultures for thousands of years.

The ingredients for cultish change are always there: first an appealing ideology with emotional, spiritual foundation to capture/bind/blind God Modules to the cause; followed by 'scientific' verification; the media to communicate the cause; and, finally, sufficient public patronage to promote change. Because Christian and Muslim cultures adopted the Image of God Thesis at a time when both could provide the 'scientific' logic to justify the linkage along with devotional, royal patronage capable of dispensing that knowledge by controlling the media and educational institutions, Christianity and Islam flourished, big time.

What allows Christianity and Islam the big "Tribalism on Steroid Award" is the global impact they had on the human condition. A condition that came about when humans realized they were material reflections of an all-mighty God with God Modules energized to elevate the man-over-nature philosophy to a dominant state of governing: a state of affairs that turned into an intense, mind-altering, compelling phenomenon funneling millions of ignorant serfs onto Christian and Islamic principles and rationalized reasoning.

During their medieval reign, there was little or no opportunity for these millions with their addictive minds to be energized by any formula other than Muslim and Christian doctrine. The result was to support God Module sensitivity, both genetically as well as culturally, to eliminate Aristotle's objective thinking from the moral/ethical equation altogether.

It's difficult today to appreciate the sensitivity of God Modules to deities in the human form the Christian and Muslim religions provided. At a time when mass communication and travel were primitive, Christianity, in a few short centuries, spread across the Continent, North Africa, and the Byzantine Empire. In the short span of 100 years after Muhammad's death in 632 AD, Muslims conquered all the lands along the Mediterranean from Morocco in the West to Tunisia in the East, and in 711 AD, Berber and Arab Muslims conquered Iberia to the north, establishing a cultural bond, however tenuous, with the continent for 800 years.

Chapter 13

Colonialism Manifest Destiny and Social Darwinism

The multiplier effect is a major feature of networks and flows. It arises regardless of the particular nature of the resources, be it goods, money or messages.

- John Henry Holland

As the Holy Roman Empire blossomed and ripened into dominance and Feudalism failed, it insured the decline of democratic values and Aristotelian thinking. The Image of God thesis was so successfully infused into tribal intelligence that sanctified man remained the governing force for centuries. Democracy was out! Kaput! Not until the later part of the 19th century would the humanists' vanguard in Europe separate itself from religious dogma and move Western cultures in a more democratic direction.

Effectively, Feudalism was the very juvenile stage of a secular/religious cult trying to gain footings in Western Europe that failed due to its inability to maintain a strong devotional attachment to either a secular or religious ideology. The Divine Right of Kings simply lacked any of the devotional aspirations essential to inspire the average God Module. In the end, Charles I, along with a host of other nobles, found themselves dead or, in the case of their God Modules, out of work. All the entrenched royal memes that survived generations of trial and error would slowly but inextricably find themselves non-adaptive.

In the year 2000, noted thinkers from around the world were surveyed to name the most influential person of the past millennium. The "Man of the Millennium" distinction was awarded to Johannes Gutenberg who, in 1450, invented the Gutenberg Press. Much of the chaos in the following centuries is attributed to Gutenberg whose press helped introduce the spiritual endeavors of the religious Reformation and the intellectual endeavors that made possible the Italian Renaissance and revolutions throughout the sciences. A period collectively known as the Age of Enlightenment.

One thing the Enlightenment did well was provide for an up-and-coming middle class of skilled worker who plied their many talents into vibrant communities. Utilizing local resources, new technology, new science inventions and improved trade routes, these towns became vibrant city states. By the 15th century then, numerous European nations were testing new Atlantic trade route to lands unknown, driven by the "Manifest Destiny" philosophy that espoused the expansion of Western European cultures around the world being both justified and inevitable.

The new enlightened sciences provided not only gun powder that thwarted the Mongols, but produced new armament and navigation technologies that moved sea powers like Italy, Spain, Portugal and England to go on a colonization rampage around the world with a first stop by Columbus in the Americas. Today, the European discovery of America is known as the "Columbian Exchange," because of the what America gave to Europe and what Europe gave to America, which turned out to be a grossly lopsided exchange.

Starting with Columbus, wave after wave of smallpox, measles, influenza, bubonic plague, diphtheria, whooping cough, chicken pox and tuberculosis brought countless millions to their knees or to their graves. Whole cultures become extinct. Those few spared by immunity or luck would be absorbed into the emerging colonial fabric. Although initial population figures are still debated, most scholars agree the European invasion of the Americas was the greatest calamity in human history. So, while the Enlightenment surfaced democratic thoughts, they remained there as superficial hopes and wishes while despotic and tyrannical God Modules held sway.

Spain must hold the record for imperial tribalism in the Americas, where it took only a hundred and thirty years (1492-1618) for Mexico's initial population of some twenty million to be reduced to about 1.6 million. A hundred and thirty years to annihilate some 18 million people! In 1562, the Spanish friar Diego de Landa Calderón signed a decree that all Mayan books be destroyed. In the process, they burned all historical records of the Inca, Mayan and Aztec people. The work was carried out so thoroughly that of the hundreds of books found, only four somehow escaped the holocaust.

These disasters were part of a justified expediency to civilize paleolithic savages by destroying all traces of their unorthodox lifestyles and religions. As a result, we have little knowledge of their religion or the science they applied to building roads, calendars, temples, water systems and the like, thousands of years of hard-won memetic knowledge lost to humanity forever.

During this early colonial and pioneering period, Manifest Destiny also drove America's political and economic engines. *In Guns, Germs, and Steel,* Jared Diamond estimates a similar pattern occurred in North America during the same period when only five percent of approximately twenty million Native Americans survived. Most of the deaths in southern portions of North America at that time were due to smallpox introduced by the Spanish. Almost all the great Indian civilizations along the Mississippi Valley vanished. Except for numerous burials, ceremonial, and midden mounds scattered throughout the eastern and central portions of the United States, we know little of this vibrant mound-building culture that flourished for thousands of years.

No less absolute were the politics of the migrant Shakers, Calvinists, and Baptists who migrated later to North America to get away from the religious turmoil occurring in the British Isle and on the European continent. For them, the move was an opportunity to express their tribal beliefs in a free world, a world where man though born in a state of original sin and a world filled with temptation could exercise freewill, overcome temptation, and achieve happiness. For others, migration was simply freedom from hunger, a search for adventure or an opportunity to climb the economic ladder. For all, it was man against nature in a land of opportunity. By 1900, all Native American tribes west and north of the Mississippi would be defeated and resettled on remote reservations. In a sense, our ancestors were back in the Stone Age, with small clans and tribes struggling for survival against an unforgiving Mother Nature.

These devastating episodes, like all great wars before and after, often included killing without the slightest intention of doing wrong, and torture with the full intention of causing great pain. In *The Lucifer Principle*, Howard Bloom details numerous historical examples of whole cultures getting emotionally and psychologically seduced into marching off to cleanse the world of tyranny, only to see their addictive worldviews cast into the trash bin of history. "Viewing the scene from a celestial seat, one could only assert man was driven into a bloody battle to the death for prestige, the outcome of which was a divided society into a class of masters, who willing risk their lives for King and Country and a class of slaves, who give in to their natural fear of death."

Social Darwinism

It wasn't until the late 19th century that some elites began to question the brutality of classic tribalism that was Manifest Destiny. And, as so often happens when conscious or unconscious guilt needs exposure, people lie or transfer the guilt. But this was not the case with Manifest Destiny. The justification here lay with classic tribalism itself being accepted as normal social behavior. Manifest Destiny was simply an early rendition of the theory, "Social Darwinism" that lent support to the mass migration and destruction that occurred during this period.

With its publication in 1859, Darwin attempted to dispel popular man-centered philosophies by placing man in an ecological context of being one with nature and should, therefore, act as guardian of Earth's resources. Ignoring Darwin's inclusive, ecological principle, leading intellectuals saw the new science as license for tribal domination by man over lesser men and nature.

From the public debates that followed, this racist form of Darwinism emerged. Within weeks of publication, God Module thinking took over and the ideals that "might is right" and "survival of the fittest" became newspaper gospel. In brief, the doctrine claimed we should look to nature for what is good and real. Thus, any institution built on the theory that the strong and rich, as well as the weak and the poor, deserve their status in life is justified. Although Darwin made no such connection, these simplistic theories of man as nothing more than a drone to his instinct devoid of cultural constraints, caught the public's imagination.

The philosopher Herbert Spencer is credited as a major player in this movement. The fact that he was largely self-educated with little training in natural history did not deter Spencer from his selective use of evolutionary theory in promoting social causes. Through a series of books, he concluded that ruthlessness and aggression were morally necessary and beneficial. The social Darwinian writings of Nietzsche, the most influential philosopher at the time, also had an enormous impact on the movement. Nietzsche felt living things could not be healthy, strong or productive except by living within a certain set of values that are accepted absolutely and uncritically. Statements such as "No artist will paint his picture, no general win his victory, no nation gain its freedom, without set values," validated the attitude of the times.

English journalist Walter Bagehot agreed with Nietzsche. In his 1872 book, *Physics and Politics,* Bagehot claimed that nations evolved principally by succeeding in conflicts with other groups. Tribalism in its purest form was the general mindset of European leaders, a survival of the fittest mindset, a dog-eat-dog mindset lacking any moral footing or social responsibility in the New Worlds. An enlightened mindset that ended in the early 20th century with two world Wars and countless millions of casualties. All normal inside/outside bubble behavior. It was classic tribalism. Powerful tribes competing against one another with absolutely no regard for those harmed in the process. Brutal, brutal classic tribalism

Summary Part 2

The autocratic governing during the Historic Period was normal objective tribalism thinking on steroids. Conservative thinking on the order of the STM where community responsibilities suppressed the Freedom/Equity Module demands. Except, the autocratic loss in community solidarity opened the door to rebellion between liberal rebels demanding their freedom and equity rights, and the conservative establishment refusing to comply, as with Feudalism.

Feudalism was not only a reflections of a failed governing model that survived in Europe for some eight hundred years, but a reflection of things to come throughout Western civilizations. Classic Feudalism failed because tribal devotions was split along liberal nobility lines and conservative papal lines. The spirited disputes between kings and popes sapped and scattered the collective energies needed to keep a tribe together. Classical Christianity also started it decent into hundreds of uncontrollable factions. All the result of tribal infighting that actually started and destroyed the early great Greek and Roman civilizations and would come to play a major role in growth and destruction of modern civilizations as well.

But democratic change was on its way. Especially in the vast lands of opportunity west of the Atlantic Ocean, in North America; a land that would become a breeding grounds for Modernism and enlightened democratic thinking that would result in The Greatest Generation during World War II; a breeding grounds for formulating and implementing more humane ways of controlling public opinion; and, a breeding grounds for Postmodernism that would result in The Greatest Generation divided by identity politics and President Donald Trump as president.

PART 3

BIRTH of a POSTMODERN CULT
- The Enlightenment-

The most perilous moment for a new government,
is one which seeks to mend it ways.
-Alexis de Tocqueville

Chapter 14

PHASE ONE -A RECEPTIVE PHILOSOPHY- HUMANISM To SOCIALISM

The first man who, having fenced in a piece of land, said "This is mine," and found people naïve enough to believe him, that mans was the true founder of civil society. From how many crimes, wars, and murders, from how many horrors and misfortunes might not anyone have saved mankind by pulling up the stakes, or filled up the ditches, and crying to his followers: "Beware of listening to this imposter; you are undone if you once forget that the fruits of the earth belong to us all, and this earth itself to nobody.

- Jean-Jacques Rousseau

This long Postmodern effort that ended with President Trump had its beginnings with a shift in God Module thinking. Recall, the purpose of God Modules was to addict tribal members to an ideology; provide the emotional biased energy in promoting the ideology; provide the emotional energy in blinding members to contrary ideologies; and finally, act as a damper on member's Freedom/Equity Mandate by limiting those energies to facilitate community solidarity. During the Age of Enlightenment, the function of the Module limiting Freedom/Equity Mandate energies to facilitate objective, community solidarity was reversed, to promoting those energies in a more subjective, democratic fashion of thinking with some cultures. As a result, the Age of Enlightenment was nothing but a confusing era where humans found themselves stumbling around searching for some form of community solidarity.

This fumbling shift in tribal thinking came about as the young natural sciences and their rigid methods of testing and retesting were being directed at politics. One of the few efforts the young natural sciences were to take in understanding how politics works was with the Motivational Force Theory. First came 17th century philosopher Thomas Hobbes who expounded on tribal thinking by claiming our base motives are biological. Later, David Hume addressed the role emotions played in overriding reason, followed by Immanuel Kant asserting our rational and intellectual makeup was designed around universal, tribal precepts. Georg Hegel went a bit further by suggesting that ideologies were incomplete logic and led to bias and conflict.

All of these men are considered some of the greatest minds of the Enlightenment Period who were followed later in the 20th century, by Ludwig Wittgenstein, Russian Philosopher Alexandre Kojève, German Friedrich Nietzsche and French political writer Alexis de Tocqueville. All famous thinkers. Prominent throughout the world in extending the Motivational Force Theory by proposing that all men need status, recognition and power, fruits derived from one's labor.

Unfortunately, their tribal efforts dealing with *objective, democratic, political thinking* (individual rights subservient to community rights) came to nothing as the moral authority in the field of politics was left to social science philosophers who began to think more along *subjective lines of democratic governing* (community rights subservient to individual rights). By 1500, then, European social science philosophers have, for better or worse, called the political tune we dance to, a reformation dance that began with "Humanism."

Humanism is another one of those Great Leaps Forward, with one tenet *focused on the individual rather than the collective*; another on the use of freethinking, impartial reasoning rather than objective secular or religious dogma; and, lastly, a doctrine supporting universal, biological man rather than idealized, made-in-the-Image-of-God man. Humanists like Desiderius Erasmus began the long march to modernity and representative government by questioning divine order and redirecting thinking toward human potential. Though ordained a priest in 1492, Erasmus was more involved with promoting art and literature than expounding on theoretical discourse that might get him, at the very least, a date with the Inquisition. Eventually, though, he and other humanists began to question the infallibility of the Catholic Church, a theme later pursued by social reformers like Martin Luther.

Luther, himself an ordained priest, initiated the Reformation in 1517, a transition from one Christian church to many, by detailing the corruption of the Church in his Ninety-Five Theses. In the process, Catholicism, with its stranglehold on defining heresy for centuries, became itself a heresy, resulting in violent infighting between peevish religious groups, with all sides becoming persecutor and prosecutor of witches and heretics. According to the Study of Global Christianity, by 2012, the Catholic Church eventually fragmented into approximately 40,000 *individualized* denominations scattered around the world.

Although the Reformation was considered anti-intellectual, resulting in the decline of monolithic Christianity, the subjective thinking promoted by the social philosophers was groundbreaking. Slowly, such social theorizing became a guiding source of moral authority resulting in Humanism which, eventually, became the foundation for modern Western political thought. At the time, social science as a truth meme remained within the realm of those few philosophers with access to knowledge considered reliable "truths," who had the ability to impose their beliefs on the powerful, who had the ability to enforce the "truths."

So then, while natural philosophers were exploring man's inner tribal virtues, romantic Humanists like Jean Jacques Rousseau were weaving man's natural inclinations (his oneness with the land) with his outer virtues (his civil rights, his freedom and equity needs under democratic rule) into the Romantic Movement. In *The Social Contract*, Rousseau claimed humans were inherently good and that this goodness was a communal reflection he termed the "will of the people" where the good of the whole, would outweigh that of the individual or any one entity *if done correctly*. He also makes a strong case for civil liberty by defending the collective will against divine right, and individual will against the absolutism of church and state. To this end, Rousseau trusted majority rule to make the all-important political decisions and provide the theoretical support for the civil unrest sweeping Europe at the time.

Rousseau was the first to air suspicions that autocratic society with its restrictive paraphernalia was designed to keep the majority in bondage. He was also among the first to sense that a power lacking theological foundations and conceived as power over other competing groups, was inherently unstable. He considered leaders promoting freedom, justice and equal-opportunity for all were only lures invented by clever autocrats or by base flatterers to impose themselves on the Haveless.

It was during this period, the 18th century, that Rousseau crystalized some of the perennial questions all humans ask themselves: Can humans really define themselves, if not, what holds societies together and what divides them? Why do the under-privileged majority erupt in revolt against the privileged few? And, what roles should intellectuals like himself, play in these conflicts?

A bit later, in the mid-19th century, a group of young German Rousseau scholars gave definition to one of his core beliefs about the importance of *objective* communal living A lifestyle they defined as the 'Sparta Lifestyle' which they believed to be the ideal governing model. To that end, the scholars started a movement of a small organic community model, they called the "Volk," a model united by a distinctive language, a way of thought and shared traditions driven by collective folklore.

One of their influential writers, Johann Gottfried Herter refocused the Sparta model within the context of his Spartan-like, Germanic ancestors, a culture he claimed was marked by social harmony and moral clarity. Eventually Herter went one step further by expanding the Volk into a spiritual and aesthetic ideology that included distinctive forms of language, architecture, music, art, cuisine and religion. Like the natural science philosophers who recognized the inherent value of tribal behaviors being recycled over and over again, the young Germans were expounding their inherent desire to recycle the paleolithic STM into the Volk.

Immanuel Kant put the frosting on the romantic, democratic cake by asserting humans are emotional, moral beings and, therefore, occupy a special place in creation, and have *individual categorical rights* he called categorical imperatives, from which all duties and obligations derive. He defined imperatives as any proposition declaring a certain action to be necessary. It was not a question of should or maybe or perhaps? It was a summons, a maxim demanding public acceptance, a rule of moral conduct directing us to follow absolutely, regardless of our inclinations. Unlike hypothetical imperatives that satisfy the need to eat or drink, a categorical imperative is an unconditional requirement, a maxim that becomes universal law should an individual wish it.

It's within this enlightened yet confusing environment where governing became more diversified along socialistic, democratic lines in classless, "collectives" where all are equal, and commerce and industry are controlled by the state; or along capitalist, democratic lines where trade and industry are controlled by private owners for profit rather than the state. Both were attempts to balance community rights (objective thinking) with individual rights (subjective thinking) as millions of migrants settled the Americas searching and testing the evolving brands of governing for their brand of democracy.

Chapter 15

PHASE TWO RECEPTIVE ENVIRONMENT

Man is a reasoning animal rather than a reasonable animal

> \- Alexander Hamilton

The confusion surrounding efforts to stabilize subjective and objective demands during this Age of Enlightenment carried with it numerous growth pains. Some physical, some psychological that showed up as classic wars between nations and internecine civil wars, interspersed by thoughtful interludes when a Declaration of Independence, a Bill of Rights and a Constitution were articulated and made reality. But all those adaptations took time. Something on the order of our ancestors coming up with their STM except more rapidly along cultural time lines and not genetic time lines.

This was true especially in America. Unlike Europe at the time where classic and internecine wars raged, those ships capable of navigating around the world and replacing thousands of small paleolithic tribes, also dropped off European migrants onto virgin landscapes, rich in resources and political opportunity, intent on making life better than what they left behind.

But …. that took time. Several hundred years.

And …. Time to see what works politically.

Throughout the carnage that was Colonialism, the doctrine of Manifest Destiny remained alive and well in North America where territorial expansion was not only inevitable, but ordained.

Given freedom, equal opportunity and an unspoiled wilderness, our forefathers set out across North America to grow hundreds of small organic communities—something on the order of the German Volk—with majority rule and values centered around a Sparta lifestyle.

A lifestyle that ever so quietly supplied the opportunity for settlers to experiment with the fledgling Postmodern cult theorized by fellow European philosophers. It was a cult like those started by men like Joseph Smith, Jesus Christ, and Muhammad around an inherent spiritual need. A need for ideological freedom and equity that lay smoldering in the minds of thousands of our immigrant ancestors who survived medieval times and found freedom and equity in America during the Age of Enlightenment.

Like the opportunity it provided Joseph Smith, America's colonial period offered settlers a politically uncluttered space to experience capitalist and democratic ideals. It was in this rarified environment where democracy grew from a spark to a flame, ever so slowly, here and there, as the settlers expressed their rendition of freedom with no intellectual elites telling them they were wrong.

It was a young political movement moved by lumbermen, miners, dam builders, and the millions of immigrants needed to drill wells, build roads and river boats, realign rivers, cut cross-ties and lay track for the million miles of rail lines coming and going to lumber camps, mines and booming cities. Therefore, unlike Europe, where intellectual elites ran the political lobby with a focus on civil disorder, the lobby in America, was run at the grassroots level by amateurs who, at first, focused their emotional efforts in a rather calm and utilitarian manner onto whatever ideas and beliefs that felt right and comfortable at the time.

Where the new natural sciences influenced public policy by dissecting nature into smaller and smaller under- standings with clarity and reason, the environmental romantics energized public policy with a hunger for an undissected, idealized nature in which God was present in every rock and waterfall, a nature attuned to the subjective and inward experiences where landscapes stirred the imagination, inspired wonder and rustled the emotions. For romantics, whatever happened in nature was a freedom-equity life force.

From the beginning, then, American romantics pressed for a benevolent government that would limit exploitation, restrain free markets and preserve large areas of land as national parks and national forests. No more Manifest Destiny. It was the beginning of a progressive movement, led by men such as John Muir, Asa Gray, George Perkins Marsh, Henry Senger and William D. Armes who presided over the establishment of Yosemite National Park in 1872 and the formation of the Sierra Club in 1892.

These men were aided in their pursuits by a number of influential writers who idealized unspoiled nature and Native Americans. Men like Washington Irving, James Fenimore Cooper and the much-celebrated Walt Whitman and Henry David Thoreau. These writers, along with a number of frontier artists sounded the first public alarms about *equal rights* for endangered Native Americans, wildlife, plants, despoiled rivers and wilderness.

Their efforts did not go unnoticed. In 1876, the US Forest Service was created and in March of 1891, President Benjamin Harrison established the nation's first timberland reserve: 12.25 million acres next to Yellowstone National Park. The Soil Conservation Service was instituted to aid farmers and to administer soil and water policy. National park lands were placed in the hands of the US National Park Service while the US Bureau of Land Management administered millions of square miles of Western lands leased to individuals and private corporations.

Until his death, John Muir (*Time* magazine's "real father of conservation") wrote and spoke eloquently on preserving wilderness areas and wildlife from commercial exploitation and destruction. Muir embellished his eloquent rhetoric in passionate prose for what he saw as outright stupidity in cutting down sequoia groves that predated the

Christian era, and permitting sheep and cattle to destroy unique and rare habitats in the Yellowstone Valley. His many writings include *The Mountains of California, Our National Parks, My First Summer in the Sierra, The Yosemite* and *Travels in Alaska.*

So, as the land was settled, the grinding forces driving Manifest Destiny slowed down and a more benevolent form of tribalism came in play. This progressive surge for bigger government to protect a despoiled nature and its inhabitants was aided by big-game hunter, President Theodore Roosevelt, who believed that natural resources formed the basis of our nation's economy and were, to a large degree, limited. Under the rubric of science, professional conservationists like Roosevelt would lead the way in ridding Manifest Destiny of all its plundering features, while attempting to balance rights with responsibilities.

At the same time, a new *social media* emerged as a growing number of restless writers, poets and artists concerned about social and environmental issues were flexing their romantic muscles in an effort to instill into Roosevelt politics a Rousseau-like concept of man in tune with nature. A media that would become a driving force in the embryonic Postmodern cult with the nation providing equal right to not only Native Americans but all life forms, a media stymied for a time by *The Great Nature Faker Debate.*

Fake News has been around forever, although it was never journalistically defined as such until President Roosevelt jumped into a contentious debate between nationally recognized liberal and conservative writers that came to dominate public opinion at the time. Like Muir, the liberal challengers were admired nature writers who found their flowery, emotive style popular with children and non-hunters. Several noted scientists quietly challenged the romantic trend terminating in America's first public test of nature-ethics between amateur and professional conservationists.

Self-righteous God Modules have always been a force to reckon with, especially when folk of stature slug it out in the media which, at the time in 1903, consisted of magazines and newspapers that eventually labeled the controversy "*The Great Nature Faker Debate.*" It all began with an article in the *Atlantic Monthly* when nationally known sportsman John Burroughs attacked nationally known writers like Ernest Thompson Seton, Jack London and the Reverend William J. Long as 'sham naturalists' for stories giving animals human reasoning abilities. One story had a porcupine—when nudged by a cougar—trussing itself into a protective ball and then rolling downhill. Several had woodcock or ruffed grouse purposely casting broken legs in a combination of mud and feathers. Another had a fox diverting the interest of hounds by jumping on the back of a sheep. Some books had animals talking with each other. Some reviewers criticized the writers for such sappy, maudlin writing, but Burroughs was one of the few people who had the stature and credibility needed to capture public attention

Living in a post-Disney world, and fed a steady diet of cartoons and movies in which all animals—including dinosaurs—are given human qualities, we might find such controversy humorous, but things were different then. Many in positions of authority found the stories infantile and an affront to the very fabric of social intercourse. As a recognized outdoor leader, Burroughs felt he had a moral responsibility to respond and set the record straight.

His concern was for the effect the emotion-laden fiction might have on children and persons not familiar with nature. In an article titled *Current Misconceptions in Natural History*, he states this concern: "Never before in my time have so many exaggerations and misconceptions of the wildlife about us been current in the popular mind." He was concerned such tales would revive medieval bestiaries traditions by hijacking nature as a source of moral narratives, a direction Richard Dawkins—the famous geneticists—in his 1998 book *Unweaving the Rainbow* called "bad poetic science."

The debate went on from 1903 to 1908, during which time Burroughs focused most of his wrath upon Reverend Long who continued to match article for article with Burroughs. For Long, nature study was nature of the poets, prophets and thinkers. A vastly different thing from the study of the natural sciences. His science was like psychology and history, where emotions are more real than facts and therefore more righteous than the facts. He continued irritating Burroughs with stories of how animals bandaged their wounds using pine pitch, spruce resin or clay to knowingly prevent infection and how adult kingfishers coached their young with practice sessions in diving for fish.

As president, Theodore Roosevelt was reluctant to enter the fray, but in 1907 when he discovered the books were being used in schools, he wrote a series of articles ending with the *Nature Fakers* that dealt a killing blow to the contest. It seems he was especially upset knowing the books were used in public schools and worried about the damage they were doing to children. In that context, he focused not on animal psychology but the distorted facts being published and the responsibilities of parents, school boards and publishers for permitting such emotional quackery to occur. The debate established a new standard of accuracy for responsible journalism and, for a time, limited the supply of romanticized nature books and articles.

While the debate was a defeat for romantics, it served as harbinger for an endless series of contentious battles between America's two great liberal and conservative forces. Time and again, amateurs, with no economic stake in the outcome, and resource harvesters with an economic stake, would clash over a piece of the natural world. They would carry their fight into the streets or nearby woods, newspaper, shopping center, and through the courts.

In a sense, it was the first step in a rather long series of steps by journalists, psychologists, and politicians in gaming emotional support to justify their tribal reasoning with the voting public. *Though a looser, it's important to note that Long's logic, claiming his reasoning was no different than psychologist and historians using rationalized emotions rather than rigid facts, would come to be the very essence of political, Postmodern thinking well into the 21st century.*

Reasoning the romantic progressives would find very useful in the up and coming Environmental Movement, an absolute essential in the Equal-Rights Movement, and the growing Postmodernism cult that would divide and threaten the very fabric of America. Reasoning Burroughs defined as rationalized exaggerations, and misconceptions to emotionally sway public opinion away from reality.

Chapter 16

PHASE THREE FREUDIAN PSYCHOANALYSIS

In our age there is no such thing as keeping the peace. All issues are political issues, and politics itself is a mass of lies, evasions, folly, hatred and schizophrenia.

- George Orwell

Survival for any cult depends on four elements coming to fruition: an appealing ideology with an emotional, spiritual foundation to capture God Modules to the cause; "science" to authenticate and validate the ideology; an authoritative leadership capable of defining, redefining and enforcing new tribal standards; and four, a membership capable of working together tirelessly, ruthlessly, and remorselessly.

To a degree, the Environmental Movement had all these features which, over time, seemed to generate a broader stirring in the nation calling for a new religion, a spiritual grounding that would include not only a passionate respect for Mother Earth and all her creatures, but an extension of that passion to include freedom and equity for all humanity.

What the romantic writers brought to that table was emotions, the addiction currency, the God Module glue that captures, binds and blinds. Now, what the romantics needed to go from environmental causes to an equality movement, was a *practical, scientific* process to authenticate and administer Long's logic of using psychological theory. A process that took some time. A problem to which dozens of enlightened social philosophers in the early 20th century spread their theoretical wings and flew off in every direction the stormy political winds blew.

Considered the scientists of their time, these social philosophers were the first to fill the ruptured moral process their religious predecessors left behind with a vast number of fledgling theories, most of which were vague and ambiguous, resulting in decades of debates on how to separate *outdated social theory* from the new theories generated by the *young natural sciences.*

At the time, what turned young people away from old social philosophy as a profession was the debate over linguistic logic. Ludwig Wittgenstein was a young natural scientist who argued that language is composed of complex schemes that can be broken down into less complex schemes. In like fashion, the world is composed of complex facts that can be worked into less complex facts. For example, breaking a thought down into smaller and smaller facts until the "real" fact emerged as the "truth" could solve any confusion over word meaning. From this analysis, only real-world themes acquired with reason, intuition or perception were considered meaningful. Metaphysical and ethical statements were not meaningful assertions.

Not to be outdone, the social philosophers stretched linguistic philosophy to the point of obscurity by claiming words and language were not capable of defining reality or truth in any fashion. They alleged that words are rationalized, mental states with no footing in reality, and any word—or by extension, idea, value or action—can exist only in a mental state. Therefore, words and our behavior built around language may not exist at all, except in the mind.

Here is where the old philosophical chestnut by George Berkeley came into the discussion: "If a tree falls in the forest and no one's around, does it make a sound?" In his *Confessions of a Philosopher*, philosopher and member of English Parliament Bryan Magee supported the theory by insisting: "If all I experience, and all I ever can experience, are mental states, what warrant do I have for believing that anything exists other than mental states? Indeed, what warrant do I have for believing that there are any mental states other than mine?" From that logic, many assumed there's no sound produced when tree falls in the forest.

This old, philosophical logic of individuals defining no other mental states other than their own, did not make much sense at the time to the new natural science philosophers. It was considered nothing more than abstract thinking looking for a cause.

But! …

But! ….

But! ….

Such rationalization did fit in with Rousseau's Humanism framework: a focus on the individual rather than the collective; freethinking, impartial reasoning rather than objective hard-core dogma. While causeless at the time, the philosophy took on a solid 21st century Postmodern cause, actually a Postmodern foundation, with the advent of Freudian psychology.

It was with Freud where the question of how to *manage* and *formalize romantic logic into a scientific-application process* began to show signs of resolution. Given the public's perception of how cultures should be structured along lines of individual, foundational precepts, rather than natural science logic, Freud psychology provided the first step in that direction.

Considered one of the great reasoned thinkers of the 20th century, Freud afforded the romantic movement with that reasoned logic the progressive cult needed to capture, bind and blind. The subjective thinking was a rejection of logic devoid of ethics as the natural sciences proposed, and an acceptance of *the old progressive view that most any form of moralized ethics was righteous criteria in solving social problems as long as they were practical, meaningful, and worked.* Considered a new exciting idea by many, it essentially was just a new rendition of Aristotle's old rationalization philosophy that turned out to be a philosophical study of immense scope.

By talking to patients about their childhood, Freud offered degrees of sympathy previously unavailable. First came schizophrenia, then autism and homosexuality. This made psychoanalysis a popular and practical service when the alternatives were a deep barbiturate sleep, insulin coma, a lobotomy or electroshock—all unpleasant, addictive or dangerous treatments in use at the time. By emphasizing memory repression from childhood, psychoanalysis gave patients a ticket out of the asylum. Indeed, psychoanalysis offered its services to those who were not so much ill as unhappy, and who would pay well for the chance to recount their life story while lying on a couch.

In his analyses, Freud asked patients to say whatever came to mind, no matter how embarrassing or irrelevant the answer might seem. Through this method of free association, he found that what we say and what we do are two different things. Much in the mind is unconscious, such as professed love, repressed hatred, flagrant anger or concealed guilt. Although psychoanalysis is notoriously bad at changing people, it's correct in its premise that there are such things as formative experiences that are learned early, stay in the subconscious to influence intuition, and are hard to reverse, pre-adaptive sexual modules and God Modules for example. Plus, it provided the young, Postmodern cult with a semi-scientific allure.

Although repression formed the cornerstone of Freud's philosophy, he came under fire for using *repression* and *deception* in his work when a number of researchers friendly to Freud judged much of his early work, published in *The Etiology of Hysteria*, as a failure. Wryly, Freud himself acknowledged to friends that duplicity of a kind was essential if his enemies and hostile critics were to be kept at bay.

It was a kind of duplicity generated by contradictions that results in cognitive dissonance. The result, a kind of "Constructive Lie" that 21st century psychology refers to as "Projection." One of those functional flights of fantasy that lead to a self-defense mechanism in which a person: 1) identifies a conscious or unconscious problem that generates guilt; 2) transfers the guilt to another person or process; and 3) reaps the guiltless psychological benefits. Example: Think of the media projection FBI Director, James Comey used to justify his involvement in the Trump/Russian Collusion plot that resulted in a failed 2½ year Mueller investigation.

It was rational, practical "whatever works science" our paleolithic ancestors used to solve all political issues. A theory that became accepted by elites as the only way of understanding how social interaction works. A very successful pattern of thinking that became gospel among late 19th century philosophers who were preaching the theories of "functional psychology" and "pragmatism." Thus, the public began to see Freud's analytical process helpful as a *personal defense mechanism* by helping to identify conflicting mental issues; rationalized understandings with constructive lies; and being pragmatic in reducing relationship conflicts by redirecting unconscious anxieties and guilt. All of which opened the door to a lucrative business model.

Actually, what Freud did was take the viewpoint expressed by the Reverent Long in the *Great Nature Faker Debate*—who claimed his rationalized thinking no different than the study of human behavior by psychologists and historians using emotions rather than real facts to move people and give the process "scientific" validation. Because of his world-wide fame, Freud effectively authorized the use of rationalization and obfuscation to solve or redirect many social issues.

Actually, Freud would be surprised to know his constructive lie would become an economic windfall for the youthful science of psychology. And, his three-step process of transferring guilt would become a dependable warfare strategy, a never-ending Gotcha Game of identity politics, played out daily in the up and coming struggles Postmodern romantics would face in their quest for individual freedom and equity.

Chapter 17

PHASE FOUR RADICAL BLANK SLATE PSYCHOLOGY

In short, if there were one wisp of wisdom that we could pluck from the mind of Freud it might be this: those who are unaware of their feelings risk becoming puppets of those feelings.

— Tina Rosenberg

While flights of fantasy oversaw the decline of Enlightenment philosophers, their rebirth as practical enlightened psychologists did manage to energize subjective, democratic thinking at a time in both Europe and America. The Russian Revolution stimulated by both the French and American Revolutions added to the subjective democratic drift in which individual rights were being examined within a communal context.

In turn, Freudian psychology justified subjective thinking to an individual level as a *personal defense mechanism* against repressed feelings and actions that didn't quite reflect existing conservative standards. In the process, it allowed for public acceptance of an individual-rights ideology which, although lacking in hard-historical evidence in large cultures, gave life to the devotional psychology movement as potable science on a much broader social level.

The only concern with the new psyche movement was whether the empirical sciences would *accept* the values and crusading strategies needed to move an embryonic-rights cult to maturity. Many in the rights movement were still smarting over their romantic values being relegated to step-sister status by Teddy Roosevelt in the Great Nature Fake Debate. They would not make the mistake of lacking scientific validity to support their cause, again. So, while the Greeks were able to decipher human thinking into scientific, technological and phronetic processes, it took psychologists to separate the sciences into *two scientific processes* with distinct thought patterns: the social sciences and empirical or so-called natural sciences.

At the time there was little to differentiate the two, but slowly lines of demarcation became evident and contentious. The combative nature of the disunity centered on how to justify quarrelsome shifting, moral issues. Since Teddy Roosevelt argued science should be practical, and the social sciences had become invested in "pragmatism," they argued: "What was more practical scientifically than doing what comes naturally, like belittling your opponent and, if that doesn't work, send a mob to smash his printing press like Mormon James Smith did to solve one of his political problem."

Their difficulty with the empirical scientific method was it required rigid observation, formulating hypotheses, testing measurable evidence, verifying and modifying hypotheses as new evidence comes in, all carried out with no regard for moral clarity. Actually, the acrimony came to a boiling point in mid-20th century, when the social science community realized it didn't want any interlopers messing with its centuries-old philosophical status as tribal expert on human behavior, a status achieved via the "Blank Slate Theory."

The idea of the mind as a "Blank Slate" is attributed to 17th century English philosopher John Locke, who wrote that the mind is like a white paper, a blank slate void of all character where *learning by association* explained all thought, feeling and behavior. It became official doctrine with intellectual elites during the first half of the 20th century to counter the widespread discrimination against women, Jews, non-whites, and non-Western cultures, as efforts like eugenics and Social Darwinism gathered momentum. The movement reached its zenith later in the 20th century with partakers in the Sixties Revolution claiming the Freedom/Equality Mandate their major social goal.

In all cases, the assertion was that *culture alone* influenced behavior which was supported by Freudian psychology claiming man is superior to all other life forms, has conscious control of his behavior from birth to death and, therefore, is responsible for his actions. Locke's theory fit especially well with the American affection for Manifest Destiny, responsible for stoking Colonialism and our economic engines from the 16th through the 20th centuries.

Needless to say, any contrary hypothesis was considered a threat to these most basic tribal tenets. Although Freudian psychology was shown scientifically lacking and many argue its current validity, Freud's psychoanalytical theory on human behavior is considered one of the most influential theories of the 20th century. Hence, Freud is generally acknowledged as one of the century's great creative minds and a major contributor to the Blank Slate Movement.

The main reason blank-slate thinking prevailed for so long was because the empirical sciences had given little thought to the subject and because people had only an obscure idea of what the mind was and how it worked. Thousands of sound evolutionary studies were carried out during the 20th century, but they focused mainly on how physical traits were passed from generation to generation and the role genes played in this transmission.

By 1950, however, scientists in genetics and neurobiology in particular, made theoretical connections suggesting behavior schemes exist in the brain that gather, analyze and catalog incoming stimuli, a process a blank-slate mind cannot do. Something must be present to translate a sentence into conscious thought or distinguish a smile from a frown.

The first step was taken in the 1950s by Norm Chomsky who argued that neurology theory should replace blank-slate philosophy. As a linguist professor at Massachusetts Institute of Technology, Chomsky developed the theory that the mind cannot learn unless it has the rudiments of innate knowledge. In a famous rebuttal to the celebrated behaviorist B. F. Skinner—who claimed that language is acquired in much the same way that rats learn to press a bar for food pellets—Chomsky demonstrated that it was impossible for children to learn the rules of language as quickly and as effortlessly as they do without some innate, pre-adaptive mechanism to which the vocabulary of the language fit. He was one of the first to claim the human brain is a product of evolution and is hardwired to learn certain behaviors.

While this debate was a significant first step in down-playing blank-slate theory, it didn't generate much attention or criticism among social scientists or the public at large. It was Edward Wilson's seminal book *Sociobiology* that generated a fire storm of debate from sociologists and the religious right. There were 26 chapters covering the biology and behavior of animals, but in the last chapter he speculates on a possible genetic connection to traits like compassion, aggression and other behaviors long thought to be subject to freewill and thereby only under conscious control.

The reaction to such heresy was instant and vicious. By then, the fields of psychology had gained wide inroads throughout the medical field and society at large, so, the blank-slaters felt the book a surprise slap down they didn't quite appreciate. Although criticism by clergy was expected, the ferocity of the attack from colleagues came as a surprise and served to emphasize the cognitive bias and blindness within the two tribal fields.

What occurred to cause the animosity was psychology had gained enough tribal stature as a functional ideology to permit bold-faced *deception and violence* into their though-control formulas. Released from the stigma of a hard-core science bound by rigid methods of formulating, testing, verifying, modifying, and retesting, they now had at their disposal their whole range of *tribal cognitive fluidity* including mob violence to control any opposition, and do so with authority.

Political correctness and identity politics crept in and Wilson was called a sexist and a capital imperialist, his book labeled a right-wing plot to continue the oppression of the oppressed. Colleagues at Harvard excoriated him as a racist, and fifteen scientists damned him in a letter printed in the *New York Review of Books* for subscribing to the same views that "led to the gas chambers in Nazi Germany."

The criticism did not stop with baneful verbiage. Mob tactics kicked in and Wilson had a bucket of ice water poured on his head at one meeting. Others with similar research like IQ scientist Arthur Jensen needed a bodyguard at his lectures. Police investigated racial-difference scholar J.P. Rushton for six months. A mob of protesters beat up Britain's most prominent psychologist, Hans Eysenck, and the University of Edinburgh fired IQ researcher Chris Brand despite 26 years of tenure. Apparently, opponents felt strong language and mob action were needed in stamping out, once and for all, the seeds of genetic determinism.

What's significant about this mob behavior is the degree to which tribal psychology had progressed in its devotional bias and blindness to justify attacking contrary ideologies. The amazing feature of this violence was the fact, behavior psychologists were responsible. When in modern times did "scientists" agree with mob tactics and physically assaulting a fellow scientist? The whole concept of modern science was built on the premise of intellectual debate until a problem is resolved. Now though, veteran social scientists felt confident enough with their psychology credentials to skip fooling around with some silly debating, and simply threaten the opposition physically and be done with it.

What *Sociobiology* did was show the empirical sciences for the serious threat they were to psychologists and, therefore, deserving of the elevated violence for infringing on their business and threatening the very essence of their ideology. Essentially, it was the first time *a scientific group* in America used identity politics, political correctness, obfuscation, duplicity along with a touch of physical mendacity to ward off the enemy.

But …. only a touch of rational violence.

A weak primal scream.

A mild case of Trump Derangement Hysteria.

Yet a bold Freudian defensive slap down.

Rather than suffer with guilt given the lack of concrete scientific evidence to support their cause, they simply *transferred the guilt* by *projecting* the upstarts as sexist, capitalist imperialists, modern Nazi's and empirical science bigots, pushing false conspiratorial theories designed to distract psychologists away from their democratic rights. Then, when all was said and done, they sat back *enjoying the benefits* of watching the astute opposition slither back into their academic caves.

Thank you! Mr. Freud.

Cruel! Sure! But what fun.

Here is where psychology's rendition of Aristotle's phronetic rationalization came into play as an unusually efficient crusading strategy to ward off the empirical sciences from muscling in on their tribal territory. Like the Image of God Thesis that sanctioned exploitation of non-believers by Christians and Muslims to inquisitions and burning at the stake, the social sciences had reached that level of using vengeful god-like rhetoric and mental inquisitions to castigate non-believers who dare threaten their brand of science.

Using such political tactics on fellow scientists at this time was unheard of, especially when an abundance of sound empirical research showing much of man's behavior driven by pre-adaptive modules in the brain was available. From a tribal standpoint, the shock-and-awe tactics was quite remarkable. Not good at civilized warfare, the empirical scientists did not crawl back in their caves but did stay out of the fray by barricading themselves within their cloistered university walls. They had learned their lesson: Don't screw with the new progressive social sciences. A lesson that would last well into the summer of 2020.

Chapter 18

Phase Five VERIFYING POSTMODERN CULT

Many 'hard' scientists regard the term 'social science' as an oxymoron. Science means hypotheses you can test, and prove or disapprove. Social science is little more than observation putting on airs.

- Michael Kinsley

While Freudian theory had numerous connections to the field of neuro-science, few if any were followed up as was the case with the Father of Modern Psychology, William James (1842-1910). James identified a list of inherent human impulses that included the actions of babies crying, smiling, sucking, standing, walking and grasping. He claimed there emerged in older children a fear of heights, dark places, strangers, spiders and snakes along with predispositions for shyness, cleanliness, modesty, shame, jealousy, love and distinct play preference between boys and girls.

James insisted that ideas, moral beliefs and values—what psychologists called "truth"—must pass the test of biological consequence to be significant. James was inspired by Darwin's views on how perception, cognition and emotion evolved as biological adaptations. He was part of that American tradition that turns its back on thought for thought sake. But here, again, the Postmoderns showed phronetic thinking the "science" for solving political issues.

It would take several decades before a single legitimate spokesperson for social science to acknowledge the Blank Slate Movement a failure. It occurred in 1991, when Diane Halpen, a PhD past president of the American Psychological Association (APA), began writing *Sex Differences in Cognitive Abilities*, and changed her mind about sex differences being due to blank-slate socialization. Why? Because after reviewing piles of empirical articles and books that countered the blank slate idea, she concluded the brain being a sex-typed organ with distinct anatomical differences in neural structures, scientific data that was too enormous to ignore.

Regardless, romantic psychology was not dead. It seems Dr. Helprin's voice, along with that of Freud and the Father of Modern Psychology, William James, was just another voice in the wilderness. By then, the Freudian art of mind-control, the ability to capture, bias and blind humans to a cause, was just too addictive, an emotional addiction beyond any known drug or reeducation facility to remedy.

Tribalism was working well within the confines of the psychology tribe. Perhaps the weak fightback they got from the empirical sciences to their mob tactics was enough to ignore the one or two warning voices like that of Ms. Helprin. The reality is, unless forced, human addicted to a philosophy that governed for several hundred years, will simply reject any divergent ideology.

To solidify the phronetic approach as sound science, Bent Flyvbjerg wrote a book, *Making Social Science Matter: Why Social Inquiry Fails and How It Can Succeed Again*. At the turn of the 21st century, Flyvbjerg was one of the leading figures in the widespread movement against the idea that the social sciences should model themselves on the empirical sciences. In the book he was definitive in proposing social sciences be modeled on Aristotle's concept of phronesis, suggesting "decisions related to human behavior be made according to practical reasoning," and "focus less on established scientific theories and universals and more on common sense, experience, intuition and wisdom." Essentially, like Freud, he was claiming the many forms of *emotional rationalization* their right and responsibility.

Around the same time, but in a much different manner, a number of eminent and not-so-eminent environmentalists were working to *emotionally* help move environmental legislation being proposed by Congress. What eminent and not-so-eminent environmentalists brought to the table was not only emotions, but *a wide range of emotional-scientific validation*, simply by their presence. At the time, the not-so-eminent validations came from individuals advocating Gaia Theory, Deep Ecology and Ecopsychology.

A range of influence is evident with Gaia Theorists claiming the earth a single, living, and breathing organism. In Greek mythology, the Goddess of the world was named Gaia and in the late 1960s, James Lovelock, an atmospheric geochemist, used the name in his Gaia hypothesis to posit the world as a super organism.

Sometime later, Arne Names, a Norwegian philosopher developed a theory holding that the natural world had an innate, native self-worth, a theory he called Deep Ecology. Naess called for the development of community therapy in order to heal our sick relationship with Mother Earth. Advocates see Deep Ecology workshops as community therapy where participants learn that the world is not a commodity to plunder, nor should we tamper with the grand sweep of evolution by destroying habitats or driving species into extinction.

Both Gaia and Deep Ecology theories blend well with the field of Ecopsychology. Using Freudian, Jung and Gestalt psychology, ecopsychologists claim people have an "ecological self" that, integrated with the "Freudian self," motivates them to sympathize with the non-human planet. Some claim our collective myopia to world danger is a psychological defense against witnessing world pain and we should use our sensory capacities of taste, touch, sight, smell, and hearing to get back in touch with the world.

The problem here is that street folk and many academics view such rhetoric as just so much cultish psychobabble, rich in aphorisms and illusive solutions. Speaking and writing in metaphor about having widespread psychological distress, witnessing world pain and expressing psychic numbing and depression as manifestations of cultural imbalances, are touching moral clichés, indeed, but are more reflective of their authors' emotional temperament, then they are of social reality. Here, as in talk therapy, Freudian psychology gave life to the romantic movement by their adopting emotional-phronetic science on a much broader front.

Consequently, it might have been easy to ignore such mawkish views. But their popularity as mental therapists, gave the ecopsychologists not only a scientifically valid platform to preach from, but generated those addictive *emotional glues* so necessary to capture, bias and blind to a spiritually charged cause, much like the writings of early theologians St. Augustine and St. Aquinas who granted 'scientific' momentum to man-over-nature with their version of Christian and Islamic theory.

The eminent scientists validating Postmodern thinking are a host of renowned individuals like Edward O. Wilson and Jared Diamond, whose works in the fields of sociobiology, population genetics, biology and biogeography are recognized all over the world as the epitome of sound science, impossible for anyone to marginalize. Given the gap in reliable research separating the empirical and social sciences, one would think a marriage between the two impossible, but strange things happen when people in the empirical sciences realize that Gaia, Deep Ecology and Ecopsychology have their fingers not only on the pulse of ecology but on the heartstrings of Americans as well. It was a reality check illuminating the fact humans, given the opportunity to choose between a cold, objective science-based political movement or a warm, subjective, transcendental movement, most often choose the latter.

Yet, Wilson shines in his validation. In his book, *Consilience*, he admits that even while science wins the mind of men, transcendentalism continues to win the hearts of men. To his credit, he continued his call for earthly considerations in his 1984, *Biophilia*, a small but interesting book claiming every living organism is priceless, to be learned and cherished and never to be surrendered without a struggle. By "every living thing" he included invertebrates and microbes, "the little things that run the world."

Wilson estimates that the current extinction rate for both plants and animals is one thousand species a year. He believes this figure will rise past ten thousand a year (one species per hour) up to one million in the next 30 years. Data released by the World Conservation Union indicates that of the approximate 4,600 species of mammals known to exist, more than 1,000 are classified as being at risk for extinction.

Several decades after the science community ostracized him for writing *Sociobiology*, Wilson won two Pulitzer's for *On Human Nature* and *The Ants* along with being named to one of the most prestigious professorships at Harvard and elected to the National Academy of Sciences. Further, he was lauded as the world's most eloquent biologist and "Father of Evolutionary Psychology," a field of genetics and cultural evolution he explored in *Sociobiology*. For the hardcore Postmodern, the entrance of such a renowned empirical scientist into the various movements was heaven sent. Without it, their subjective, faith-based agenda would not only be heavy on emotions, but heavy on reason. Now, there was validation with impeccable credentials.

Before the 1970s, the romantic, ecology-minded crowd received little national attention. Though articulating strong emotional elements, their views were slow to catch on because they simply didn't appeal to independent, self-reliant Americans. After the 1970s, in the short span of a couple decades, with a media focused daily on such issues, people were finding traditional social and international policy emotionally sterile and opting for a more sophisticated, urbane politic, one with a global heart and vision.

The equity idea became so intoxicating that by the end of the 1970s, Marxists, hippies, environmentalists, and housewives were joining hands and marching against nuclear power, while milling crowds were busy advocating civil rights and animal rights. Their conscious effort to protect nature and humanity exceeded all expectations.

Equity was so compelling an idea, the public soon began to feel comfortable giving equal rights to women, minorities and illegal immigrants, as well to water, soil, air, wolves, eagles, mice, owls, wetlands and wilderness. Darwin would have been pleased. Social Darwinism was out. Environmentalism and Equal Rights were in. What the theoretical rambling of enlightened philosophers, Freud's constructive lie and talk therapy, blank slaters' mob tactics, and the eloquent and not-so-eloquent scientists did for the equal-rights movement, was: Provide the emotional energy of their brand of science, and a unified direction to the romantic, equal-rights endeavor.

Summary Part 3

****

This change in governing philosophy could only have occurred at a time when Old World philosophers were searching for a more humane governing process; immigrants in the New World were searching for the same; and the broad field of psychology and political science were recognized as professional tribes to 'legalize' any political actions they deemed normal, appropriate behavior. This long gestation period the young Postmodern cult went through was necessary for human minds and their God modules to be reprogrammed at supporting individual rights over community responsibility, the Community Mandate subservient to the Freedom/Equity Mandate.

In the process, these energized, romantic elements would, in the coming years, coordinate their values with those of other liberal groups to support a Postmodern movement that would reach out in an extremely dramatic fashion, and show just how effective the constructive lie, identity politics and political correctness can be in the hands of committed Postmoderns.

PART 4

PRE-MODERN CULT TO POSTMODERNISM

I am extremely conscious of tribalism. And when you talk about tribalism, you talk about living in a white world. I mean, Native American tribalism sovereignty, even the political fight for sovereignty and cultural sovereignty is a very us versus them. And I think a lot of people in this country, especially European Americans and those descendent from Europeans don't see themselves as tribal.

\- Sherman Alexie

Chapter 19

MODERNISM TO POSTMODERNISM

The Western world has lost its civic courage. Such a decline in courage is particularly noticeable Among the ruling and intellectual elite, causing an Impression of a loss of courage by the entire society.

> - Aleksandr Solzhenitsyn

Many historians describe the President Woodrow Wilson era as the beginning of a rather unique form of liberal capitalism. Unique, because a balance seemed possible between unrestrained free enterprise, environmental concerns and the fair and equitable distribution of wealth. To a large degree, the assessment of this unique balance would, over the next six decades, prove correct. It was the period historians call "Modernism" which began with the romantic philosophers of the Enlightenment and eventually led to the most powerful nation in the world.

Other historians see this era as the outset of social democracy, the beginning of powerful federal and state bureaucracies along with a welfare state. To this end, government institutions worked ever so slowly in consort with a rising class of intellectuals embedded in academia, labor unions, a liberal media, growing social sciences, and an expanding liberal judiciary. In 1908, newspaperman Arthur Fisher Bentley published *The Process of Government*, a long, theoretical work describing politics as a never-ending struggle among shifting coalitions of self-interest groups, a process Bentley called "pluralism." In the book, he suggested little had changed during this era other than setting the groundwork for bigger government composed of liberal interests rather than free-market interests.

While America's consciousness was tracking increasingly toward meme complexes associated with a global form of socialism, much of it was lost during World War I and World War II. Although Franklin Delano Roosevelt's New Deal was a major step in that direction, Hitler and Stalin dampened big-government enthusiasm for a time. Another thirty years would pass before environmental concerns would coalesce into the Equal Rights Revolution, a movement that by 1980 would have strong Postmodern trends.

So, it was after World War II that America took a hiatus from the wants and needs of the emerging Postmodern cult, as the economy boomed, and conservative pluralism dominated US politics. Political dissonance, at a minimum, also put a damper on any radical displays of tribal infighting. It was a time when capitalism, the industrial/military complex, manufacturing, international trade, mass production and mass consumption took on real meaning. In the political struggle that was brewing, the US chose to balance Roosevelt's wise-use management and capitalism over equal rights.

From the standpoint of a modern United States aging successfully through its juvenile and mature stages, one could say America had arrived, standing tall and strong after the two world wars, led by the likes of so many of its young citizens who returned from warring theaters in Europe and the Pacific. And, like so many of these young men and women of 'The Greatest Generation,' the nation had been tested and had shown itself capable, confident and mature, ready for the next tribal test, the Cold War.

The Cold War not only showcased autocratic and democratic values on a world stage, but demonstrated a shift in warring tactics where clever diplomacy replaced bombs. Given the fear of atomic weapons and an expanding communication technology, warfare became propaganda warfare, playing with people's heads, where a large part of the strategy was gaining power over emerging third-world nations with threats, counter threats, trade embargos and blockades. In essence, it was Aristotle's fine art of phronesis once again rehashed in various forms of rationalization and obfuscation to see which tribe would dominate on the world stage. Warring tactics America had some experience with during the Blank Slate War.

At the same time, young progressive intellectuals were knocking around the Rousseauian thesis of subjective relativism within the context of its freedom and equal-right postulates. Stimulated by opportunities from an explosive economy, all the ingredients for advancing such a Postmodern cult were there: an ever-increasing cadre of K-12 teachers promoting student-oriented classrooms; universities infiltrated with Marxist intellectuals who fled Europe with Hitler's rise to power; a liberal television industry driven by ABC, CBS, and NBC; liberal trending Democrat and Republican Parties, as well as a liberal trending judicial system. For better or for worse, post-World War II America became *the perfect breeding ground* for Postmodern-styled, social engineering.

And why not, with the economy booming and the nation enjoying a sense of euphoria, anything romantic was not only righteous but possible. Plus, the national elation was such the public even learned to appreciate those ecopsycholigists speaking and writing in metaphor about widespread psychological distress, battling world pain, while expressing psychic numbing and depression as manifestations of a cultural imbalance. Not only was the poetic wisdom appreciated, but the claims also accepted as challenges that would come to define the basic foundation of the young Equal Rights Movement.

The underlying challenge was to alchemize all tribal sub-sects into a singular national identity, a new ideology. Then, build a "New man," forge a "New Nation" by persuading several hundred million people to renounce social standards and traditions that endured for two-hundred years, cast aside their *national sense of authority*, and undertake a gamble to create a modern global collective.

This was the Postmodernism Movement that was actually well into its juvenile stage by 1980. Recall, the cult's embryonic stage germinated way back with Teddy Roosevelt's successful conservation programs and the romantics' poetic writings. The next nugget of good fortune was the environmental movement when, between 1963 and 1976, twenty-six environmental acts became law, the 1960s riots that highlighting the Vietnam War as evil, and the discovering of a nation lacking in civil rights.

The largest nugget of good fortune catapulting the movements into its juvenile stage was the symbiotic relationship that slowly matured between the television industry and a progressive paper media. During this period, national outlets reflected the broad appeal of liberal values highlighted by only three outlets: ABC, CBS, and NBC. The result was a united media platform from which corporate executives shared liberal values promoted by well-respected TV commentators like Walter Knonkite, Charles Kuralt, Robert MacNeil, Jim Lehrer, Ted Kopel, Dan Rather, week after week. Trends all highlighted by the major new papers like the *New York Times*.

Postmodernism and The Gang of 5

By 1980 then, America became the most powerful nation in the world and, driven by a liberal form of capitalism, the Postmodern cult metamorphosed into a scrappy juvenile. Also, except for the Middle East where industrialization resulted in social unrest, much of Europe, the Far East, and America enjoyed a calm economic upswing resulting in a powerful economic class of "Income Elites." With bank accounts on par with some developing countries, these elites came to dominate politics to the exclusion of all others.

Much of this domination was nested in capital cities around the world such as Moscow, Beijing, London, Brussels, Paris and America's east and west coasts. Aside from the money, what made these "Income

Elites" a powerful political force in America, was the conjugal relationship that evolved between them and the liberal elites in the media, academia, the social sciences, and the Democrat and Republican Parties. The remarkable thing about these five entities is they became uniformly radicalize to function as a single entity, definable here as "The Gang of 5," responsive to solidifying Postmodern goals.

Therefore, by the late 20th century, Postmodernism became officially contextualized as a movement that looked upon the grand dramas of the past as having burned up their fuel and, with energy spent, proclaim these dramas passé. The implication being the modern age had ended and the country had embarked upon a new age, governed by a new intellect, forging new assumptions and new sensibilities. One assumption, tribalism's out, individualism, diversity, and cooperation are in. Another, no theory however noble, can escape the prejudices that encompassed and produced it. The effect was to declare all political stereotypes as irrational, morally irrelevant social constructs, including our lifestyle, codes and creeds, our Constitution and borders, and, therefore open to wholesale revision, a fact we should not only acknowledge, but celebrate.

Spiritualized by such all-embracing political thinking, liberals came to realize anything was possible and set about resolved to be more audacious, more action oriented and, to that end, step out front with a new image. Hence, they dropped liberalism from their lexicon because its original definition of freedom from social rules and regulations, had been taken over by libertarians and did not reflect current progressive values.

The spillover from World War II horrors also gave socialism a bad name. The trick, then, was to deny any connection to socialism, ignore the term liberal, change their cause to a "progressive movement" and step forward into the future with a new public image. It took a few decades, but by 1990 they succeeded. Progressives not only changed the public's perception of their image, but masterfully succeeded in changing the perception of their agenda as well, by applying a heavy dose of obfuscation to personalize the words freedom and equity.

To the great conservative trustees of political freedom, freedom meant freedom from coercion and the arbitrarily powerful. The new progressive freedom meant freedom from want and need. To the same conservative trustees, equality meant equal opportunity, whereas the new progressive definition became equal outcomes for minorities, illegal aliens and women in housing, the workplace, in education, in health care and so on. Their goal: Equalize all disparities. Make it personal. Make it emotional. Focus on the individual, not the tribe.

Who could disparage that? And to their credit, their messaging was amazingly successful. In the process, they had become experts at cognitive capture, the first step in constructing a fail-proof mature cult. Fact is, their all-around efforts at rebranding was a stunning success, and hard to overstate its importance, because it set the political stage for decades of progressive achievements on a revolutionary scale. Its appeal to the addictive, compassionate mind was on the order the Image-of-God thesis had on human thinking that catapulted Christianity and Islam into dominance as world religions.

Dressed up as freedom from want and equity of outcomes, the progressive campaign took on the full-fledged trappings of a religious orthodoxy with a James Bond license to wipe out the opposition. Immediately, community activists sent out spiritual edicts to proclaim the remarkable transformation. All of the ingredients were there for a Great Leap Forward: a bevy of equal-rights groups demanding equity on all fronts; flocks of academic intellectuals, social scientists, and judicial reformers ready to provide the 'scientific' verification; Hollywood and the media ready to disperse the information; and, finally, government agencies ready to supply the patronage and political clout. Who could lose with such backing? The fix was in, a Big Bang ready to be heard around the world.

The movement turned into the Equal Rights Revolution that produced several years of rioting, burning and killing (including President John Kennedy, his brother Robert and Martin Luther King), culminating in a new political narrative for America. A new political ideology governed by principles of equity for all and generational sustainability for all life forms. It was Modernism on steroids. In essence, man, stripped of his Image-of-God status and no longer idealized, was downgraded to only one among many, no longer sanctioned to hold dominion over other men and other life forms.

To appreciate the significance of this equity movement one must remember that, from historic times, the goal of individual rights and freedom from oppression was a failure in Greece, Rome and all the great medieval cultures due to internal fighting. And here, after several hundred years, America, the most powerful nation in the world was adopting a similar brand of subjective relativism—Postmodernism—with all the mind-control mechanics to achieve the same negative results.

Change was coming. Where but a few decades earlier, the Greatest Generation was reflective of hard-working immigrant men and women who, to a large degree were uneducated, but highly skilled in all the essentials of building a great nation. That national reflection was to change as the Postmodern Gang of 5 elites would come to symbolize a ruling class of "intellectuals" with degrees in the "Higher Ed" liberal Arts. A divide that would begin to show itself in a dramatic fashion with Identity Politics.

Chapter 20

LEGALIZING IDENTITY POLITICS

"When you find people who tolerate your quirks but celebrate them with glad cries of "Me, too!" be sure to cherish them. Because these weirdos are your tribe."

-Sweatrpants & Coffee

The democratic STM was an emotional, intuitive, impulsive and—from the outside looking in—an irrational process humans use in their search for freedom and equity. The Equal Rights Movement was no different. As a maturing cult, the Postmodern ideology remained impulsive, intuitive and righteous. But it was different in one very important way. It was grounded in a desperate, urgent anger, a God Module outrage over being denied what many perceived to be their God-given birthrights.

It was 'fire-in-the-belly' anger that in times past produced duels, gunfights, hangings, witch hunts, and the Inquisition. Yet, it is one thing for a political party to be fired up for freedom and equity, it's another to meet those goals with strong judicial support, along with some means of disparaging the conservative opposition steeped in long-held American traditions.

By 2006 the Democrat Party became the embodiment of this emotion-driven psychology and the party's progressive firebrands, experts at implementation. Although, their remarkable success could not have happened without several cultural trends that had slowly evolved since President Teddy Roosevelt's time: the ground swell of euphoria after World War II that spilled over as an overwhelming yet lighthearted communion by Americans of all stripes with social and environmental causes; and the symbiotic relationship that slowly matured between the political parties, media, social sciences, academia, and income elite—the Gang of 5.

To their credit, though, serendipity had little to do with the tactical success the Gang of 5 had in recognizing and taking advantage of these trends. By making causes personal and emotional, progressives were able to expand the yardstick of moral justice to include a wide range of hither-to-neglected minorities who quickly became victims and reliable voting blocks. Identity politics was underway.

Victimhood though, was only part of a larger plan that included: controlling emotional narratives; staying on offense; preaching and demanding party purity; harassing scapegoated Republicans; never going on defense; and, being obedient, disciplined, tenacious, ruthless and tireless. The goal was to generate anxiety, guilt and depression among opposition ranks while keeping loyalist emotions raw and sensitive to maintain that fire-in-the-belly. It was a muscular social agenda that would require a muscular thinking judiciary to enforce.

Like the prospector getting his deed to a rich claim, progressive's deed to legally expanding the moral yardstick of equal rights came with the judicial system adopting Immanuel Kant's categorical-imperative theory that pushed the US over the threshold into a big-government welfare state. Like the Image-of-God Thesis fueling Christianity, Kant's moral theory super-charged the Equal Rights Movement by placing the intelligence of Postmoderns above that of science and non-believers to define accurately or marginalize. In effect, legalizing individual rights over community responsibilities.

The theory was that wise, benevolent leaders with public interest in mind and no axe to grind would define the pure categories. In turn, wise, benevolent legal experts with public interest in mind and no axe to grind would translate the intellectually pure categories into just laws. For example, although we can readily understand the utility of harvesting resources like oil, timber and wildlife, the total implication of harvesting is unknowable and, therefore, caution is required in all related actions. Hence, the goal of resource management should be long-term, generational sustainability like "Ecosystem Management" presently being implemented across the US.

Although an old application of Cicero's natural law, categorical rights provided the guiding principle central to legalize memes like individual freedom and equality as not only morally righteous, but legally demanding and untouchable. In his well-known book *A Theory of Justice*, John Rawls claims categorical rights are not subject to the calculus of social interests by which other human values are measured. Categorical imperatives command us to put our Freedom/Equity Mandates aside and act according to the mandates of third-party intellectuals.

The key to such success was allowing the judicial system the power to expand the yardstick of moral justice to third-party intellectuals who, as we have seen, can be anyone able to use his or her linguistic gifts to mesmerize an audience into thinking he, she or they have rights beyond the ability of science to marginalize. All that was needed for a right to become a birthright was to sprinkle a cause with some emotional reasoning, a bit of guilt and social compliance followed.

But none of these intellectualized rights could hope to reach stardom without media's support. Therefore, the only member of the Gang of 5 capable of putting traditional US morals and beliefs aside, and have Americans act according to the mandates of third-party intellectuals, was the national media that quickly adopted and played *the major role* in nudging the judicial system to approve Kant's theory.

It's important to understand that this action on the part of the media was a rebellious act. No government can survive without a media biased toward its ideology. China has media biased to communism. Same with Russia, all the Muslim countries and most all non-Western nations. That means an objective news media as well as an objective legal system only exists within the tribal context. If they did not reflect tribal values and standards and were working to negate traditional standards and values, they would, by definition, be considered a radical, rebel force. Consequently, from 2000 on, the national media played *the major role* in advertising ideas, moral beliefs and values Postmodern leaders would claim America's new truths to be believed, or else.

Thus, Postmodernism progressives not only had the Gang of 5 supervising the movement, but the judicial system and media moving the population in the right legal direction. Within no time lawyers, legislators, judges, clerics, academics, government officials, union leaders and numerous other activists were in the business of inventing rights, and, in the process, reconstructing our body of law around an ever-expanding ring of equity legislation.

Given free reign, the God Modules of those so infected and inflamed were super-energized to believe wholeheartedly their rights were God-given and beyond the ability of science to marginalize. Almost overnight, several thousand years of ethnicity rule, objective common tribal law was undone by subjective relativism. Postmodernism was becoming America's spiritual ideology.

It's difficult to over emphasize the importance of energizing intellectual rights as categorical imperatives that are beyond the ability of science to marginalize. Such devotional power gave progressive the spiritual right to evangelize and like all successful prophets, progressives took on the cloak of spiritual curates, where, from their politically-correct pulpits, began defining right from wrong, vice from virtue. With their super-charged God Modules, their equal-rights narrative became their religion.

So energized, progressives were able to tune political correctness into a finely pitched instrument of intimidation by which any expression or action perceived to exclude or marginalize the physical, psychological or intellectualized rights of a person, group, or creature could be charged as being politically incorrect and, thus tainted, the interloper stigmatized as homophobe, Islamophobe, animal hater, xenophobe, tree hater, chauvinist pig, religious zealot, sexist, white supremacist, xenophobe, racist or bigot.

What political correctness gave progressives was a civilized rendition of the wolf-pack warfare Mongols used to subdue their enemies for some 1300 years. In like manner progressives learned to never launch a bold frontal attack on enemy ideas. They study the opposition's values, history, and family interests then make a concerted and sustained media attack showing some aspect of that lifestyle morally suspect. Habitual traditions for conservatives were their affections for the traditional family and marriage, religion, a strong self-defense, balanced budgets, legal immigration, border enforcement, civil discipline and responsibility, the Constitution, free speech, the English language, free enterprise and the rule of law. All, low-hanging fruit to be picked and pared as exclusive and dangerous to someone or something. Thereby offering a never-ending supply of insensitive clods to savage along with an equal endless supply of victims to fold into their flock.

Once progressives expose an agenda as being politically incorrect, they, like the wolf pack, cull out leaders and, with the help of a complicit media, relentlessly smear them in some fashion. The goal is to diminish faith not only in the leaders, but, by extension, faith in their ideology while being careful not to attack moderates who may be swayed by the scapegoating from joining the progressive flock. Supreme Court nominee Robert Bork, Supreme Court Justice Clarence Thomas, Independent Counsel Kenneth Starr, President George W. Bush, Vice President Dick Cheney, Governor Sarah Palin, and Congresswoman Michele Bachmann are but a few of the many individuals, who were chastened early on and maligned. The millions that make up the Tea Party were eventually included in the scapegoating as extreme right-wing crazies.

The beauty of spiritualized inter-tribal warfare of this nature is that it handcuffs the opposition with charges of victim apathy, a quasi-legal method of vilifying the opposition and generating guilt. If effectively managed, guilt will nullify any aspiration the guilty opposition has in extracting revenge and, when layered on thick enough and fast enough, the guilty find themselves living in a constant state of cognitive dissonance, become guilt-ridden, emotionally drained, insecure, a bit squeamish, easy to manipulate and, therefore, make easier the need to drive a philosophical wedge into the heart of the American spirit.

Tribal infighting is usually predicated on finding ways to end an opponent's ability to continue, physically or psychology to control the media. In civilized society that's not an easy task unless dutifully carried out by the media controlling the narrative on a daily bases, and vilifying the opposition as grievous threats to Postmodern victims. But it happened, and turned out to be an extremely beneficial maneuver in keeping loyalist emotions raw and sensitive to any feelings of humiliation, jealousy and envy they might be feeling by pointing out the opponent's elitist and inconsiderate feelings. Like a love bubble, political bubbles can shrink, or collapse should that 'fire-in-the belly' driven by hate grow cold, therefore, generous reminders of class envy and resentment are needed to maintain a steady state of anger, hate, indignation. This takes experienced professionals with known credentials.

A good example of how effective and generational victimhood can be is the racism and sexism that emerged after the late 60's riots when blacks and feminists had the upper hand in controlling the equal-rights agenda. After this heated period, black preachers and leading black spokespersons were relatively free to make moral judgments against whites, where similar judgements against blacks, were severely chastised. The same with feminists who were equally free to make moral judgements against males.

By the late 20th century, professional scapegoating activists found both feminist and racial causes endless sources of income and professional enhancement. Television came to dominate the news, so its long-held progressive slant was not only sympathetic to the Postmodern cause and its proponents, but its public appeal an obvious source of income to keep the cause and cable networks operating.

What made the powerplay by victims and their activist promoters so deplorable to many, was the obvious mendacity and greed involved. For many it was seen as a charade after millions of ethic migrants, from dozens of nations had battled political bondage of one sort or another back home, including itinerant conditions in the US, only to eventually assimilate peacefully and prosper in America.

One example: During the great Italian immigration of 1900, many northern Italians came to mining states where they survived as itinerant miners: living in company houses; shopping in company stores; and visiting company doctors with lungs blocked by mine dust and bones broken by falling timbers and rock. In each case, company largesse with company house, store, or doctor, was paid for with meager wages.

While many of these multi-shaded immigrants had much to complain about with living standards, most didn't, because they were better off than where they came from; saw the many opportunities available; cherished the benefits of their hard labor; and in a generation saw their children prosper. They didn't see themselves as victims. Consequently, many grew resentful of the never-ending preaching by victimhood advocates.

This simmering resentment by a rising class of rural conservatives put the focus on Postmodernism for the extremist cult it was. Until then, old leaders of The Greatest Generation remained sympathetic to not only environmental needs but obvious civil needs as well. But after decades of non-stop identity politics, these elders also began to see Postmodernism as a cult determined to replace Americanism and all its hard-fought benefits.

Such conservative opposition came primary from the rise of conservative talk radio in the late 1980s which began to highlight the union of the mainstream media, judicial system and the Democrat Party as an incestuous cabal. The rise of conservative talk radio was, itself, a successful mini explosion because it reflected the views and values of a rising tide of Americans the Tea Party concerned about where the country was headed.

Although the rise of conservative talk radio along with the rejection of progressive talk radio came as a surprise to many in the media and the Democrat Party, it was too little, too late. By then any suggestions nightly news narratives had a progressive slant fell on deaf ears. Left-leaning narration had become something like baseball, an American pastime and negative charges considered disingenuous.

Throughout the rise of Postmodernism, the cognitively-challenged Republican Party unwittingly became the foil in the progressive con game. Unwittingly because they seem not to understand you don't get to the Super Bowl by being unfocused, undisciplined or nice to the opposition. They simply didn't recognize they were at war. Thus, exposed as straw men, they became the party of fall guys, whipping boys and scapegoats the rights revolution needed to blame for its ever-growing list of right-less victims.

To keep emotions raw on the good-guy side and subdued on the bad-guy side, you need a scapegoat like the Republican Party that was short on warring zealots and, therefore, totally ignorant at combating inter-tribal warfare. For any successful con to work the mark must believe the scheme as rational or at least reasonable. This was true with the Republican Party. Their success as mark was in thinking progressives were reasonable and rational and, therefore, reason and logic on their part would prevail to mediate differences.

They were wrong!

Like all zealots, ideologues are only rational within the framework of their ideology, the bind-and blind, tribal groupthink demanded by their God Modules. So, bound they were blind to the unintended consequences of Postmoderns' unrelenting appeal for more and more of the social pie and bound to their daily need to evangelize and demonize. Like St. Augustine, Muhammad and the New England Patriots, they were immune to rational thought beyond their tribal reasoning to win, and to win at all cost. But, President Clinton's problem with women provided an opportunity for the Republican Party to unite and show some political muscle, and for a short while they did by impeaching the president.

All the animosity and anger that surfaced in the highly polarized atmosphere with impeachment had the signs of a religious war epitomized by tactics developed by James Carville and George Stephanopoulos who knew we were at war, and in their War Room they strategized daily, using scapegoating and political correctness to neutralize the negative press during President Bill Clinton's hearings. The ceaseless fighting over impeachment only added fuel to the political soap operas being played out daily in the media. Hard-line, inflexible polarization became reality when the US Supreme Court gave George W. Bush the 2000 presidential election.

The problem with this form of warfare is that it destroys any working relationships between tribal entities. No longer does polarized thinking work to balance the needs and wants of communal interests. Moral outrage replaces common sense as polarization becomes more strident and the never-ending sophistry more degrading and obvious.

The carnage left behind after weeks of rhetorical warfare and legal maneuvers was a country divided equally along lines of hatred for Mr. Bush or love for Mr. Bush. From then on, Washington politics experienced take-no-prisoner tribalism at its best, where charges of 'politicopath' gained substance. A politicopath is analogous to a sociopath who, like many politicians, is clearly seen as a pathological liar, intelligent yet dishonest, irresponsible and unreliable, cunning and manipulative, impulsive yet shallow and charming while totally lacking in emotional insight and remorse. This inflexible polarization is a noteworthy example of addictive minds driven by Freedom/Equity Mandates super-charged by highly active God Modules that were designed to work well against opposing tribes, not against in-house tribes.

None of these tactics could have been so successfully carried out without the liberal public accepting Postmodernism as the liberal orthodoxy governing all ethical and moral values in the US during its 50-year reign. It's not much of a stretch to state that in America, by 2010, the progressives enjoyed a virtual monopoly in the media, education and the law. Reminds a person of the thousand-year monopoly the Catholic Church enjoyed, where all men of learning were priests who defined all learning, controlled the media and legal activities within a firmly established Christian context throughout Western Europe.

What we have here is tribalism warfare in its most civilized form: An absolutely brilliant campaign by the Gang of 5 to promote a Postmodern brand of globalism. Throughout this period, one can only imagine Mother Nature sitting on the sidelines, looking down, smiling and whispering: "Civilized Inhouse Warfare! Who would have thought? What happened to bombs? No interference needed here! These refined folks have bias and conflict down to a science, with very little bloodletting and only a few surface bruises. Yes! Yes! Yes! Scapegoating, mendacity, duplicity, capitalism, socialism, cronyism, feminism, racism who cares? Those old, reliable God Modules energizing addictive minds are working just fine. Thankyou America!

Chapter 21

CONTROL THE NARRATIVE
-WEAPONIZE GUILT-

The worst guilt is to accept An unearned guilt.

— Ayn Rand

As with all secular and religious ideologies, Postmodernism is fraught with hypocrisy, irony, duplicity, and mendacity. So successful were the progressives in promoting Postmodernism that most national standards such as the traditional family and marriage, religion, a strong self-defense, balanced budgets, legal immigration, border enforcement, civil discipline and responsibility, the Constitution, the English language, free enterprise and the rule of law, were dramatically altered. Under the guise of equal-rights, a political/media revolution, just as formidable as Russia's takeover by the Bolsheviks, was underway. Sadly, many Americans were too immersed in feeling guilty from being smeared as inconsiderate boobs to realize or even question what was happening.

Then came 9/11 to add to the guilt and anxiety. The firestorm of passion resulting in the collapse of the Twin Towers in New York City by hijacked airliners again pointed out the fact that not all is morally relative. There is good! There is evil! For Westerners, evil is generally considered any intentional behavior that causes physical and/or psychological pain. For terrorists, evil is not pain, suffering, or even death, which they seem willing to suffer, but rather living among infidels.

In the case of suicide bombers, not only is such behavior repulsive to the Western mind, but there is no way the national psyche can reason the use of children as weapons of war. How does this happen? How, in the 21st century, can the addictive minds of leaders so warp the collective conscience of entire cultures that they willingly sacrifice men, women and children hoping their God will rain fire and brimstone on the idolaters?

Though fairly hardened by a media reminding us daily of rape and rampage, we cannot comprehend the inner dementia needed to commit such vile acts. It is evil incarnate. Writing in *National Review,* Victor Davis Hanson details the outright insanity that occurs when tribal equities clash:

> Paradoxes of civilization are seen in a more sinister context in the Middle East, where a sophisticated and modern society like Israel's is racked by suicide killers right out of the Dark Ages. For such leeches of civilization, it only takes a modicum of cunning and little skill, rather than real education or intellectual accomplishment, to strap on imported explosives and blow up women and children. Dismembering a child is easier and quicker than nurturing and educating him; exploding a bus involves less work and training than building it.

Hanson went on to state that confronted with such elemental nihilism, all the sophisticated policing, electronic security, preservation of human rights and civil liberties "can disappear in moments."

Just how palpable the fear of terrorism was at the time is evident in the panic caused by the presidential plane, Air Force One, flying low over New York City eight years after 9/11. *The Staten Island Real-*

Time News reported that on Monday, April 28, 2009, the plane, escorted by military fighter jets, zoomed low over the Manhattan skyline just before the workday began. The purpose, to take publicity shots. For a half hour, the Boeing 747 and F-16 jets circled the Statue of Liberty and the Financial District sending startled workers streaming out of their offices fearing a repeat of 9/11.

At the time it seemed President Bush was just as odious a threat to humanity. With no weapons of mass destruction found and the war in Iraq bogging down with Muslim infighting, progressives saw an opportunity to ratchet-up charges against President Bush with mismanaging the Iraq War. They claimed the war was started by him under false pretenses. Although Saddam Hussein had killed thousands with poison gas and both Democrats and Republicans, including President Bill Clinton and Senator Hillary Clinton, and US intelligence networks, supported the atomic-weapons claim, the progressive media were successful in painting Bush the villain.

The charges only added to the confusion and cloud of guilt hanging over Americans, which increased as progressives continued their propaganda onslaught by pummeling the public with endless politically correct questions about the war. Did the president lie about the war? Were we right to invade? Were we wrong? Is the war just? Is the war unjust? Are we responsible for all the deaths? Does it warrant the killing of coalition soldiers and Iraqi citizens? Will others think of us as liberators or invaders? Is waterboarding legal or illegal? Should terrorists be kept in the Guantanamo detention facility in Cuba? Are they being treated humanely?

Identity politics is nothing but Freud's Gotha Game used to transfer feelings of guilt and anxiety of suffering victims to the opposition. Just as important was the media arm of the movement and their endless negative attack, attack narratives. So effective were these tactics that popularity polls during the spring and summer of 2007 showed President Bush with a 30 percent approval rating, and the Congress with ratings in the teens. The ratings reflected a public frustrated and befuddled by endless news of Americans and Iraqis killed and maimed in the most inhumane fashion, while our leaders and the press squabbled over how to treat prisoners of war humanely; how to conduct a war humanely; how to treat thousands left homeless by Hurricane Katrina humanely; how to treat millions of illegal immigrants humanely; how to handle the threat of global warming; and how to deal with an exploding national debt. No matter what action taken to solve a problem, the public was fed a steady diet of conflicting messages, designed to elicit fear, guilt, submission, and paranoia. Such acrimony gave rise to the question of whether this generation would be called "The Most Divisive Generation."

Fear and guilt are powerful motivators and Americans are no exception to their ply in trade. Fact is, because of their caring nature, Americans make excellent scapegoats. Blamed for the sins, crimes and sufferings of humanity at home and abroad, Americans had become confused, cynical, politically polarized and riddled with guilt over questions of right and wrong, good and evil. By themselves, the problems associated with climate change, the War on Terror, immigration, political corruption and the economy were insufficient contributors to the equity overkill, but, topping years of endless infighting over fetal rights, gay rights, women rights, religious rights, animal rights and a host of other categorical rights, the total effect was wearing.

The remarkable thing about scapegoating is not only does it generate guild and anxiety among Republican Party scoundrels, but guild and anxiety among a good percentage of those 60 percent independents who shift left because they believe the Republicans are the cause of their guilt and anxiety. With no clear definitions of right and wrong, humans find living uncomfortable. Guilt ridden, they become physically and emotionally drained from riding nonstop, emotional roller coasters. Once guilt became firmly established in the collective consciousness, national unity started to erode. Throughout this endless cycle of moralizing, our Constitution was ignored, long-held ethics recalibrated, traditions forgotten.

The fact scientists can put a man on the moon but others can't figure out our divisive behaviors only adds to the severe case of cognitive dissonance our nation was suffering. By 2008, half of America was seen as an unjust, tyrannical culture bent on suppressing minorities, destroying the environment and subjecting other cultures to its whims and wishes; and, the other half claiming America the world leader in promoting minority rights, preserving the environment and a universal beacon for freedom and prosperity. America was a guilt society suffering from compassion fatigue: a symptom where people are troubled by a disturbing guilt, a neural guilt, that turns on feelings of shame for having done something terribly wrong, where confusion and depression reign because people are not sure what it is, they did wrong.

Living in a constant state of cognitive dissonance and nowhere to turn for help, the squeamish, guilt-ridden, emotionally-drained and insecure American public, like the residents of Nazi Germany in the 1920s, began a search for an alternative source of comfort and security. In 2008, they elected the unknown but attractive Senator Barack Obama as their 44th President. A trained political activist. A man who expressed a wish to fundamentally change America along Postmodern lines. A man who knew well the power of the God Module to capture, bind and blind and how to escape any negative after effects.

Chapter 22

PRESIDENT OBAMA = TRUMP

A certain prince of present times, who is not well to name, never preaches anything but peace and faith, and is very hostile to both. If he had observed both, he would have had either his reputation or his state taken from him many times.

\- Machiavelli (The Prince)

Not only did Kant's moral theory buttress Postmodern doctrine of individual freedom and equity, it gave credence to the claim mankind reached an evolutionary summit of thinking in which enlightened intellectuals are no longer subject to Darwinian restraints. They believe their old reptilian brain and their newly evolved 21st century brain embrace equity and empathy over bias and competition as forces driving humanity. Thus transformed, those Postmoderns rising to the top of the political ladder are the latest incarnation of aggressive, rational, intellectual beings, setting agendas and defining rights and responsibilities with devotional energy beyond the ability of science to marginalize.

The problem for conservative America soon became obvious. Rational, intellectuals capable of looking beyond their sticky preconceptions are rare—if they exist at all. We need look no further than our Supreme Court for proof that addictive minds drive the highest court along liberal and conservative lines. Chosen from a profession that, by definition is supposed to offer objective justice, most on the court vote their tribal values. It's true, blinders are there, but they are more like horse blinder that, unless forced to look in another direction, offer a narrow tribal view of the political landscape. Conservative failure to recognize the Kant ruse for what it was became Mr. Obama's ticket to the White House.

The 2008 election clearly defined that drift to the left and his administration accepting the challenge with age-old Machiavellian designs for supporting and expanding the progressive agenda. Looking back at his record, it's obvious the path Mr. Obama—as a self-proclaimed community activist—chose to do was fundamentally change America with the goal of shifting America's slow drift to the New Left into high gear. Given such a task, he and his Chicago teammates knew their efforts to be massive and, to their credit, their endeavors were not halfhearted. They went for the whole enchilada in classic activist style.

In a mere eight years, Postmoderns philosophically energized progressive God Modules to: Increase activism in the universities to sensitize the public to idealized Postmodern goals; Solidify gay marriage as a cultural norm; Radically change the ethnic demography of the nation, the Democrat Party and Congress; Change the sexual demography of the political parties and Congress; Successfully define transgenderism to fit Postmodern goals; Successfully defined right/wrong, vice/virtue, normal/abnormal to fit Postmodern goals; and, massage the main-stream media to censor, aggravate, and impede Republican and Conservative values.

These events could not have occurred without the aid of a unified progressive media, executive orders, decisions handed down by activist judges, and the entrenched far left Income Elite on the east and west coasts. Most important, throughout the past-six decades, the Gang of 5 was brilliant in stopping any effective opposition by the Republican Party with their Orwellian identity politics warfare.

As it turned out, Postmodern progressives could not have elected a better leader than Obama. He was the frosting on the Postmodern cake. As a true ideologue, he was blessed with an extreme sensitivity to socialist theology while being insensitive to the America spirit and its traditions by youthful indoctrination to socialist ideology. A devout believer, he was the Messiah progressives had been looking for.

So programmed, he seemed undisturbed by the unpatriotic barbs thrown his way and seemed to relish the many controversial tactics he utilized in his change efforts. Obama was also a better student of human nature than his opponents. He understood the biology behind ideology addiction. How addictive minds works. How to play with human minds and the enormous value ideology addiction had in supporting his cause.

Not only was President Obama ideologically shielded by cognitive blindness while encapsulated in a socialist bubble, his administration also got a free pass from its political stumbles by a media that had turned into pack journalism with a far-liberal bent. In the process President Obama became a cult figure, confident the major news outlets would, by their silence, support any social endeavors he embarked upon. The *Washington Monthly* listed some 50-plus achievements of the Obama presidency they considered his legacy, of which many enhanced the liberal agenda and international globalization efforts. Other achievements such as ending combat missions in Afghanistan and Iraq, improving US image abroad, reducing the threat of nuclear weapons, an anemic annual economic growth, the massive increase in student debt, securing the removal of chemical weapons from Syria, and avoiding scandals have proven questionable. Nevertheless, poles showed he went out a beloved winner.

Pander politics has been around forever as a form of soft despotism. Mushy Republicanism failed because it maintained its socially liberal, fiscally conservative goals in the face of a well-orchestrated scheme making them cultural bullies. It was a gentleman's shortcoming illuminated by presidential candidates such as John McCain and Mitt Romney who acted as if they would rather lose—which they did—than put up a spirited fight. Such laxity was seen not so much as un-manly weakness but an effort to avoid being labelled one of the proverbial racist, sexist, homophobe, nativist, or xenophobe. In the mêlée, the populist

Tea Bag movement seemingly went by un-noticed, or possibly, ignored, by the country-club Republican elites, as an insignificant, marginalized bunch of far-right conservatives sticking to their bibles and guns. Reminds one of the ideology differences between feudal religious and secular leaders during medieval times that lead to the demise of Feudalism.

One can only assume the Republicans knew the media fix was in, so chose not to counter with sulfurous tactics they simply were not good at. Plus, unlike the progressives who were emotionally bonded to their liberal ideology, the Republicans lacked a cohesive narrative with leadership radically divided along liberal, libertarian and conservative lines. So, they walked away from the Postmodern legacy battle, losers, and deservedly so.

On the surface, then, it looked as if America's slow but steady drift into Postmodernism had been successful. Not only was the American public guilt ridden and confused, they were ill equipped to stop the movement. In *The End of History and the Last Man*, University of Chicago philosopher Yoshihiro Francis Fukuyama describes man's need for self-actualization and his benevolent nature as a paradox, with his altruistic tendencies constantly threatened in contemporary society by the very principles of liberty and equality on which they are based:

> According to the Anglo-Saxon theory of which the United States was founded, men have perfect rights but no perfect responsibilities. Their duties are imperfect because they are derived from their rights, his community exists only to protect those rights. Moral obligation is, therefore, entirely contractual. It is not underwritten by God or fear for one's eternal life or the natural order of the commons, but rather by the contractor's self-interest in fulfillment of the contract by others.

By this time people began to realize that—like 18th century Rousseau—societies promoting freedom, justice and equal opportunity for all "were only lures invented by clever autocrats or by base flatters to impose their own brand of governing on the haveless." In *Soft Despotism, Democracy's Drift*, Paul Rahe was one of the first to describe this progressive drift to the left as the "French Disease" by which Americans surrender "their destinies and liberties to bureaucracies." Like Fukuyama describing man's equity need and benevolent nature as a paradox, Rahe argues "that the effects of living in a democracy render the continued survival of democracy increasingly doubtful" because "its citizens gradually embrace habits and dispositions that treat freedom as a burden and reduce self-government to a hollow ritual in which wards choose between interchangeable sets of wardens."

The idea of surrendering one's liberties to bureaucrats as a French Disease was not new. Catherine The Great of Russia, in 1791, after careful study of what happened with the French monarchy during the French Revolution, described the upheaval as a "French Poison," putting the blame at the feet of certain liberal philosophers stirring up a rising mercantile class and belligerent, ignorant serfs. This at a time when she herself helped promote influential philosophers such as Voltaire and a rising middle class of intelligentsia (doctors, lawyers, writers, architects and poets) who were only a few short years earlier, uneducated ignorant serfs.

The amazing feature of this drift is that most other social movements had largely disintegrated worldwide by the 1990s. After the Berlin Wall fell, communism behind the Iron Curtain collapsed, and China moved a bit toward capitalism. It seemed Marxist socialism was reduced to a couple floundering South American countries, the insulated halls of Western universities and Western news agencies. But the Equal Rights Movement proved that theory wrong. The soft despotic tactics skillfully used by progressives showed socialist change can be achieved if leaders work from within using identity politics.

In the Postmodern drift, America became divided along ethnic, cultural, educational, sexual, economic and religious lines as hard-core progressives tore the Constitution and Bill of Rights to shreds with their impossible demands for freedom from of want and need and equity of outcomes. They gave it their best shot by building an entitlement class with identity politics and political correctness. Under Obama, they reached their apogee, but left a large section of the population poorer economically and psychologically.

And …. Then came Trump!

Chapter 23

THE TRUMP DERANGEMENT SYNDROME

*He who brings trouble to his family will inherit only
the wind, and the fool will be servant to the wise.*
- Proverb 11:29

Obviously, any selection process elevating the rights of one group over the rights of another generates conflict. Consequently, the tribes best able to focus their cognitive skills at promoting tribal wants and needs, while directing tribal aggression toward those with different beliefs, survive to pass tribal genes onto future generations. The result is an enduring biology in which the primal forces that drives humans ever onward is conflict between and within tribes.

Unlike classical warfare between tribes that battled each other to the death or capitulation, tribal infighting is more reasoned. Should needs go unmet, social smarts kick in and attempts are made by individuals to remedy the situation with dinners, free tickets to the ballgame, plane rides to the convention and so forth. If gentle persuasion doesn't work, threats, face slapping, nose punching, strikes, lawsuits, sanctions, marches, politically-correct bullying, flag burning or riots might be tried. When all else fails, impeach someone or declare civil war.

The irony is, as social animals with several million years of evolutionary experience, one would think mankind had reached a point where peace and tranquility, love and compassion would prevail, but an hour of TV news tells a different tale where civil conflict, envy and hate reign supreme. A quick review of one such inter-tribal scenario scripted out to conflict perfection is what occurred during and after president Obama's administration.

From the very beginning, his administration had all the trappings of a personality cult with a fixation on Mr. Obama revitalizing and speeding up America's trend toward Postmodern globalism—which he did skillfully, ending with high hopes and assured confidence Mrs. Clinton would continue his efforts. Yet, even with majority support of the Income Elites, mainstream media, Hollywood, the social sciences, and academia, his presidency ended with a stinging 2016 party defeat. It seemed the Democratic Party's focus on identity politics came back to sting them when a disillusioned working middle class, spear-headed by the Tea Party, gave Republicans 12 state governors, 69 house seats, 13 senate seats, 900 state legislature seats and Donald Trump, a political outsider, a businessman as president.

It was an election that stunned the Democrats to the point of mental breakdown and a flaming desire for revenge. Like flash mobs terrorizing local markets or a raucous group of Brazilians after a lost soccer match, the progressives' reaction to the Trump presidency exhibited an interesting but not well understood behavior known as lateral mind behavior, a form of collective mob behavior where many minds work as one with party wishes unstated.

At first the Washington attitude was one of, how dare some fly-by-night playboy think of joining "The Club" without being recognized as having shown the proper modesty, dignity, politeness, and respectability that comes with the cherished invite? How annoyed were they then to see their chosen Mrs. Clinton, along with a dozen or so elite republican candidates, quickly defeated in a rather deplorable fashion, by one devoid of all political protocol?

To regain the initiative, Democrats began to play with public heads by claiming President Trump a dupe, a dunce and a dangerous threat to America. Essentially, their response was a media blitz that was nothing short of a first-of its-kind media revolution to rid the world of an elected president. Hollywood, late-night talk show hosts and comedians chipped in with malicious commentary.

In the meantime, more than 50 progressive organizations united in opposition to Trump, and congressional Democrats setting out to create a 12-member Oversight Commission on Presidential Capacity to determine whether the President was mentally able to do the job, and if not, use the 25th Amendment to have him removed from office. Noted authors and intellectuals wrote books or flooded the airwaves and editorial pages with scathing rebukes. A Missouri state senator called for Trump's assassination. Dr. John Gardner at New York University started a petition stating, "We, the undersigned mental health professionals (please state your degree), believe in our professional judgment that Donald Trump manifests serious mental illness that renders him psychologically incapable of competently discharging the duties of President of the United States." The petition garnered some 41,000 signatures. Next, the Gang of 5, supported by innumerable unverified rumors, claimed Russian hacking influenced, with Trump's aid, the presidential election. The process went well into 2019 with senate, house and a special council set up to investigate the many accusations.

Several news commentators labeled the hysteria "The Trump Derangement Syndrome." Dan Gainer of Fox News described the media's reaction to the election as a "Primal Scream." A Harvard study in late 2017 showed CNN, CBS, NBC, MSNBC and ABC with an 80 percent plus negative coverage of the Trump administration that included numerous fabricated stories.

Annoyed and dumfounded, one could almost feel the palpable hysteria building daily among the Gang of 5 as they struggled to control the narratives of their many campaigns to take Trump out, only to be let down time and time again. The remarkable surprise was the depth to which emotions had embedded themselves into the progressive fabric. Yet, after decades of controlling the equal-rights narrative by way of identity politics, it was understandable that one half the US voting population believed, at a spiritual level, their democratic religion was inviolate, untouchable. And, anyone with contrary opinion be defined as bigots or Fascist pigs and their rights to free speech eliminated, especially that of the devil himself, President Trump with his stupid "tweets."

In a nano second of that presidential defeat, Postmodernism became an admitted terrorist cult set out to not only reform the entire US, but take out, in any fashion, a duly elected president and the whole Republican Party as well. Without thinking of the consequences, all semblance of propriety was set aside, and their decades of Marxist theory was revealed as the real deception behind the daily fodder of false rumors and news stories needed to feed the masses of ignorant serfs.

What these humiliated were expounding was their tribal sense of conscience, that moral sense of self-interest our ancestors founded in our neural makeup some 100 thousand years ago, an equity conscience that will not be denied unless severely censored or suppressed. Except for a first-of-its kind US media revolt, there was nothing new in the Trump/progressive confrontation. It was simply inhouse tribalism carried out in a modern democratic style with one party gallantly trying to regain some dignity from a seemingly assured victory that somehow went terribly wrong.

The election was tribally informative because both sides in true tribal fashion believed their beliefs, values and actions as rational, righteous *truths*. To an interested party ignorant of tribal behavior, it would seem one side or the other delusional, but they were not. Rather it was classic, internecine tribalism at its best with two tribes, one liberal and rebellious, the other conservative and traditionalist, struggling in a no-holds-barred battle for supremacy. It's within this *search for truth* where American politics would get very messy, with both sides claiming the other of conspiratorial narratives to bolster their rational democratic ideologies.

Summary Part 4

****

Trump came because Postmodernism is anti-traditional tribalism in all respects. At the time, it was a form of globalism with no physical borders or traditional social standards. As a cult, it used the emotions of identity politics to divide the nation to gain popular support, resulting in not only economic stress, but guilt, anxiety and confusion that many felt was something on the order of a sexual assault. Like being stripped naked of their traditional way of life and violated of those underlying community feelings their ancestors implanted in their heads, by accusation of bigotry, homophobia, xenophobia and the like. A sense of community solidarity that cannot be replaced by Postmodern fantasies.

Postmodernism went far beyond what the tribal mind had been programmed to deal with. Classic paleolithic thinking was relatively minimal in logic construction, simple moralized standards, and a simple, rational language evolved to meet the demands of a relatively small number of compatible individuals and their rather simple theology. Even through medieval times, autocratic governing was driven by simple logic, codes and creeds, and a rather simple, direct, language built to meet the demands of uneducated, compliant individuals emotionally attached to their simple theology.

So…. Postmodernism was a revolt, Catherine The Great would have called an "American Poison," resulting in the Trump presidency, and the nation divided into two cultures: one top-heavy with "income" elites, living comfortably in their cloistered DC, New York and California bubbles; the other, bottom heavy with rural folks scattered across the country, where many were forced to deal with austerity, poor housing, and mass immigration. A serfdom composed of mining, lumber, agricultural, and manufacturing communities where assimilated ethnic neighborhoods thrived in non-affluent complacency; simple people lacking Higher Ed degrees living in places like Detroit, once the very essence of labor's heartland in American. Stable, close knit communities of multi-shaded migrants with a burning desire to have their children live a more prosperous life then they.

Now, in a divided country, the serfs were bewildered, disorientation and, inexcusably, dismissed as casual racists, white supremist, and bigots. Yet it wasn't their sense of race that had been violated by the sudden upheaval in their community, it was their sense of order. A divided country where they were told to get with the movement. A country increasingly atomized, where millions were feeling a sense of isolation, their conservatism increasingly incompatible with Postmoderns' "woke" politics that was, effectually, a coup to take over the US government.

PART 5

POSTMODERN PATHOLOGY (AKA – PMP)

Extremism in defense of liberty is not a vice, but I denounce political extremism, of the left or the right, based on duplicity, falsehood, fear, violence and threats when they endanger liberty.

\- George W. Romney

Chapter 24

THE TRIBAL VIRUS

If you spend time with crazy and dangerous people, remember their personalities are socially transmitted diseases; like water poured into a container, most of us eventually turn into — or remain — whoever we surround ourselves with. We can choose our tribe, but we cannot change that our tribe is our destiny.

- Stefan Molyneux

No one could have imagined that the onward march of a quasi-religious, political belief in continuous progress out of the early 20th century would, by the late 20th century, produce Postmodernism which, in turn, produce some 60 million anxiety-ridden serfs who, in turn, produce President Trump. For many, an unattainable, anxiety-ridden injustice. Actually, not so. As early as December 9,1841, Ralph Waldo Emerson gave a lecture called the *Conservative* at the Masonic Temple in Boston in which he expounded over his anxiety about the destructive nature of internecine tribalism, and his fear of a civil war to come due to inhouse fighting. A small portion of which follows:

"This may stand for the earliest account of a conversation on politics between a Conservative and Innovator [Liberal], which has come down to us.

Two parties which divide the state, and have disputed the possession of the world ever since it was made. This quarrel is the subject of civil history. The conservative part established the reverend hierarchies and monarchies of the most ancient world. The battle of the patrician and plebeian, of parent state and colony, of old usage and accommodation to new facts, of the rich and the poor, reappears in all the countries and time.

The castle, which conservatism is set to defend, is the actual state of things, good and bad ...whilst innovation is always in the right, triumphant, attacking, and sure of final success. Conservatism stands on man's confessed limitations; liberalism on power; one goes to make an adroit member of the social frame; the other to postpone all things to the man himself; conservatism is debonnair and social; reform is individual and imperious. We are reformers in spring and summer; in autumn and winter, we stand by the old; reformers in the morning, conservers at night.

The war rages not only in battle-fields, in national councils, and ecclesiastical synods, but agitates very man's bosom with opposing advantages every hour... It is the primal antagonism, the appearance in trifles of the two poles of nature."

Emersion understood classic tribalism between nation states. What puzzled him was why intelligent people could not resolve their in-house problems without resorting to the civil-war hysteria he was witnessing. This lecture preceded Darwin's book by several decades and, although evolutionary ideas were being tossed around during the Enlightenment, Emerson probably lacked any insight on the democratic values our paleolithic ancestors evolved. So lacking, Emerson was wont to blame the inevitable infighting for much of humanities woes throughout all of human history, rather than a *flaw* in the large cultures that matured during historic times.

For those of us, like Emerson, concerned about such civilized behavior, it's necessary to look back over the last 100 years, and try to understand WHY and HOW Postmodernism became the kind of in-house rebellion capable of such fractious infighting. Let's remind ourselves that tribes are made up of diverse, creative individuals. Individuals who are spiritually bonded together by family and friends to a unifying cause, an ideology, based on moralized beliefs, codes, and creeds. Individuals who coordinate their individual skills to function as a single organism to compete successfully among other tribes of diverse, creative individuals.

Yet, any such vibrant collective can cease to exist if enough members demand their individual rights. Such selective thinking was contrary to that of our highly success paleolithic ancestors with their STM, that focused tribal energy on the community, not the individual. Postmodernism was a rebellion reversing that process, making the Community Mandate subordinate to our Freedom/Equity Mandate resulting in the internecine tribalism that Emerson was so concerned about. Liberal and Conservative tribal members beating up on each other. "Classic Internecine Tribalism." A house divided. Each side claiming their ideology the true morally righteous road to salvation.

To a degree, what Emerson defined as a "tribal quarrel," Catherine the Great defined as a "French Poison," Fukuyama and Rahe a "paradox," was actually such a reoccurring practice that deserves being labelled a "Tribal Virus:" An intelligent attempt by inhouse rebels, to replace established conservative moral beliefs, traditions and ideology with new tribal moral beliefs, traditions and ideology; a cyclical tribal disease that, over time, resulted in codes, creeds, the ten commandments, and vengeful gods to control the rebellions; a virus with a very long history.

An interesting study supporting the tribal virus theory, appeared in the March 20, 2019 edition of *Nature* that was something on the order of what came first, the chicken or the egg. In this case it was what came first, large, complex societies or the belief in vengeful gods? The scientists analyzed 414 societies from 30 regions over the past 10,000 years for their size and legal codes that included four measures of supernatural moral enforcement codes. Their findings showed that vengeful-gods came later at, approximately, the million-person level. The purpose for later was vengeful gods—which God Modules are especially good at generating—helped enforce moral codes that increased as liberal, rebellious behavior became more prevalent. Such a conversion at that time in history supports the tribal virus theory that conservative efforts were made to staunch the internal flow of spiritual energy rebellions generated.

As a historic conversion, it sided well with the Greek civilization, peaking around 500 BC, where creation myths supporting gods in animal form, shifted to vengeful gods in human form, culminating in the Christian doctrine of a single vengeful God as the Roman Empire declined. It was a slow process, carrying with its bits and pieces of cultural lore into subsequent generations. A number of authors for example, describe the tenets of a divine trinity (Father, Son and Holy Ghost) in Jewish, Christian, and Mosaic theology as forming a noticeable part of narrative thinking by the Persian, Hindu, Babylonian and Egyptian religions, all preceding Christianity by hundreds of years. Later, human-like gods like Jesus came to drive Western theology during Medieval times.

Tribal infighting requiring vengeful gods was not how the human mind was designed to work. A tribe can't be devoted to two ideologies, two iconic gods, etc. God Modules simply don't allow for such tribalism, and yet infighting has this long history There are numerous passages in Greek literature of murderous civil wars (stasis) between oligarchs and democrats, of laments on how conforming morals and laws are destroyed in a cycle of madness, depriving both parties of sanctuary when the tide one day turns against them in their effort to achieve short-term gain.

Even the ancient civilizations of Egypt, China, India, and Persia engaged in the philosophical study of the underlying psychology involved. Understandings that grew in China from the philosophical works of Laozi and Confucius, and later from the doctrines of Buddhism. Classic Chinese internal medicine for example, identified the brain as the nexus of wisdom and sensation, including analyzes of mental disorders and destructive social uncertainties. Yet today, all these nations with their long philosophical histories find themselves struggling with the same social uncertainties as they did throughout their long historic past.

A modern, psychic effort was undertaken to address the virus issue in 1920 by the German's Goering Psychotherapy Institute. At the same time, a similar Russian psychology was heavily promoted by the Bolsheviks in their effort to engineer the "New Man" by way of socialism during the Russian Revolution. The countless millions who died throughout the 20th century are stark reminders of what infighting disasters those German and Russian psychologies to cure the tribal virus turned out to be. Lacking neural knowledge of the God Module connection we have today, these civilizations were unable to fully grasp any consistent behavior pattern that controlled the destructive yin/yang, liberal/conservative forces at play. Forces that are actually interconnected and complementary but crippling when used to destroy from inside.

That the tribal destruction is there for everyone to observe is the truly amazing feature about the tribal virus: Liberal-leaning forces replacing the existing conservative government with their brand of governing by using classic psychological strategies to change the thought patterns of a majority of the population to support a new ideology. A tribal virus working like an influenza flu virus that, instead of causing lung issue to function abnormally, causes God Module neurons to function abnormally. Instead of God Module energy being directed at promoting tribal solidarity, the energy is redirected at promoting individual wants and needs.

The procedure Postmoderns used to divide the country was a slow, tedious, heartless pathology from the very beginning, carried out by thousands of zealots in education, politics, science and philosophy using classic identity politics throughout that ended with Trump. Given Trump seemed immune to the *Postmodern virus*, the Gang of 5 was forced—like a flu virus mutating into a more infectious coronavirus— to mutate into the "individual diversity virus" capable of infecting a larger population of victims *demanding their individual rights*.

But before that could happen, a truly remarkable *thought-control strategy* had to be undertaken. The Gang had to redefine the term "normal," to fit their concept of individual normalcy, and to do that, the term "individual diversity" had to be recalibrated. Remarkable because, for countless centuries, normalcy was recognized as any behavior supporting tribal solidarity and survival, and individual diversity recognized as Mother Nature's insurance policy undertaken to ensure a tribe has a great variety of genetic diversity available should social or physical environment change radically and established tribal norms fail to meet the challenge. Two definitions, neither of which fit Postmoderns' hysterical needs at the time.

So, progressives simply rejected those realities by recalibrating humans as unique individuals and their diversity redefined as *free-ranging individuals* to justify their own wants and needs as *tribal norms*. It was a simple proclamation claiming existing community norms passé and individual norms rule the day. With that simple proclamation, Postmodernism had reached a true pathology status as a Post-Modern Pathology (aka-PMP).

A pathology is defined as any social construct exhibiting *mental, social* or *linguistic abnormalities* contrary to established mental, social and linguistic norms. The *mental* addiction of God Modules with Postmoderns promoting a contrary, *social* construct that depends on rationalized *linguistics* to destroy established mental, social and linguistic norms, illustrates how Postmodernism exhibits all three abnormalities.

So weaponized, the Gang of 5 bombarded the public daily with their brand of normalcy, a pathology in which Trump was only the latest target of its materialization. A pathology that would claim the Republican Party guilty of dividing the nation by trying to keep its traditions, beliefs, values and spiritual ideology while, from the very start, the Gang's main intention was to divide and conquer from within.

****

To fully appreciate just how the Gang of 5 planned from the very beginning back in the 60s to divide and conquer, let's once again, take a walk down memory lane and examine the How and Why this viral pathology evolved to destroy America from the inside. To do that, it's necessary to go back and 1), examine the mental indoctrination ideology introduced within the US educational system by German Marxist and American social-reform academics; 2) review and provide examples of the *social* organelles (fields of philosophy, psychology, academia, media and politics) used to promote and certify the socialist movement; and 3) provide in detail the many *linguistic* strategies and tactics used to drive the process. All, when looked at from the standpoint of a once thriving American culture, exhibited pathology abnormalities generated by a socialist tribal virus. To justify the duplicity involved in promoting rights over responsibilities, the Gang simply set about redefining and recalibrating community norms. A Post-Modern Pathology (aka-PMP) as Post-Truths enforced by Post-Politicians, Post-Academics, Post-Scientists and Post-Philosophers.

Chapter 25

PMP WAR TACTICS

Collective fear stimulates herd instinct, And tends to produce ferocity toward those Who are not regarded members of the herd.

- Bertrand Russel

For a mature pathology to survive requires personalized reasoning to attract sensitive God Modules along with a liberal dose of spiritual energy to bias God Modules to the ideology and blind them to contrary ideologies. For young Postmoderns that was not an easy task given it was a new-age philosophy, governed by a new intellect, forging new assumptions and new sensibilities that eliminates not only borders but all old traditions and ideologies. As such, it should have been considered early on an extreme cult with harmful overtones. If so, The Greatest Generation might have gone to war, again, to stop any such movement as would most all its European friends and allies.

But that didn't happen.

A new spiritual force replacing tested beliefs that made America the strongest nation in the world, simply did not register with the public. It was after World War II that America took a hiatus from the wants and needs of the emerging Postmodern cult, as the economy boomed, and conservative pluralism dominated US politics. So, cult leaders were faced with orchestrating all the tribal emotions the God Module and freedom/equity modules would require for a bold inhouse type of warfare using a more sophisticated inventory of linguistic-war tactics.

Whereas in classic tribal warfare, any and all warring strategies and tactics can be used to physically destroy the opposition, inhouse warfare had to be more humane. The bits of anger, spite and resentment that drove the blank slaters resulting in baneful verbiage and a bucket of ice water poured on someone's head, would not suffice. The polarized rationalization and obfuscation, mob mentality, anger and enthusiasm had to be repackaged in a more acceptable fashion that normalized Postmodern standards, spiritualize its goals, while effectually neutralizing the opposition.

The earliest known overt recipe of such crusading came to them from an essay written by Quintus Tullius Cicero, circa 65-64 BC, as a guide for his brother's campaign for consul of the Roman Republic. In it, Cicero develops several basic guidelines: 1) Identify opponents as scoundrels by constantly reminding the public of what villains they are, and to smear them at every opportunity with crimes, sexual scandals, and the corruption they bring with them; 2) Always control the narrative by using any and all assets to spread your goals to the widest audience; 3) Preach the gospel of hope in simple vague generalities, and; 4) Assure the public you will always be at their sides and, remember, that lies are better than refusing to speak.

Cicero was a great writer and orator who represented liberals and moderates in the Roman Senate. At the time, he was convinced by fellow politicians to use his vast influence to pass a resolution requiring Julius Caesar to disband his armies, and forgo his imperium (power to command), leaving Caesar open to prosecution for treason. But Caesar crossed the Rubicon River and entered Rome with his army intact.

Tumult and violence followed with the death of Caesar along with numerous plots backfiring on Cicero and his allies. Eventually Cicero is killed on the direct orders of Octavian Caesar who had Cicero's hands nailed to the senate doors. Soon after, Rome returns to an imperial state and Octavian Caesar its first Emperor after surviving a rousing campaign against Mark Anthony, in which both blamed each other with degrading origins, cruelty, cowardice, oratorical and literary incompetence, debaucheries, drunkenness and other slanders.

Over time, these concepts of defining the opposition as villains, controlling the media narrative, preaching in simple vague generalities, and promoting lying as warring tactics were expanded upon by any leader of substance. In 1315, Niccolo Machiavelli, the Italian Renaissance political philosopher and statesman simplified Cicero's, theory in *The Prince* with: "Never attempt to win by force what can be won by deception." Not surprising, a similar thought-reform strategy was expanded upon in *Mein Kampf* (*My Struggle*) by Adolph Hitler while in prison for political crimes in 1923.

The book was an autobiography in which he outlines his political ideology, future plans for Germany, and the roll propaganda must play in winning the hearts and minds of the German people to support his political views. Such a vision stemmed from the fact he believed one of the reason Germany lost World War I was because the British had a better propaganda machine than the Germans. In *Mein Kampf* he describes the simplicity of controlling tribal member:

"The function of propaganda is not to weigh and ponder the rights of different people, but to exclusively emphasize the one right which it has set out to argue for. Its task is not to make an objective study of the truth .... its task is to serve our own right, always and unflinchingly .... The great majority of a nation is so feminine in its character and outlook that its thought and conduct are ruled by sentiment rather than by sober reasoning. The sentiments, however, is not complex, but simple and consistent. It is not highly differentiated but has only the negative and positive notions of love and hatred .... But the most brilliant propagandist technique will yield no success unless one fundamental principle is borne in mind constantly and with unflagging attention. It must confine itself to a few points and repeat them over and over. Here, as so often in this world, persistence is the first and most important requirement for success."

Any warfare creates anxiety and guilt within the aggressor's populations. For Hitler, that meant the Jewish people were essential as scapegoats for transferring anxiety and guilt. With a Doctor of Philosophy degree, highly trained and practiced as a public speaker, as well as a devoted friend of Hitler, Joseph Goebbels became Reich Minister of Propaganda in 1933 and quickly obtained full control of all newspapers, radio stations nationwide as well as the film industry. The end result was Hitler became chancellor of Germany one year later. Then came World War II. And throughout, the Jewish people persecuted without mercy.

While such mind-control tactics have always played a significant role in political history, their significance had little public exposure until World War II when Hitler and henchman Goebbels added the great Prussian military general and theorists Carl von Clausewitz's battle tactics to their control theories, and converted them to a more brutal brand of thought-control warfare.

In her Pulitzer Prize winning book, *The Guns of August*, Barbara Tuchman describes in great detail the von Clausewitz battle tactics: Seize the initiative; Control the battle by staying on offense; Attack. Attack. Attack; Push to the limits with no second thoughts; Be obedient, disciplined, tenacious, ruthless, tireless in pursuit of your goals and, forget defense. Carl von Clausewitz was also a great writer who before he left Prussia to join the Russian army, left behind these simple tactics in an essay for the sixteen-year-old Prussian Crown Prince Friedrich Wilhelm who, later as King of Prussia put the clear and simple advice to good use.

As a rule, the Postmoderns in Western cultures tend to ignore the many shadowy characters that influence their philosophical foundations. Although people like Cicero, Hitler, and von Clausewitz are only a few among many who played a role in designing successful warfare strategies, they remain ghostly reminders of the deception and devastation that can occur. Given such a history, what these tactics boiled down to was an *identity politics/scapegoating formula* that proved to be enormously successful and became the signature strategy with the Gang of 5. For some 60 years we saw this formula of identity politics used time and time again to capture the minds of the masses and destroy the minds of the opposition by forgotten or invisible men.

Invisible Propaganda Men

Once students leave mandatory public-school systems, invisible propaganda men continue their education by way of gossip, reading, watching television, or interacting on the Internet. In all cases, they are subject to propaganda, usually defined as information of a biased or misleading nature to promote a political cause or point of view. We are victims of propaganda, a public form of academic education, taught by professional politicians, the media, and propaganda corporations.

As early as 1928, the Father of Public Relations, Edward L. Bernays wrote *Propaganda,"* with the thesis "that 'invisible' people who create knowledge and opinions rule over the masses, with a monopoly on the power to shape thoughts, values, and citizen response." He went on to state that "the conscious and intelligent manipulation of the organized habits and opinions of the masses is an important element in democratic society. We are governed, our minds are molded, our tastes formed, our ideas suggested, largely by men we have never heard of."

He compiled materials for his book from social science literature that explored the psychology behind manipulating masses and the ability to use propaganda to influence politics and effect social change. At the time, he suggested propaganda would be very useful in lobbying for gender and racial equality. (The Reverent Al Sharpton, Jesse Jackson, Gloria Steinem and Betty Friedan must have read *Propaganda*.) He went on to suggest that propaganda techniques would become increasingly effective as scientists became better at discovering hidden motives. (Here, Bernays must have been familiar with Freud's work.) He also suggested the term propaganda was too negative and so created the term "Public Relations" with a "PR" alternative. Since then, PR has become a multi-billion-dollar industry driven by any number of Silicon Valley-like corporations using every conceivable rationalized strategy to manipulate public opinion.

Probably the most shadowy person in the Postmodern movement was Herbert Marcuse, a German associated with the Frankfurt School of Critical Theory who immigrated to the US in 1943 when Hitler came to power. As philosopher, sociologist and political theorist, his first job in the US was with the Office of Strategic Services (predecessor of the Central Intelligence Agency) where he criticized and worked to undermine the Communist Party and its ideology.

Later, in 1952, he began a teaching career as a political theorist, first at Columbia University, then at Harvard, followed by a time at Brandeis and finally at the California University of San Diego. From these academic bastions of progressive thinking, he reverted back to his base, socialist foundations, and set about critiquing the American capitalist system in several books that resonated strongly with socialist movements at the time.

His *Postmodern claim to fame* revolved around his theory of fomenting class warfare in well-established and powerful nations like America, by *fomenting a coup from the inside*. A divide-and-conquer strategy he theorized could be achieved by dividing the culture among *groups of "victims."* The fact that charges of racism and sexism played a major role in the 60/70 riots and received popular support, lent sustenance to the victimhood logic. It was a personal, emotional strategy with the potential to effectively destroy long-established norms like top-down distribution of wealth, the family, religion, community responsibility, traditional legal systems and the like that were cornerstones of capitalism.

In essence, he was a professional PR academic, who remained invisible for his efforts because of the need, over the decades, to hide his Marxist influence from the public. Even after the universities were teaching the various elements of Postmodern socialism, they refused to publicly advertise any aspects of higher ed as being socialist oriented, or credit Marcuse and his friends for their role in the Postmodern, education movement.

In 1971, another shadow individual, Soul Alinsky, fired up the movement with *Rules for Radicals: A Pragmatic Primer for Realistic Radicals* as a guide for community activist in uniting Haveless victims, in order for them to gain social, political, legal and economic power. Alinsky had been active in community organizing from 1939-1971 when many of his rules for radicals were influenced by philosophers like Marcuse who became known as the "Father of the New Left," and Alinsky considered its first "Community Organizer."

The fact early progressive politics picked up on these inhouse warring tactics and strategies advocates for direct contact by Marxists-leaning academics like Marcuse and especially Saul Alinsky with politicians like Mrs. Clinton who was offered a job working for Alinsky. She turned the job down, but as a close friend, Mrs. Clinton wrote her senior thesis on Alinsky's revolt methods. In the thesis, Mrs. Clinton rejects Alinsky's views on destroying America from without by violence, and claimed the Marcuse strategy of *revolt from within* the more practical scheme. Some years later Mr. Obama was trained in community organization under Alinsky's guidance.

The modern propaganda tactics to emerge from this marriage of Roman-Prussian-German theorizing to cognitively capture, bias and blind the public, while destroying the opposition, consist of the following steps the Postmoderns pick up on and mastered:

1. *Make things personal with identity politics where possible.*

2. *Identify scapegoats and vilify in every manner possible to relieve ingroup tension.*

3. *Truth is irrelevant: rationalize and obfuscate where necessary.*

4. *Define normal and abnormal and preach normal party purity.*

5. *Control the narrative with simple emotional principles.*

6. *Be disciplined, tenacious, ruthless, tireless, never go on defense, deny negatives and Attack. Attack. Attack.*

It was within this context of a coup from the inside by dividing the culture among groups of victims, that the early Postmodern movement took on a pathology context. Recall, a pathology is a "mental, social, or linguistic abnormality. As Postmodernism matured it would exhibit all three of these abnormalities: Mental from the standpoint of God Module addiction; social abnormalities due to its primary goal of restructuring a nation; and linguistic abnormalities by way of the linguistics used in the rationalization, duplicity, obfuscation and mendacity required in identity politics.

Chapter 26

PMP Education

A liberal education... frees a man from the prison-house of his class, race, time, place, background, family and even his nation.
                                    - Robert M. Hutchins

While most political historians credit President Woodrow Wilson for starting the liberal movement, seldom ever mentioned is the fact Postmodern thinking started in K-12 schools, a decade or so earlier in Roosevelt's time. For the young PMP cult this was a true blessing because to survive and grow, God Modules require indoctrination early, in formative years, and later with young adults finding themselves exposed to a world of tribal thinking in the sciences, arts, politics, and religions where they will become addicted to one or two for the rest of their lives.

And, as luck would have it, public school classrooms across the nation were changing from traditional teacher-oriented classrooms to student-oriented classrooms when, progressive philosopher and psychologist, John Dewey, got the ball rolling by claiming students thrive in an environment where they can experience and interact with the curriculum by actively participating in the learning process. It was one of the first steps of Americans getting deeply intrenched in Rousseau's theory of subjective relativism. This child-centered classroom fit the early cult prescription of freedom from oppressive tribal traditions and standards, including bossy tribal teachers and degrading testing.

A prolific writer, Dewey's books on educational reform became must-reading for any teacher entering a "normal school," an early term for institutions training teachers, a term that lasted well into the 1950s. Dewey's theories during those fifty years provided the solid foundation in progressive thinking for not only K-12 teachers, but fit well with university academics throughout higher education who were working in the same direction teaching the teachers.

Dewey was also decades ahead of the Postmodern crowd, who—like Freud—was one of the primary figures endorsing the philosophy of 'pragmatism' and 'functional psychology' which, at their simplest, claim something is true only if it works. The irony being, later in life, Dewey became alarmed by the many excesses that accrued with child-centered classrooms lacking the proper supervision by both parents and school officials, but it was too little and too late. Students and parents learned of individual rights, how to express those rights and, many learned to demand those right, at any time, any place, with anti-social behavior. His reform measures are still with us at the K-12 level with poor showings on international-polls ranking the US in the 20's and 30's in science, reading and math.

By 1970, this Dewy-styled education became synonymous with higher education where the slow but steady saturation of Marxist dogma was being perpetrated by Marcuse-Post-Normal styled academics. Here, Dewey's axiom claiming higher education promote individual involvement in social reform to better mankind, was willingly adopted and endorsed across the Higher Ed spectrum, suggesting Post-Academic elites define, redefine, and foster universal moral and ethical standards.

Although Freud received much more public acclaim for his theories and practices, Dewey's impact on Postmodern thinking far outweighs Freuds efforts in what goes in and what comes out of all public educational institutions. Given the liberal drift America experienced after World War II, our universities became literal bastions of progressive thought. By controlling Postmodern curricula, as well as hiring practices, Dewey advanced socialist theory across the entire social science spectrum.

Limiting the Moral Yardstick of Speech

A large part of the PMP movement must reside with the Post-Academics using Marcuse's advice to generate revolt from within via generating large voting blocks of activist students and, selling their totalitarianism as "partisan tolerance" for victims of capitalist aggression, while promoting *"intolerance for those opposed."* Though an unscrupulous political platform, it lay hidden behind the enormously popular Environmental and Equal Rights movements at the time that peaked with Postmoderns redefining normal.

Of the numerous attempts by academic elites to promote the Postmodern religion, their intolerance of free speech strategy has been most successful, and interesting tribally for its obvious duplicity. Not so much for its first amendment challenges or duplicity, but for the interesting manner in which sheltered professors become Postmodern Academics in adopting the Postmodern agenda as tribal ideology. Most surprising tribally, is the blind, zealous devotion expressed by the vast number of academic institutions promoting speech limitations as normalcy.

All such indicators are wonderful examples of the success old intellects—hardened to a tribal cause, with God Modules driving them to evangelize—can have on young minds. Essentially, the academics were showing their expertise at tribal warfare with well-worn indoctrination schemes that are easy to identify and fascinating to follow: addicted professors operating like a well-disciplined orchestra, doggedly subscribed to tribal doctrine; and, like Post-Sanctuary City mayors, all unblushingly following classic propaganda strategies with no regret or remorse for the duplicity and mendacity involved. Nor is there any remorse it seems with that 'fire-in-the-belly' promoting bullying tactics and violence during contentious gatherings. "Whatever works for the Party" became a Postmodern Academia reality in liberal universities. Meek and mild academics exhibiting "unbridled ambition, weak ethics and excessive patriotism to justify nearly any action of questionable rightness" in their Postmodern drive. Who would have guessed meek elite academics being haughty, zealot tribalist?

But that happened.

The appeal of youth to action-oriented causes, and the harden God Modules of entrenched professors, are but steppingstones for professors and student to sell their Marcuse'-styled *tolerance* and *intolerance* totalitarianism. After all, what's the sense of promoting a cause if you can't enforce it, plus, for the young and adventurous, intolerance can be exciting. Thus, since the 2016 election, youth violence has increased, rapidly. One tribe, suspicious of another tribe's intentions, sets out to criminalize its cult-like behavior and, by direct or covert action, its demise.

On August 12, 2017, one such provocation occurred when a permit was issued in Charlottesville, Virginia, to a group—defined by the media as White Supremacists—to rally in opposition of plans by the city to remove a statue of Robert E, Lee from a park. Next, an opposition group showed up dress like the White Supremacists in helmet, shields and clubs to march in approval of the statue's removal. To the shock and dismay of local officials and the press, violence erupted resulting in three deaths and 20-some injuries. Who would have guessed, another Ruby Ridge debacle? Classic blind, biased mob hysteria.

By 2019 the PMP became even more radical with the University of Michigan establishing a *Bias Response Team* to handle alleged acts of "bias" violations. At the time, more than 200 American campuses had established similar administrative offices that were ready to investigate any and all charges of bias. An outsider looking for "alleged bias" might find it difficult to identify the many shades of bias which, turned out not a problem for academia. U of M advised students that "the most important indication of bias is your own feelings." It then urges "them to report on their peers, anonymously if they prefer' and, to "encourage others to as well." Under U of M rules, "the most sensitive student on campus effectively dictates the terms under which others may speak."

The team warns potential offenders that bias "may be intentional or unintentional." Complaints at the time centered on social-media posts, drawings, comments, and phone calls. The Bias Response Team also had the ability to investigated speech or other expression even when it occurred off-campus. Students found responsible for a bias violation faced discipline, ranging from training sessions to suspension or expulsion. In short, students are encouraged to report their peers for anything that makes them feel bad, even if unintentional.

Talk about a slippery slope, especially in an institution where free speech was the very corners stone of its foundations when I went there. One has to wonder what the Michigan Bias Response Teams' response would be to a bias charge in which a brilliant Muslim student claims a female student "a shameful women" because of the way she dresses and her "living with another women." Behaviors extremely sinful and illegal in his culture. Would the team consider training sessions like the Chinese do with Muslims who fail to assimilate, or suspension for a year, or recommend expulsion?

Decisions!

Decisions!

From then on, limiting speech became the thing to do. Within the month of November, 2019, the following academic protests were but a few that occurred:

November 6, former Attorney General Jeff Sessions spoke at Northwestern University in Illinois where he had to be escorted under heavy guard after student demonstrators tried to stop him from giving the speech. Later the student paper covering the speech apologized for "retraumatizing students" with coverage of the event.

November 15, according to Portland's KATU2 NEWS, 100 students walked out of class to protest the West Linn High School's decision to allow a Chick-fil-A food truck sell chicken sandwiches during a football game. This came amid other incidents which some claim made LGBT students feel unsafe.

November 20, a speech by conservative commentator Ann Coulter at the University of California, Berkeley, drew hundreds of protestors, where at least seven people were arrested.

November 23, the Harvard and Yale football game was interrupted by students rushing the field during halftime to stage a climate change protest that disrupted the game for an hour, causing the game to finish in near darkness.

One of the most ominous and also successful aspects of this diversity movement was—and remains—the callous way empirical science was seen as a threat driving liberal activists to shut down diversity of speech. An example of dragging science into the fray is what happened at Evergreen State College, Olympia, Washington. In an op-ed published in the *Walled Street Journal* on October 2, 2017, Heather Heying, the wife of embattled professor Bret Weinstein, argues progressives rejected the basic principles of science to justify their new political philosophy. In 2017, Heather and her husband—both progressives—found themselves at the center of a national media story and their jobs threatened when protesters complained of Bret's criticism of a controversial activist event. Heather claimed much of the negative collegiate activism at the university stems from diversity policies that, "despite their well-meaning intentions, only serve to silence those who disagree with the progressive orthodoxy....an autoimmune disease of the academy...weaponized and repurposed to catch and cull all who disagree." Evergreen made it clear they wanted Bret gone, thus, "allowing their diversity narrative "to be fully unhooked from any expectations that they be put to the test of evidence."

In September of that year the school agreed to pay Bret $500,000 in response to a claim alleging the college failed to protect its employees. In February 2018, President George Bridges of Evergreen State sent a shock through the campus community by telling them they could expect a drop in their fall registration by some 20 percent and a reduction in staff.

In October of 2019, an Ethnic Studies Advisory Committee, under the Seattle Public Schools Superintendent, published a preliminary Math Ethnic Studies document for their district representatives that explains math as a racist study used to oppress students. Basically, it claimed: "Who are you to insist two plus two equals four?" If a student says two plus two equals eight and you correct his faulty math, you can be found guilty of discrimination.

The framework, created by various statewide districts attempts tackling how to deal with four themes: Power, Oppression, History of Resistance and Liberation. The belief seems to be that "Western" math is viewed as the only "legitimate expression" of math identity and that it's used to "disenfranchise people and communities of color" and, consequently "erases the historical contributions of people and communities of color."

What's interesting here is the math our ancestors around the world used in solving the many physical mysteries in nature, or in the production of millions of products that made life comfortable, has nothing to do with Power, Oppression, History of Resistance and Liberation. Math is an innate, SciTech way of thinking humans use to solve concrete, inflexible variables found in nature.

A similar event occurred on November 16, when the Ohio State House of Representatives passed the Student Religious Liberties Act, which prevents teachers from penalizing students for giving incorrect answers on schoolwork that is scientifically wrong as long as the reasoning is religiously accurate according their religious beliefs.

Separation of Church and State

Such moralizing ineptitude could not have saturated the educational system as it has without interference by the Supreme Court creating laws and enforcing those laws with numerous ruling since the 1960.

Rulings that put a clear wall between secular activities and religious activities, such as no literature, or ten commandments, or Christmas scenes, or praying on public property, including public schools. The unintended consequences of these ruling by the Supreme Court is one of the most fascinating aspects of the academic entrenchment in Postmodernism, via the *Supreme Court breaking the law*.

The metaphor, "Separation of Church and State," is probably one of the most misunderstood concepts for, not only the average citizen to understand, but for the average politician to understand. The phrase is not found in the U.S. Constitution, Bill of Rights, the Amendments, or in any legal document in the United States. Under the present governing context, the 'Church' is that power which represents authority on matters of faith, duty, ethics, spirituality, morality, right and wrong; the 'State' is that power which represents taxation, policy, military, rule and governance. Yet, even though all tribal ethics and standards, codes and creeds, responsibilities and duties have moral foundations, spiritualized by citizen devotion to the American capitalist ideology, the Supreme Court—whose job is to enforce all such beliefs—violated its own mission by ruling to restrict devotional, moral expression and confine it to only religious places of worship or at home—a clear violation of the U.S. Constitution.

Where the Court went wrong is assuming devotion to a secular ideology is altogether different than the devotion to a religious ideology. The unintended consequences of these actions opened the door for Postmoderns to foster their brand of religion as a secular ideology while hinged to the God Modules that drives Postmodernism.

Fact is, the God Module does not distinguish between religious or secular, it's the caretaker of both domains. While the Supreme Court had no understanding of God Module as inherent motivating force at the time of its rulings, it should now. The devotional, God Module glue binding mankind to its tribe's secular or religious ideology has been "The Essential Motivating Political Force" practiced in public since prehistoric times. It only applies spiritual devotion to the tribal cause, whatever that cause may be.

On January 18, 2020, President Trump took steps to provide easier access for religious organizations to get federal programs, and reaffirmed students right to pray in public schools.

The role teacher unions also played in stifling any attempt at change should also be mentioned. While teachers' unions were a necessity in providing teachers with pay raises that were badly needed—and remain so—they lack the desire to adopt any reforms, at any level, and most all remain committed to Postmodern reform. None of this should be a surprise, because, depending on the poll, liberal professors outnumber conservative faculty 5 to 1 in a *Washington Post* 2014 pole, or, 12 to 1 in a *Washington Times* 2016 pole. Findings that would probably be more extreme in K-12 schools, where Postmodern thinking remains devotionally excessive.

Chapter 27

POLITICAL PMP

*Don't pursue something with a vengeful heart, Or
it will destroy you. Hate wraps a cold hand
Around your heart that hollows you out.*
- Dannika Dark

In every country unfettered by revolt, populism is expressed as people worry about traditional values and national sovereignty. People who don't want blowhard bureaucrats in Washington DC, or the European Union, making decisions their representatives should be making back in their community. Everywhere, always, people worry about their cherished traditions and are concerned about the forced injections of foreigners demanding their rights be adopted. Hard-working, multi-colored people who despise overbearing bureaucrats or snobbish elites beating out a steady diet of how they should live their lives, open their borders, what their sexual orientations should be, preaching their God is dead, and forced to grin and bear the transgender restrooms.

When you break it all down, the internecine tribalism going on in America today is a battle between *tribal rights* and *tribal responsibilities* in which Postmoderns learned a bit of such diplomacy from China. China is a very old tribal culture that understands how classical tribalism and internecine tribalism works. It also understands the in-tellectualized duplicity that comes with the Roman-Prussian-German Prescription and its many forms of deception, dishonesty, disloyalty, unfaithfulness, treachery, fraudulence, betrayal, deceitfulness, and dishonesty very well. China understands because it has some six thousand years of playing around with tribal infighting.

Perhaps, after several thousand years of experimenting with various forms of autocracy, socialism, communism and democracy, China's political elites came to realize their present form of government of balancing individual rights with community responsibility with carefully set borders is working, and has room for a diversity of Muslims *but, only if* they assimilate. If not, they spend time in re-education camps, camps they rationalize for Western media benefit as Vocational Educational Centers. Camps that, however operated, will hopefully be more humane than Mao Tse-tung's re-education practices that lead to some 65 million Chinese deaths. The shocking range of duplicity China uses in its problems with democracy-loving Hong Kong and its problems assimilating Muslims, as well of its criminal handling of the prononavirus epidemic that gave rise to a world-wide pandemic, seem to indicate Mao Tse-tung's re-education practices are still in play.

Like the Chinese, Postmoderns have a similar problem with rights and responsibilities made visible by what they preach and what they do are two different things. In reality, they are interlopers promoting a radicle, foreign pathology of individual rights over community responsibility. Why tribal America didn't respond quickly to stifle Postmodern thinking, only makes sense if we credit the none-response to the slow but steady change in liberal governing that started with Teddy Roosevelt, matured with the 60's riots, and ended with President Obama.

Plus, unlike the Chinese, the modern conservative establishment had no experience with rebellious forces and many were ambivalent about the rights trend. Though some could see the vast potential for problems, they were also conscious of its popularity and potential for good, and therefore reluctant at moving too quickly at prevention. Also, unlike the Chinese, Americans, didn't think in terms of cultures using slow-creep terrorism to revolutionize a nation. Duplicity tactics

Chinese and the Muslims are becoming famous for and continue using to cause conflict around the world.

The Cancel Culture

Nor did conservatives recognize the *deceptive and destructive nature* of identity politics by Post-Democrats. Hidden behind the compassion and empathy aura surrounding victimhood lay minefields where character assassination occurred. Media minefields where linguistic bombs were set by PR specialist who searched for any newsy item that could be modified with a negative slant against the opposition. Then, in military fashion, provide daily opposition talking points to a biased media that dutifully distributed the data to their paper, TV and radio outlets. Outlets where talking heads, in unison, provided a dutiful, military character assassination response against any individual or group posing a threat.

As noted, leaders early on learn scapegoating the opposition as some sort of abnormal, sinful, creature intent on destroying their efforts with their aberrant behavior are essentials. Therefore, identity politics became a twofer process with benefits coming and going. A process that allows excesses in spending and accepting radicle policies by tribal members, while redirecting any feelings of envy, resentment or fear to the hateful opposition. It works because it concentrates violence on a seemingly, hand-cuffed individual or group, while defining the ingroup as victim.

In practice, the *ingroup* which controls the media, singles out a person or group they believe deserving of negative treatment which, for whatever reason, the scapegoat is unable to fight the charges effectively. End result: ingroup achieves morally righteous victim status deserving of empathy, affection and legal standing; outgroup becomes the amoral scoundrels deserving of apathy, slander, and the burdened anxiety and guilt that comes with their obvious fomented bigotry.

In addition, the ingroup gains voters by gaming sympathy, doubt and guilt from the independents who float back and forth between the 10/20 percent liberal/conservative zealots at both ends of the political spectrum. As a rule, these swing voters are more emotionally sensitive to victims deserving of empathy, affection and legal standings. In the no-holds-barred atmosphere that the equal-rights movement created, scapegoating became so successful a practice that scapegoated individuals successfully taken out as threats, would be considered 'dead' and those responsible for their demise, 'bomb throwers'.

It was after the riots of the 60/70s, and especially after Al Gore's loss to George Bush in 2002, that progressives stopped playing the long game and shifted into high gear with a short game of identity politics, and the job of fundamentally changing America from the inside was underway. Blinded by assumptions of high-intellect, Postmoderns were convinced they were no longer tribal animals but free-ranging elitists, destine to change the world into one-big-happy family.

Recall, the original goals of Postmodernism were to claim tribalism is out, individual diversity and cooperation are in; no theory however noble, can escape the irrational prejudice that encompassed and produced it. Therefore, all political stereotype—except Postmodernism—are irrational, morally irrelevant social constructs, including our Constitution and borders. By 2008 the Postmodern movement was an established ideology all its own, a spiritual force indelibly etched onto millions of Postmodern God Modules.

We should be reminded that political tribalism in American was not always the ugly rebellion it is today. Prior to the late 60s, America's spiritual unity was evident in The Greatest Generation where rights balanced responsibilities. After the 60s' revolts, that balance shifted to more rights and fewer responsibilities. What made the quick shift in the rights/responsibility equation unique, was that 'fire-in-the-belly' over being denied what millions perceived to be their God-given freedom and equity birthrights.

Once firmly established as birthrights, it was only a matter of time before identity politics proved its worth with a long list of victims having such birthrights. After that, all the Gang did was follow the Roman-Prussian-German prescription of using identity politics to produce enough sympathetic karma over the years to smother Republicans and Conservatives in guilt and anxiety while elevating the Gang to angelic level. Here was where *truth became irrelevant*, rationalization and obfuscation became the new normal, and zealot leaders became disciplined, tenacious, ruthless, tireless, never went on defense, denied all negatives and Attacked, Attacked, Attacked.

Thus weaponized, they steamrolled all opposition with identity politics, political correctness and scapegoating into a demoralized population suffering from guilt fatigue. In the process they became very, very, very successful at intimidation. Success to the point where character assassination, redefining cultural standards and ignoring the Constitution and Bill of Right, became accepted civic practices which a few claimed unethical, but for the most part, a majority was too confused or guilt ridden to care.

The Gang's first big success came in 1987 when they methodically blocked the nomination of Robert Bork to the Supreme Court with a smear campaign, followed by the unsuccessful but brutal attempt to smear Clarence Thomas in 1991. Later, the scapegoating tactics used by James Carville and George Stephanopoulos to help President survive impeachment, were used successfully to chasten and malign Independent Counsel Kenneth Starr, President George W. Bush, Vice President Dick Cheney, Governor Sarah Palin, and others. And in all cases except for Clarence Thomas, they were successful.

An interesting tribal aspect of these successful inquisitions is the God Module mentality that evolved among the timid oppositions. Republicans were found acting like the brutalized wife trying to be the perfect spouse between beatings. In like fashion, the Republican Party showed no desire to resist fellow tribesmen. Being emotionally attached to traditional ideals and a strong capitalist ideology, the attempt to destroy such a relationship by members of the same household seem preposterous. But, like the battered wife, they were delusional, and the battering continued. Eventually the Republicans, endlessly characterized as bullies and suffering from a host of bigot phobias, found themselves in a state of denial, where even the most aggressive of the clan shied away from any victimhood challenge.

By 2010 progressives ruled the air waves by virtue of intimidation, their marriage to the social sciences, media, academia, coastal power pockets and key judges. But it was the Roman-Prussian-German prescription that made the real difference. Postmoderns were in the drivers' seat and on their way to victory. Over time the system worked so well, that dozens of instigators from the legal and academic world became sought-after political advisor and, like the news and cable outlets, became prosperous and sought after.

Even Freud's constructive lie was re-defined as a virtuous "Noble Lie" in the case of President Obama joining the gotcha game by blaming an Internet video for the 2012 Benghazi attack resulting in the deaths of a US ambassador and several US contractors. That Noble Fib was followed later when he repeatedly told the public that they could keep their doctor under his proposed health care plan. The point here is not to pick on any one politician, but to illustrate how Freud's constructive lie was weaponized so successfully during this period.

Chapter 28

SCIENCE PMP

The American people need no course in philoso-
phy or political science or church history to know
that God should not be made into a celestial
party chairman.

- Mario Cuomo

As we have seen, next to the media, probably the most devious Gang of 5 disciples to ply their Post-Modern Pathology trade must be the psychologists who choose tribalism over their responsibility as impartial, 'scientific' observers. Like many in academia and politics, many in the social sciences became Postmodern, zealot as well. Trump haters! And, as such, threatened the very fabric of traditional Americanism by using their profession to sanction the Post-Modern psychobabble in academia and politics. Mob behavior that stemmed from their reluctance, or refusal, to admit their dutiful Trump attacks were tribally biased and blind behaviors.

It's with the fields of psychology and the media where Postmodernism exposes itself as a truly Post-Modern Pathology where "scientific" pragmatism became established social science doctrine late in the 20th century, when blank slate psychology was able to maintain its dominance over Edward Wilson's *Sociobiology* threat via identity politics and mob violence. Shortly thereafter, the social sciences adopted Aristotle's phronesis theory (pragmatic rationalization) as the reasonable way of formulating theory, like Freud's functional constructive lie.

Although psychology played a major conspiratorial role in the identity politics game, its recognition as validator to the whole Postmodern movement was never obvious. While psychology always had its problems with credibility, it was a very large tribe made up of many therapeutic subsets promoting reasoned pragmatism with practical, emotional appeals. Several, like talk therapy enjoy a long history of helping understand mental conflicts. It therefore never lost its public appeal and continues to serve as an empirical science substitute in the minds of the public. But their biased tribalism was becoming ever more obvious and costly.

Take the book, *The Dangerous Case of Donald Trump*. While void of scientific logic, such an effort reflects the trend in Post-Science to use whatever tactic that has self-serving aspirations. The book, published in October 2017, was written by Yale professor and clinical psychiatrist Bandy X. Lee, and 27 other psychiatrists and mental health experts. The authors were all members of a group called "The National Coalition of Concerned Mental Health Experts," who use the Tarasoff Doctrine which claims medical experts can characterize an individual as mentally incompetent *without a personal examination* if that individual is deemed a threat to society. (A practice we will see used later by federal agents to justify their involvement in the failed Mueller Investigation.)

So tasked, they went on to diagnose Trump as hedonistic, narcissistic, bullying, dehumanizing, liar, misogynistic, paranoid, racist, self-aggrandizing, entitled, exploiting, empathy-impaired, unable to trust, free of guilt, manipulative, delusional, likely senile, and overtly sadistic. While alone, each symptom might be deemed unobjectionable, in combination, they pointed to a very, very severe sociopathic case needing immediate isolation.

They then went on to blame Trump for the negative impact the "Trump Anxiety Disorder" had on the nation's psyche. Ignored was the fact that 90% of the news coverage from the time of his election through the first year of his presidency was negative and might have had something to do with such an analysis. Not only was the reporting negative but in many cases fake news, generated by the Gang of 5. As Gang members, they dutifully ignored the fake news charges, and claimed Trump's denials of colluding with Russia to steal an election a sign of delusion, while neglecting to point out the total lack of proof that colluding even occurred. Apparently in an effort at fairness, the book also, offering zero evidence, claimed Vladimir Putin a reborn Adolf Hitler.

Although dubious as sound science, the book was influential in defining Trump early in his presidency, as one sick individual, and received enormous press and prestige for Lee, who in December of 2017, spent several days briefing members of Congress where she claimed Trump could cause the extinction of the human species. What's important with this smear effort is not the bad science involved but the *successful* motivational psychology involved in getting the public familiar with Freud's three-step *Personal Defense Philosophy* of transferring guilt and anxiety: 1) Psychologists identify problem as guilt in losing the 2016 election; 2) They transfer the problem and guilt to Trump, then; 3) They sit back and enjoy the media hysteria, and the public accepting Post-Science Psychology as a reasoned scientific process.

The downside of this story is, that on Monday, January 11, Dr. Lee backed away from those claims when she was forced to admit on a radio talk show hosted by a Dr. Drew, that other presidents, such as Abraham Lincoln and Theodore Roosevelt, also had psychological profiles that could be defined as psychotic but who turned out to be two of our most admired presidents. She agreed that such diagnosing could be dangerous and ended the interview suggesting that Trump may not suffer from mental illness at all. Although Ms. Lee suffered some embarrassment, the interview had little media coverage and, in the end, the overall effort was a great *success* for the Postmodern movement.

On January 18, 2018, Rear Admiral, Dr. Ronny Jackson, President Trump's doctor, an accomplished physician to three presidents, including President Obama, pronounced Trump physically and psychology fit to serve as commander-in-chief. In response to the book, American Psychology Association's (APA) past president Jeffrey Lieberman, in *Psychiatric News*, wrote that *The Dangerous Case* is "not a serious, scholarly, civic-minded work, but simply tawdry, indulgent, fatuous tabloid psychiatry."

Price of Post-Science Redefining Normal

While the Trump invectives in the book were considered by many as "scientific," they were but one example of Post-Science attempting to redefine normalcy. It took eons for our paleolithic ancestors to refine virtuous acts like kissing and hugging, tolerance for others, and respect for the old and infirm into behaviors that mellowed communal interactions. Behaviors defined as normal. It took the same time to refine the intuitive, impulsive and emotional behaviors that go into lying, cheating, hating, deceiving and fractious infighting. All normal behaviors that in just a couple decades, the APA redefined many as abnormal, with some reaching the level of psychopathic.

Fortunately for Postmodern APA members, tribalism is an alchemy of such contradictions designed my Mother Nature to confuse and maintain conflict: A supposedly objective media disassembles itself in hysterical fits of biased rage to take down an elected president; Empirical science elites, the crème del a crème of their professions, unable to arrive at plausible explanations to unending political discord; Enlightened Western democracies showing not only an inability at resisting anarchy but actually promoting anarchy across their intellectual institutions.

In accordance with that alchemy, Post-Scientists found themselves inventing and reveling in new theories to define who are mentally ill and who are not, as classified in the APA's Diagnostic Statistical Manual (DSM-V), often referred to as the "Psychiatry Bible." To the surprise of many, the manual published in 2013 that took nineteen years to complete, listing over 300 mental health disorders, was roundly criticized by noted psychiatrists especially from Europe. In America, several high-profile articles by Professor Allen Frances (Chair of the DSM-IV Task Force) argue the increased number of, and expansion of, existing mental disorders was vastly overdone, a process he defines as "medicalizing" patterns of behavior and mood.

Criticism also came to the public's attention after an open letter and accompanying petition representing three divisions of the APA were published by the Society for Humanistic Psychology Division. The letter argued that members were concerned about the lowering of diagnostic thresholds, the increase in disorder categories and the introduction of disorders that may lead to inappropriate medical treatment. Approximately 13,000 individuals and mental health professionals signed a petition in support of the letter and roundly criticized the manual for saying nothing about the biological underpinnings of mental disorders.

Just as disturbing was the news that some 70 percent of the panel of experts writing the manual had connections with the pharmaceutical industry. Apparently, like their cohorts in the political-advisory business who very successfully invented political victim for themselves to diagnose and cure as reliable Democrat voters, Post- Science psychologists learned the value of inventing diseases for themselves to cure by redefining normalcy, and pushing pills to relieve the underlying psychological pain.

Many in the empirical sciences and public saw this symbiotic relationship between the drug industry and social sciences, as problematic. The obfuscation needed to identify, classify and justify medical cures for questionable abnormalities, had enormous ramifications extending well beyond the field of psychoanalysis into all phases of family health care with physicians and other licensed clinicians dispersing an alarming number of drugs, at an alarming rate, for an alarming number of real, and perceived mental disorders. As cruel as it may seem, these Post-Scientists were very *successful* in redefining normalcy.

The main fear many had, was we were becoming a pill-popping, drug-loving society with each link, psychologists, pill makers, distributors, parents, teachers, doctors, hospital administrators, nurses, pharmacists, attorneys and health counselors reaping benefits. Along with the APA, special criticism belongs to Congress, the FDA and DEA for their inept collusion with drug companies and their distributors permitting the massive addiction problem to not only continue but grow. Once firmly established as "sound science," the population, in lockstep, marched to the pied-piper's tune. Eventually it became difficult to distinguish APA pipers from enablers.

The problem was that, like the victim-peddling politicians, the medical elites, whose job it was to pursue public interest, become absorbed into the very deception that victimize their patients, and began believing the misguided science. At the time there was adequate research showing why people tend to follow the lead of reliable and unreliable "experts." Yale law professor Khan refers to this influence of expert credibility as *cultural cognition* with research to show the influence "a biased way that people use to buttress their predispositions." He goes on to claim, "Since most people aren't in a position to judge quality science, they unwitting allow the intellectually powerful to dissemble conventional standards for their convenience."

One need only detail the disgraceful abuse of the drug Ritalin with young children diagnosed with Attention Deficit Hyperactive Disorder (ADHD) to show that some psychoanalysis is based on narrow, symptom-based diagnostic criteria that fails to take into account the moral constraints and dictates of the social environment; prior psychological responses to similar adverse situations; normal variations in temperament and personality; and, especially, predisposed behaviors which, in this case is normal behavior for many children. Check the Internet and discover Ritalin being available to children as young as two-years old suggesting one could argue the APA and the medical industry has ADHD in being hyperactive at dispensing drugs for questionable disorders while totally lax in their professional responsibility to meet well-established standards of scientific protocol.

On April 19, 2019 the U.S. Food and Drug Administration approved another questionable practice: a new, first, medical electric shock treatment device that emits mild shocks to the forehead of 7 to 12 years old ADHD patients. The prescription-only device, called the Monarch external Trigeminal Nerve Stimulation (eTNS) System, is available for patients who are not currently taking prescribed ADHD medication, and is intended to be used in the home under the supervision of a caregiver during periods of sleep.

According to eNeura's website, the latest version of their device, the eTNS mini, costs $750 for a three-month rental, with a new patient discount of $300 off the first rental period. The site also claims the most common side effects observed with eTNS use are drowsiness, an increase in appetite, trouble sleeping, teeth clenching, headache and fatigue. *Otherwise no serious adverse events have been associated with use of the device.* (Emphasis added)

Here, as with the whole ADHD issue, one must wonder what the long-term effects of inhouse electric-shock therapy will have on young brains in the very early stages of maturation? The very assumption that continuous shocks, no matter how mild, will produce a normal brain is scary. You must wonder what young animal they tested this device on and then assumed it appropriate for young human minds.

Again, we see Freud's three-step Personal Defense Philosophy used as a *Post-Science Defense Mechanism*. 1) Problem: In the guilt of not understanding normal children's behavior, psychologists 2) transfer the problem to bad genetics, and 3), solve the problem with pills and electric shock treatment, then sit back and enjoy the economic benefits and professional acclamations that come with such science.

Ignoring ADHD as possible normal, child behavior, is poor science that can result in mistakes statisticians call "false-positive diagnosis" errors in observing a difference or problem when in truth there is none. Like Freud who abandoned objective science in understanding the mind, APA zealots and their enablers remain adamant in their subjective approach to mental disorders. The Drug Enforcement Administration (DEA) classifies Ritalin as a Schedule II drug, meaning it has a high potential for abuse, but shows no signs of limiting its use.

According to the Anxiety and Depression Association of America, "approximately 60 percent of children with ADHD in the United States become adults with ADHD; that's about 4 percent of the adult population, or 8 million adults." Such articles go on to detail the symptoms include the inability to focus, disorganized, restless, forgetting and difficulty completing tasks, all common behavior many more than 8 million people exhibit daily on their way to happy, fruitful lives.

Such "science" can be deadly and enormously costly. In a TV appearance Vermont's Governor Peter Drumlin said his state in 2014 saw a 770 percent increase in opiate addiction since 2000. He claims one reasons for the increase is that the price of Oxycontin, an FDA-approved painkiller, is more expensive than heroin so a person dependent on Oxycontin finds heroin cheaper thereby adding to the addiction problems his state faces. Any honest official will tell you the problem is much larger. In March of that same year, Massachusetts Governor Deval Patrick outlined steps to address an opiate addiction epidemic in his state by instituting an immediate ban on certain drugs, while committing 20 million to increase drug treatment and recovery services. On MSNBC (April 2015) Senator Manchin of West Virginia stated the most serious problem he had to address in his state was that of drug abuse. Since 1999, two hundred thousand Americans have died from overdoses related to prescription opioids.

The most recent figures from the Center for Disease Control and Prevention suggest that a hundred and forty-five Americans die every day from opioid overdoses. It's the leading cause of death among Americans under 50 and, from 2012 to 2016, America taxpayers spent roughly $327 billion on drug-control efforts. Nationwide,72,000 deaths were linked to illicit prescription opioids in 2017, 65,000 in

2018 and 69,000 in 2019. On March 27, 2019, a White House Council of Economic Advisers report from 2017 put the cost of the opioid crisis between $290 billion to $622 billion in 2015 alone.

Chapter 29

Philosophic PMP

Creativity is more about taking the facts, fictions, and feelings we store away and finding new ways to connect them. What we're talking about here is metaphor. Metaphor is the lifeblood of all art, if it is not art itself.

- Twyla Tharp

Equal rights are important considerations, but the equal-rights meme colored over as Individualism has shown itself to be an endless patho-logic warring tactic of endless demand for more and more rights at the public expense, while providing endless opportunities to scape-goat the opposition with endless acquisitions of bigotry against those unwilling or unable to satisfy the endless righteous and not-so righteous demands.

A tribe divided by a million equal-rights demands has been shown for centuries to be a failure. The tribal hysteria surrounding President Trump is nothing but one of those disastrous side-effects that come with a culture addicted to opiate-like rights, resulting in unnatural family structures, children without fathers, men having babies, and no gods to hold society together. What's so remarkable is the long historical evidence of identity politics' destructive nature goes unno-ticed by our best and brightest, especially those in the hallowed halls of our greatest universities where many of the supposed best and brightest ply their trades.

A large part of that success must be given to the symbiotic relationship that developed between the Marcuse-lead academics and Freudian-driven psychologists where both depend on the other as science validators. It was a dependency not lacking in using highly questionable intellectualized jargon to validate highly questionable philosophical theories into highly questionable public policy. Yet, such expert-driven pragmatism worked well enough and often enough to be rewarded as its own brand of Post-Science.

It's in this rarified atmosphere that "Intellectual Rationalization" became a *exceedingly successful* PR art form designed specifically to make those struggling with the virus less confrontational given the "expert" reasoning of "Intellectual Evangelizing." Priests, ministers, and imams fall into this category as do public relation companies and high-level academic philosopher who deal in spiritualized, pragmatic thinking, something on the order of the golden-tablet logic the angel Moroni gave to Joseph on his way to Mormonism.

Although the phrase intellectual evangelizing itself might, on the surface, be considered another oxymoron given all forms of rationalization are open to criticism, some political theories are thought to be *intellectual truths*, obscure enough to warrant only the intellect of those chosen few in our most cherished religious and secular institutions capable of deciphering and articulating how the system works.

Tribal addicts are tribal addicts. Christians didn't accept Islam when it became popular. They went on to fight the Crusades for centuries. In like manner, similar tribal battles are underway in America. Norm Chomsky for example, who helped start the ruckus 65 years earlier in his famous debate with B.F. Skinner, gave us an early estimation of just how tribal some addictions can be, and the biased uproar to come from noted elites like himself. In *Who Rules the World*, he claims that the November 2016 election placed total control of the most powerful country in the world in the "hands of the Republican Party, the most dangerous organization in world history," a party "dedicated to racing as rapidly as possible to destruction of organized human life," with no "historical precedent for such a stand."

Wonderful examples of tribal duplicity and bias working at the highest level of intellectual evangelizing are the debates between the cognitive scientists in the social sciences and empirical sciences. In the rare cases where this happens, few if any hear about them because, if they did, they probably would never understand what was being debated. The dialogue would be too linguistically technical or saturated with superfluous jargon to warrant the effort.

Such debates often center on how psycholinguistics affects human behavior. Consequently, one must know something about the terribly complex psychological processes involving a person's mental and emotional state, the linguistics involved, as well as the terribly complex study of language, its structure, morphology, syntax and semantics. Take the word 'semantics' alone. The Oxford dictionary defines it as "the branch of linguistics and logic concerned with meaning. There are a number of branches…including formal semantics, which studies the logical aspects of meaning, such as sense, reference, implications, and logical form…lexical semantics, which studies word meanings and word relations…conceptual semantics, which studies the cognitive structure of meaning." Wow! The average college graduate could read this definition over 20 time and not have the foggiest idea of what the term 'semantics' means. This is but one of many where the *pathology of linguistics* manifest itself within the Postmodern movement

The linguistic gymnastics that can occur from this one definition alone can befuddle the best of minds. Perhaps, this is why President Clinton got a pass from the media when he was asked if the statement by his attorney before a judge "….there is absolutely no sex of any kind, in any manner, shape or form between President Clinton and Ms. Lewinsky" was truthful? President Clinton replied, "It depends on what the meaning of the word 'is' is."

Along those same lines of cognitive pathology is the dustup that occurred in the academic world when two linguistic giants duked it out in 2006. The two were Steven Pinker a world-renowned empirical scientist at Harvard, Massachusetts and George Lakoff a noted social scientist at Berkeley, California. Both very highly respected individuals in their cognitive fields.

What made the debate so interesting was the tribalism each exerted in his own chauvinistic fashion and, the charges and counter charges that started a free-for-all on science blogs. While neither side in this historical rift lives in the same political universe most people do, as noted researcher scientists, we must assume they are purveyors of objectivity. After all, they are considered the elite of the science elite.

Yet, though both are experts at linguistics, they make it hard to see any objectivity coming from the debate because they were so tribal in both scientific and political outlooks. Pinker was more conservative and objective in his traditional scientific rigidity, while Lakoff came off as a Marcuse-trained philosopher who believes in socialism and uses intellectual rationalization (phronesis), when it comes to supporting his speculations. Since phronesis is based on subjective, intuitive and emotional principles, a contentious debate seemed inevitable.

Basically, the debate was about the role metaphors have in designing and driving political thinking. Layoff's position was: Behavior can be understood in the time-worn fashion of framing wanted goals around emotion-laden metaphors. For example, in later speeches, Lakoff tells Democrat audiences they are losing elections because Republicans have controlled the political debate in America for decades.

Lakoff attributes Republican success to their adopting a *strict father family metaphor* that Republicans live by, an authoritarian convention resulting in a well-ordered world with God over man, man over nature, rich over poor, men over women, whites over blacks and similar authoritative values that trump rights. It's a Social Darwinism worldview Lakoff claims founded during the Enlightenment.

On the other hand, he claims Democrats should counter with a *nurturant parent family metaphor* that instills empathy and responsibility for all living creatures to ensure their freedom and equity rights are never marginalized in any manner. Therefore, children are born good, raised good, and nurtured to be compassionate and responsible, a theory he offers no historical or empirical evidence for in the debate or in his books.

Pinker based his behavior theories and writings on early seventeenth, eighteenth, and nineteenth centuries philosophers like Rene Descartes, David Hume, Immanuel Kant, Gregor Hegel and, later, Alexandre Kojeve and Alexis de Tocqueville. Men who theorized through long-term and near observations that inherent, pre-adaptive neural constructs (like the sex, language, and God Modules) play major roles in directing and motivating our tribal behavior—the Motivational Theory. At the time, the concrete genetic and cognitive evidence we have today was lacking to back up the theory, so mankind had to wait for cognitive scientists like Norm Chomsky and Pinker to ascertain and assemble the molecular mechanics involved in the early speculations.

Pinker's major objection in the debate was that Lakoff had little solid scientific research to validate his metaphor theory and was misrepresenting science for political aims. If the implication was that Republicans are tribalists exhibiting strict Social Darwinian tendencies like sexism, capitalism, war and racism, then the implication is old-hat propaganda used by Darwin critics for decades. The fact Lakoff uses Social Darwinism intentionally or in ignorance is revealing. Darwin simply outlined how the natural system works, he didn't say the system was uncontrollable. What he did say was humans have the cognitive ability to see the system for what it is and work within the system as caretakers of the environment, including the social environment.

True to tribal form, the charges and counter charges that followed sent the science blogs wild with further charges and counter charges, finally ending in what looked like a draw. At least half the bloggers seemed supporting Lakoff for ideological rather than scientific reasons, never mind there was a wealth of current research supporting Pinker's view.

Normally both sides in such debates exhibit such expressive bias, but here the empirical sciences are at a disadvantage. They can't use emotions or biased logic to support a hypothesis—the first criticism I received in a biology thesis some 60 years ago. According to scientific methodology, the hard sciences must be open to peer review as well as rigid testing, retesting and modifying hypotheses if need be.

Like philosophers of old, the only process social science practitioners like Lakoff need follow to cognitively capture an audience is to cleverly rationalize a theory, lather it up with a thick layer of cognitive fluidity—like glib schmaltzy metaphors—throw it against a political chalkboard and see if it sticks. Obviously Lakoff, flush in poetic citations that he judiciously translated into arresting metaphors, took the more pragmatic Cicero approach, by portraying his team as good people and the opposition as Darwinian robots, a common practice in Post-Modern Pathology.

The difficulty for scientists like Pinker with phronetic activism is, it's here to stay. It's been around forever because it's practical, and…. it works. The schmaltzy, emotive linguistics stick to the chalkboard often enough to keep trying. Could there be any better example of cognitive capture, bias and blindness than Layoff's metaphor theory which, as presented, had little or no claim to sound science, only the wonderful success the progressives were having with identity politics?

Once a tribe reaches the emotional cohesiveness that Postmodernism had in 2006, the stage was set to increase the level of civilized duplicity. From then on, it was not unusual to hear the phrase "High Rationality," "Elevated Rhetoric" or "Intellectual Rationalization" used by elite academics to emphasize the virtue of their claims while underscoring their elite status as cultural mentors.

The irony here is Lakoff's was very naive in his speeches assuming Democrats not familiar with identity politics. Metaphors resembling his "strict father family" and "nurturant parent family" had been used for decades in identity politics by the Gang of 5. Plus, the Gang had been enormously successful in the 70s and 80s, when they set about metaphorically rebranding their party's name; redefining traditional goals of freedom and equity; placing all freedom and equity rights beyond the ability of science to marginalize; and, applying political correctness and scapegoating tactics against anyone who used language or behaved in a way that could offend a person, plant or animal.

Musing about reframing the polemic debate in metaphors claiming tribal politics is something less or more than what has been, is simply that, musing, speculating, wishing, fake science. But it works! Philosopher like Lakoff are recognized political intellects. If a pole had been done to determine who won the Great Debate, the results would have been close to 60/40 and strictly along liberal/conservative lines with Lakoff the winner.

Chapter 30

CULTURAL PMP

Culture must have its ultimate in The metaphysical, or it will cease To be cultural
- Johan Huizinga

It was around the turn of the century that identity politics eventually morphed into the New-Left philosophy of free-ranging Individualism throughout Western culture with globalism a final goal, and, Post-Modern Pathology, aka PMP, a reality. A movement in which any individual or group with any gripe against the establishment could claim capitalist aggression by bigoted white supremist. Here, the community emphasized the moral worth of the individual, and promoted the exercise of individual goals, desires, feelings, independence and self-interest over state, or party. Forget working for the nation. Work for yourself. Ignore past truths. Stand up and demand your rights. Put on your Vagina Hats or hoods as symbols of oppression. Slip on your marching boots and march over the opposition. If tribal norms get in your way, simply redefine and recalibrate community norms to fit your needs.

From the individual's standpoint, the beauty of individual-styled diversity, is the tribal virus does not infect the individual who can simply ignore all liberal/conservative constraints as so much nonsense by claiming truth and normalcy is what he or she chooses them to be. Victoria Aveyard described how individual-styled Postmoderns managed the tribal virus paradox in her book *Red Queen* (September 2019) where she wrote: **"Truth is what I make it.** I could set the world on fire and call it rain."

As a rule, anything termed Post-This or Post-That is, by definition, an oxymoron, a contradiction. From the very beginning, even Postmodernism was an oxymoron—a deceptive contrivance—that really didn't reference a time period as something occurring after Modernism, but rather a new *practical philosophy*, new way of thinking and acting. Included in the recalibration were freedom, equality, and diversity: Freedom from coercion, to freedom from want and need; Equality redefined from equality of opportunity to equality of outcomes, and; diversity, redefined not as the diverse values humans bring to a community, but the diverse rights a community brings to the individual.

With tribal truth, normalcy, the empirical sciences and gods absent as restraints, Postmodernism was weaponized to expand its moralized yardsticks to any number of victims and in any direction. Although Postmodernism was a house of cards, the progressives didn't think so. They had faith the ignorant serfs were incapable of catching on, and their early experience with women and blacks taught them that they could generate endless unverified charges by simply moving the goal posts a bit left here and bit left there, when needed.

Ancient history is nothing but examples of tribal leaders struggling to maintain cultural order in large diversified cultures, a conundrum many tribal subsets deal with daily, at all levels of religious and secular diplomacy. On a small scale, modern poetry and art are two harmless, early examples of the religious fervor causing confusions, dissention, or a punch in the nose when someone commits artistic anarchy by claiming an American flag in a pile of horse manure as art, or a poem lacking rhythm, rhyme and decipherable logic called poetry.

In 1987, the American artist and photographer Andres Serrano produced a photograph labeled, "Piss Christ," (a small plastic crucifix in a glass tank of the artist's urine), that turned out a winner in the

Southeastern Center for Contemporary Art's, "Awards in the Visual Arts" competition. Since then the photograph has been on display in numerous galleries and, in September 27, 2012, Piss Christ went on display at the Edward Tyler Nahem gallery in New York. On December 2019, Italian artist Maurizio Cattelan duct-taped a banana to a wall that sold for $120,000. A day or so later he peeled, ate it, then laughed all the way to the bank.

Even music was unable to resist the lure of modern diversity. Tribal music of the Inuit Canadian people, for example, used drums in dance as far back as can be known, and only recently has their vocal style become of interest in Canada and abroad. According to a pratictoner, Paula Conlon, "The Inuit people of the Canadian Arctic share an ancient form of music called *Katajjait* (throat singing). Often improvised, women perform *Katajjait* alone, or more often in pairs standing face to face, trading off rhythmic, guttural sounds through vocal manipulation and breathing techniques, creating rhythms that reach 240 beats per minute or more. *Katajjait* texts include comprehensible words that have lost their meanings, vocables (nonlexical syllables) and mimicking of nature sounds. According to Inuit performing artists Karin and Kathy Ketter: "Anyone can do the basic sound. Just say: 'Huumah!'

Music aficionados like Joseph Stalin hearing such music, might have uttered: "Huumah," send these buffoons to the farthest gulag where ice never melts." During the mid-30's and until his death in 1953, Stalin was the only person to judge whether or not a composer's music was fit to be played. A time when numerous famous, Russian composers went to the frozen gulag where ice never melts and some to their death for going beyond what Stalin considered proper, moral, Russian music.

Post-Modern Individualism shines brightest when Post-Truth and Post-Normal justify reformatting the very foundational cornerstones of society one by one. Here is where Marcuse would truly be impressed with the Gang's ingenuity. In the him/her direction, first came the family redefined by any number of sexual combinations. Given the ease by which the family was reformatted, the very concept of male and female came next with dozens of transgender identities being cataloged. Unsatisfied with corrupting the family concept held sacrosanct for some million-plus-year, and the million-plus years the male/female concept was held sacrosanct, they set about extracting from tribal language, gender-specific pronouns like male and female, he and she, him and her.

The length and width to which transgenders stretched their concept of individual diversity is a wonderful example of the extremes that can occur in tribes without borders. The ABC website claims 58 gender options identified by ABC in use by Facebook, such as Agender, Androgyne, Cis, Cis Gender Female and male, etc. The reality is there's actually a difference between *gender*, and *gender identity*. There are two genders: male and female. Most people identify as one of those two, whereas, *gender-identity is a spectrum* of where you sit, physically and/or psychology, in relation to those two male/female points. This means that in any given population, an infinite number of gender identities are available, since every point on the male/female identity spectrum can be slightly different.

So, 58 may just be the beginning. A population of 1,000 could theoretically have 1,000 gender identities. Like the term, cognitive fluidity that humans use to rationalize, obfuscate, or generate acts of duplicity and mendacity to support a political ideology, cognitive-gender fluidity can generate an endless list of terms to support their Post-Normal transgender theology.

Expanding the Diversity Yardstick to Sanctuary Cities

Except for Islam, Post-Moderns seemed to have trouble with religion in general and Christianity in particular. Their pronounced indifference towards gods is best illustrated by their God-less sanctuary cities with roads well marked, and clear of obstruction except those lined with tents, garbage, human feces, injection syringes and the Homeless. While the whole process of redefining and re-formatting such cities was something on the order of a bizarre Sodom and Gomorra revisit, the move seemed righteous thinking with some two hundred Post-Normal mayors and city officials.

Disturbing was the hypocrisy of these Post-Normal officials allowing illegal immigrant protection, space for the homeless and mentally ill to settle undisturbed on city sidewalks, and addicts to get high in safety. Safe places where morality and health issues are ignored; Post-Normal rationalization and obfuscation defines justice; and all abnormal became normal. Disturbing, also, was the disciplined, tenacious, ruthless, tireless leadership that never went on defense and denied all negatives to such deviant policies.

It's at this level of Post-Modern thinking that offers insight into the kind of professional duplicity God Module are capable of in planning and executing a plan the size of sanctuary cities. Can anyone deny the intentional hypocrisy and duplicity involved in a movement that essentially says: "Screw the Constitution with its rights and responsibilities." Nor should anyone dispute how antagonistic and hostile sanctuary cities are to the whole concept of how communities should function. Such a places are not communities, but cesspools, discernable at several levels of organic and psychological waste, separated by gated STM communities where the wealthy live.

Recall, the STM was, and remains, a social contract, a set pattern of thinking that took over a million years to perfect, illustrating those tribal qualities that distinguish humans from other animals: freedom, equity, trust, cooperation, community, reasoned dialogue and solidarity, none of which exists in sanctuary cities. The very fact political elites willingly and purposely treat their citizens in the manner they do, is a reflection of the hard, cold indifference that comes with tribal zealots more concerned about their crusading objectives than public health or their own health.

The problem for Postmodernism was the Gang's leadership became hysterically blinded to the decaying rot Individualism brought to the movement's sense of tribal purity.

Individualism effectually created a new paradox, an inhouse Democrat virus that splits the Gang into factions: the conservative faction promoting Postmodernism controlled by the media and Democrat Party, and rebel factions allowing individuals to ignore the Party trends and do their own thing, like sanctuary city mayors. Or a group of four hard-core socialist who boldly assert nothing less than a far, New-Left cultural revolution in the US: the group called the "Justice Democrats," or the "Gang of 4," or the "Squad" consisting of Alexandria Ocasio-Cortez (D-NY), Rashida Tlaib (D-MI), Ayanna Pressley (D-MA) and Ilhan Omar (D-MN). Or the schism that would dramatically manifest itself in the Democrat pre-2020 election campaign with a dozen or more candidates spouting Marcuse' socialism.

Complex, far-ranging strategies of this deceptive nature require ingenuity and numerous war rooms to maintain fresh lines of psychobabble to keep party members in line and confuse the public as to true intentions. What the election of President Donald Trump did was strengthen Orwellian mob tactics and expose progressives' inherent tribal compulsion to disregard opposition evidence, refuse engagement in rational argument, and transfer the guilt and hatred they feel in losing the 2016 election to President Trump.

By 2018 then, Trump was fairly well established as the Great Marauder of women, blacks, illegal immigrants, homosexuals, transsexuals, and a host of other such victims. To be more precise, he was "*The existential threat to all humanity*" allowing for any necessary treachery. Since behavior norms and truths form the very fabric of society, these post-normal actions achieved one of the Marcuse' goals to destroy social norms, while satisfying the new Post-Modern need for individual expression and diversity. Although, he would be concerned about the purity issue.

Ignorant of such deceptive shenanigans, the public was left confused, politically disoriented and wondering who to believe. Given the proclivity of elite God Modules to moralize whether behaviors are vise or virtue, it's logical for the public to a begin asking: "If codes and creeds are cast aside as so much rubbish, who's to say what's truth and normal? Are those promoting flags in horse manure conservative or liberal bigots? Are those promoting Post-Politics, Modern Art and Poetry the tribal hypocrites, or those defending traditional standards? Are Post-Politics, Modern Music, Modern Art and Modern Poetry separate professions? And if so, who and what defines the boundaries?

In discussing globalism, the public needs to know if people are citizens of nowhere, are people then citizens of everywhere? With art lacking boundaries of any sort, then all visuals must now be defined as art, all sound as music, any word or phrase as poetry. And, thus art, poetry and music cease to exist as definable entities, only as "opinions." In like manner, if political news continues having a 90+ negative agenda, political news ceases to exist only as opinions with the few real news items difficult to delineate as news. And last but not least, if all rights are defined by the individual then, rights as a moral ideal has no moral standing in a culture of any size.

Chapter 31

HANKY-PANKY DUPLICITY

Nothing more completely baffles one who is full of trick and duplicity himself, than straight forward and simple integrity in another.

- Charles Colton

The fact there are some 80 words in the English language to define duplicity proves just how useful crookery, swindling, fakery, hanky-panky and two-faced duplicity are in energizing intellectual rights as categorical imperatives beyond the ability of science to marginalize. After Trump's election this emotional factor became an especially important consideration because it provided the necessary God Module energy of *elite* Trump haters, to be spiritually elevated to a level of radicalism to deny tribal normalcy and resort to classic duplicity tactics of destroying the enemy at all cost. A radical level of thinking it their *duty* to insist their theology of individual rights over community responsibilities, be adopted and promoted, or suffer the penalty of endless character assassination to Trump, family and supporters. A radical level of duplicity defined as "Mob Hysteria" that Lakoff used in his "intellectual evangelizing."

Mob hysteria is a product of like-minded tribal members coming together to elicit revenge for what they perceive a severe wrong imposed by an adversary. Plenty of research exists showing all social animals respond aggressively to any threat to tribal welfare with the full range of aggressive responses. The fact we refuse to admit any tribal connection to such tribal behavior, and, some 70 years after the Nuremberg trials, we still don't have a good definition of hysteria, suggests our nation is knee-deep in a blinding tribal virus. A time difficult to tell the truth from hoax, hypocrisy from sincerity or vice from virtue as liberals and conservatives slug it out.

The visceral hatred for Trump by the Gang of 5 and their supporters is the most illuminating example of tribal bias and blindness an educator could ever ask for. Though Emmerson so rightly pointed out such tribal infighting happened often, it never before became the daily media soap opera for billions to observe and participate in via the Internet and television as happened with the Trump presidency. It was melodramatic, over-the-top theatrics by all the major players in the Gang of 5. Theatrics that should had caught the attentions of all science behaviorists interested in how human nature works.

But …. that didn't happen.

In fact, there was little or no interest by anyone in the behavior business, except for the Trump haters acting as radicalized tribalist while denying any such tribalism. Not only was the Gang of 5 busy redefining normalcy, writing books and promoting surveys deploring Trump, the Gang's efforts became obvious as pure, unrestrained, uncontrollable hatred by an elitist class of spiritualized high-priests. A telling pathology in which devote converts found themselves caught-up in seeing their Post-Normal gospel threatened by a heretic preaching the gospel of America First, Make America Great Again and, the most hateful of all slogans: Nationalism. Converts unable to agree on a clear definition. And …. once they did, claim their behavior did not apply.

For example, absence a clear definition of " hysteria" as being normal tribal behavior, we had to deal with a host of old APA's definitions of mob hysteria starting with: "compulsive, ungovernable emotional excess;" that was abandoned by medical personnel in favor of hysteria being "a more precise 'somatization disorder,' suggesting emotional excess could cause some physical issues with hearing, walking, seeing, or a search for anesthesia."

Anesthesia?

Yes, anesthesia!

In 1980, the APA *officially* changed hysteria to "hysterical neurosis," then to "conversion disorder" and eventually to "conversion hysteria" characterized by the "conversion of a mental conflict into any number of somatic expressions with no apparent physical reason." Other literature labelled mob hysteria as collective hysteria, group hysteria, or collective obsessional behavior.

The most popular version, used by The World Health Organization (WHO), defines hysteria as a *"compulsive behavior disorder"* characterized by *"a persistent inability to control intense, repetitive urges and feelings, resulting in repetitive behavior that causes marked distress or social impairment."* Using WHO's definition, one could claim the co-ordinated effort by progressives to serve the public a steady 3-year diet of Trump mania nothing but a "compulsive behavior disorder" on steroids. Would it not be safe to diagnose CNN and MSNBC talking heads suffering from "compulsive behavior disorders," as well as the Gang's two-year promotion of Russian collusion with no evidence?

But …. that too didn't happen.

Although Trump had continually received 90+ negative press, no claims were ever made by psychologists, or anyone in the Gang of 5 including the media, that the *persistent inability to control intense, repetitive urges and feelings, resulting in this repetitive* negative press came from the New Left. Their behavior was always considered the paradigm of normalcy and, where found to be hysterical, they skillfully used projection, to transfer the guilt to Trump and the opposition. This was not good. Marcuse was probably looking down and asking if this gotcha game had gone too far. Even a couple Republican politicians were catching on to the duplicity.

The WHO definition was a definition that the social science haters refused to acknowledge, though proof of their bias and blindness is found throughout psychology literature as tribal. A 2019 review of Freudian, Deindividuation, Convergence, Emergent norm and Social Identity behavior theories showed such mob behaviors tribal:

… The hysterical mob is actually a complex system made up primarily of membership in a social group having a distinct moral ideology;

…The mob behavior becomes more salient by confrontation with a group having clear beliefs values and despised idol/s;

… Mob behavior is not irrational, but rather the reasoned, rational product of widespread popular feelings that are not wrong if all in the group agree actions taken are proper;

… As less-biased members of the community witness the hysteria via the media, they become more anxious and fearful until, convinced they have the same concerns, join the crowd acting anonymously.

There were several other popularized symptoms of mass hysteria at play here that are universal in nature and add substance to the strong tribal connection. One is that hysteria spreads by word of mouth, popular media, from old to young, and is most effective on women. Lastly, hysterical origins almost always have no bases in fact.

It's difficult to understand how anyone could graduate with a degree in human behavior without a background in basic tribal tenets supported by the Motivational Force theory. As noted, the original theory was laid down by noted 17th century philosophers: Thomas Hobbes claiming our base motives are biological; David Hume addressing the role emotions played in overriding reason; Immanuel Kant asserting our rational and intellectual makeup was designed around universal, tribal precepts; and Georg Hegel suggesting that ideologies where incomplete logic and led to bias and conflict. Later in the 20th century, Ludwig Wittgenstein, Russian Philosopher Alexandre Kojève, German Friedrich Nietzsche and French political writer Alexis de Tocqueville extended the Motivational Force Theory.

Even psychologists John Jost and Jaime Napier (Yale University) who devised the *Uncertainty–Threat Model* in 2011 claimed the general political difference between liberals and conservatives is that, with conservatives, stability and hierarchy (i.e., conservatism) generally provides reassurance and structure. Whereas, with liberals, change and equality (i.e., liberalism) is associated with disorder and unpredictability. The same relationships Emerson illuminated in his speech on *Conservatism*.

And yet, the uninformed graduate. In 2012, Social psychologist Jon Haidt gave one of the opening talks to the *Society of Personality and Social Psychology* with an audience over 1000 researcher members from around the world. When Haidt asked the members to raise their hands if they considered themselves liberal or left of center, 80 to 90 percent of the social psychologists shot their hands up. Next, how many were conservative or right of center? Only 3 hands went up. Later, Haidt estimated the liberal-to-conservative bias in the field to be 266 to 1. Psychologists, the very people who get up in arms whenever anyone makes a joke or casual remark that might create a "hostile environment" for a minority, are busy themselves creating a hostile work environment for conservatives. This could be why the APA and the media find no one in the Gang of 5 exhibiting mental disorders of any kind, yet, in all cases, APA definitions find the behavior of Trump and his supporters exhibiting abnormal, uncontrollable, mental disorders.

OK! Let's be realistic. The fact the APA refuses to admit its tribalism is obvious in all its stumbling definitions they themselves define, but never suffer from, is evidence their tribal God Modules will simply not permit such cognitive dissonance. That's why God Modules blind as well as bias. Plus, the admission would also include admitting to being a tribal radical with no freewill. Any admission of suffering from mental disorders by elite zealots is not going to happen.

The banality and triteness of anti-truth and anti-normalcy "experts" forcing their beliefs on the public was duplicity on a scale too difficult to measure. The fact these "experts" believe there is no such thing as truth or normalcy is contrary to thinking that was indelibly imprinted on our paleolithic minds a million years ago, and used by every civilization throughout history. Social animals require behavior parameters measured as truths and normalcy, a simple fact that has not changed in all that time.

In *One Dimensional Man* written in 1962, Marcuse claims "free human realization" within society **could not** be achieved from "the hard struggle for life, business, and power." Given, humans "are nothing but human," his Utopia was they be allowed to live on their own terms, characterized not by "perennial happiness" but by the affirmation of man's "natural individuality." The extension of that individuality by 2000 was Individualism, but not as Marcuse imagined. Like Kant, he assumed wise men would provide the truths and norms for individuals to reach their nirvana within communes.

But that didn't happen. Instead the very evils he fore-claimed capitalism would bring throughout *One Dimensional Man* were realized with Postmodernism: the corrosion of traditional debates and means of deterrence; the success of identity politics; the diversion success of no normal and truth; and the masterful destruction of the capitalist oppressor; then, when on the brink of total success, waste that success on excess after excess of individual trivia like transgenderism, and the endless waste of political energy on ridding the world of Trump.

Chapter 32

MEIN KAMPF DUPLICITY

"The rich ruling class has used tribalism, a primitive caveman instinct, to their advantage since the beginning of time. They use it to divide and conquer us. They drive wedges between us peasants and make us fight each other, so we won't rise up against our rulers and fight them."
- Oliver Markus Malloy

The crookery, swindling, fakery and hanky-panky behaviors also showed the media, APA and academia had no intention of playing cozy with conservative America. Their only goal as President Obama said, was to fundamentally change America. With the tribal virus door wide open to Postmodern tribalism, that hope almost became a reality.

The fraudulence was reflective of the same behavior noted early in a 1946 study by Dr. Douglas Kelly, after the first Nuremberg trial when he reluctantly concluded that an enormous number of Americans had the potential to act as the war criminals had with unbridled ambition, weak ethics, and excessive patriotism. Fact is, by early 2019, individualized Postmodernism had infected the God Modules of millions of humans.

Thus, we were no longer safe in our ideological bubbles with rights balanced by responsibilities, clearly defined. *A place where the natural laws of tribal nationalism prevailed.* We now live in a polarized tribal environment where rights and responsibilities may be true or false, vice or virtue, moral or amoral depending on who's pushing the power buttons. *A place where no law prevails.* A place where thousands of economic elites, educators, politicians, media, philosophers and psychologists make a living, working in the shadows of a Deep State, attempting to sway public opinion in the Postmodern direction.

By 2019, Postmodernism was so successful in reversing many cultural norms, the US was on the verge of turning into a Post-Modern state. Instead of tribal members working together for the benefit of all, America became an undefined land mass with no borders, occupied by numerous black-, brown-, red-, white- and yellow-skinned clans. Interspersed among these clans were several small, and large religious transgenders, economic, academic, criminal, political, judicial, Deep State, and Post- Science clans, all demanding their rights and to hell with traditional American values.

Following wolf-pack rules, Postmoderns use identity politics to separate a person from the herd, and relentlessly attack, attack, attack with real or fabricated shameful, shocking, dishonorable, appalling, or reprehensible allegations. Given the allegations are "opinions" or come from protected sources, as with whistle-blowers or secret media sources, there's little the average person can do to get his/her good name back. The result was an endless onslaught of charlatans pedaling their version of wolf-pack predation.

Such was the cultural theatre where President Trump found himself, center stage, beating back endless charges of misbehavior and mental disorders. Trump's sexual history, his personality, temperament, and proclivity at fighting back were just too disposed to mockery and ridicule by identity politics, and, left with no one to cover his back, he responded to the attacks with his own invective tweets that only added more spice to the media circus. By then, all honesty and objectivity were lost to *unbridled ambition, weak ethics, and excessive patriotism* and *a hate-filled focus to destroy Trump and all he stood for.*

It was hysterical internecine tribalism where much of the *success* in the question of "How did this civil war evolve to the degree it had?"

can be attributed to devoted PR teams generating malicious, media narratives, repeated ceaselessly to capture, bind and blind. Repeating salacious charges over and over is a Cicero PR practice learned early on in his battles with Julius Caesar. A tactic Hitler expanded in Mein Kampf claiming "the most brilliant propagandist technique will yield no success unless one fundamental principle is borne in mind constantly and with unflagging attention. It must confine itself to a few points and repeat them over and over."

Throughout the Russian Collusion Campaign, House Committee Chairman Adam Schiff claimed near daily of having proof of Trump's collusion. The fact he never produced any proof was not important. The fact he repeated it constantly with media coverage, was the important fact. During the same period, numerous Democrats took turns claiming little children being pillaged repeatedly in some manner crossing the border; showing pictures of beautiful polar bears becoming extinct with global warming; our youth having only 8-10 years to live due to climate change.

As noted, numerous activists make lucrative livings promoting the many "Ism" generated by identity politics. Two of the more lucrative Isms in terms of attention grabbers and reputation enhancements are racism and sexism. The House committee's trial at nominating Kavanaugh to the Supreme Court was a classic smear campaign using a few salacious points and repeating them over and over. For several weeks the media covered the nomination from top to bottom, side to side with unverified allegations of sexual misconduct. When one female charge ran dry, another seemed to appear out of nowhere.

Feeling the coverage so successful, another sexual distraction was manufactured the following year to show how great a threat Kavanaugh was to approaching abortion rulings. To that end, an artful display of PR surfaced when the *New York Times* printed a story from a book written by NYT reporters Kate Kelly and Robin Pogrebin that …. just happened to be on the market the following Tuesday, and …. just happened to have a sexual claim against Bret Kavanaugh. Only problem was, the supposed claim came from a girl who had no recollection of the alleged event, which was noted in the book, a quote the *Times* …. just happen to leave out in its reporting. But that fact didn't matter. Like Chairman Schiff's knowledge of Russian collusion, what mattered was the media ran with the sexual charge for days while leaving out the victim's disclaimer. Even before the Mueller investigation, there were months of 90+ negative and fake news that only increased to intellectual blurring, veiling, and shading the truth by the talking heads on CNN and MSNBC.

What makes such slander a brilliant, masterful revolution of tribal conformity and puts them in the "pathology" category is the endless supply of negative opinions lacking authentication. Throughout, *The New York Times* and *Washington Post* were disciplined, tenacious, ruthless, tireless, never went on defense and denied all negatives. The tribal virus Ralph Waldo Emerson found so troubling a behavior, became a hard-fought political reality. Something like what happened in the short span of 15 years with Joseph Smith's Mormon religion. Only this time on-a-much-larger-scale with tens-of-millions revolting against their host tribe. All achieved by elevating individual rights over community responsibility. A truly amazing feat!

The Gang's radical efforts became accepted inhouse warfare, and the feeble-minded Republicans, the enemy to be annihilated. Though much of the unconventional Post-Normal defining and redefining bordered on the bizarre, one must assume leading Democrat politicians in DC and states like New York, Oregon, Washington and California, were buying into the New Normal with the rapid birth in sanctuary cities and open borders that seemed to go along with the same logic of men having babies. These inexplicable behaviors contrary to all historical norms can only be explained by Postmoderns' having reached the point of being spiritually addicted to the religion of Postmodernism. At that level of spirituality, any and all irrational moralizing of their behavior was permitted.

Though many reveled in their success, hope of success would have been fruitless without a dedicated pack media. By 2019, the media was essentially the only Gang member willing, capable and enthusiastic about controlling manufactured narratives. And with good reason, their past ability was not only remarkable at feeding the public a steady diet of identity politics, but in consigning an aura, a halo of 'expertise' around themselves. Plus, it was profitable.

So enlightened, these men and women became *the experts* at the Bait-and-Switch game where they, in lock-step, could orchestrate callouts for a prescribed week that a journalist is killed by barbaric Saudi Arabians friendly to Trump, while failing to note any of the dozen or so journalist killed yearly in Mexico, our friendly neighbors to the south. In like fashion, how do you describe the media callouts after every shooting for more gun control and defining the events as acts of terrorism, designating the shooters as "white nationalists" motivated by President Trump and the NRA, while completely ignoring the thousands of shootings resulting in thousands of deaths each year throughout the many urban cities across America. Except for dedicated bias, how else do you explain the complete absent of time covering the plight of the homeless, mentally ill, drug addicts and poor that frequent West-Coast cities; the rat-infested condition they live in; the medieval diseases they are exposed to; or the thousands that die under such conditions?

The media also were *the major players* in the character assassination that came with the hysteria over the Stormy Daniels case; the 2 years of the Russian Collusion; the Covington Kids fiasco; Two Kavanaugh rape schemes; Tax Returns! Recession! Racism! Even the once admired, Attorney General Bill Barr, became a favorite target. Barr's November 8, 2019 speech at Notre Dame on the battle between Christianity and Secularism focused on "The imperative of protecting religious freedom was not just a nod in the direction of piety. It reflects the framers' belief that religion was indispensable to sustaining our free system of government," At the annual meeting of the conservative Federalist Society on November 16, Barr stood up for President Trump stating that Democrats are "using every tool and maneuver to sabotage the functioning of the Executive Branch." For tribal conservatives, the content of the two speeches could not have come at a more critical juncture in the unfolding crisis in our country, nor could the carefully researched and expertly developed arguments have been more needed, more appropriate.

True to their bias and blindness, *Times* columnist Paul Krugman called the Notre Dame speech "religious bigotry." The Washington Post declared Barr "clueless" and that the Federalist Speech was "bizarre." They asked, "What universe does William Barr inhabit?" Professor of Law at Georgetown University Jonathan Turley called it "dangerous" and "incendiary." Esquire called the speeches "crazy" and said Barr "embarrassed himself." The Huffington Post called Barr "authoritarian." Others called the speeches "aggressive," "dangerous," "infuriating," and "a disgrace."

In summary, to prevent any raise in the polls for Trump, the media religiously ignored the many Trump achievements in the economy, energy, unemployment, judicial appointments, deregulation and tax reform, while hiding the extreme counter-agenda proposed in the Democrat debates by their candidates running for president. They were also religiously negligent in failing to point out the role socialists like Marcuse and Dewey's had, and still have, in America's educational institutions, as well as the role Alinsky's and other community activists' play in promoting socialism as public policy.

Perhaps these revelations will finally lead to a realization about how rogue and dangerous these individuals and organizations are, and how urgently needed is serious media reform. None of these journalists have acknowledged an iota of error in the wake of their biased reporting, because they know that lying is not just permitted, but encouraged as long as it pleases and vindicates the political beliefs of their benefactors. Until that stops, credibility and faith in journalism will never be restored, and their despised status to any opposition will be fully deserved. To their credit, though, their behavior was exemplary tribalism, and should Postmodern come to dominate American politics, the men and women driving the media rebellion will, like all rebel leaders, have their faces embossed on tee shirts next to Shea Guevara.

Chapter 33

IMPEACHMENT -A Party Gone Mad-

Any philosophy study shows humans are exceptionally complex, rationalizing creatures who live in a world full of irrational ideologies and, therefore depend on rationalized, an irrational reasoned language for mental-health reasons.

- Author

Actually, things were not that rosy for the Gang. True, there were many manufactured narratives to take out Trump that grew and metastasized in public brains over a period of 3 ½ years, but the failure of the $30 million, 2 ½ years Mueller report, showing no collusion or obstruction between the Trump organization and Russia, opened the door to all the duplicity involved, and punctured the Postmodern bubble.

Essentially, the downfall started when the Gang recognized their failure to blame Trump for the mob-hysteria they themselves created, and their failure to change public opinion via the Mein Kampf strategy using endless false narratives over and over again. At this level of tribal duplicity and suffering Told-You-So pangs, they were left with impeachment, and Americans were faced with the question: "Has this party gone mad and, if so, who will judge whether or not the actions to take down a duly-elected president were criminal in intent or heroic displays of warrior patriotism." This was not an innocuous case of situational ethics with Louis Farrakhan receiving inspiration for his radical actions from deceased black leaders he met when beamed up to a spaceship. Or a relatively harmless case of hypocrisy where a group of dewy-eyed psychologists claim Tarasoff Doctrine rights to savage a president. This was a case of noted persons at the highest levels of the government being involved in a coup.

Even before the Gang's big Ukrainian impeachment effort, the President and a few Republicans were calling for special counsels to investigate the investigators. "I became President of the United States in one of the most hard-fought and consequential elections in the history of our great nation." President Trump wrote, "From long before I ever took office, I was under a sick & unlawful investigation concerning what has become known as the Russian Hoax. My campaign was being seriously spied upon by intel agencies and the Democrats. This never happened before in American history, and it all turned out to be a total scam, a Witch Hunt, that yielded No Collusion, No Obstruction. This must never be allowed to happen again."

House Intelligence Committee ranking member Devin Nunes, (R-Calif.), said he was preparing to send eight criminal referrals to the Justice Department regarding alleged misconduct by DOJ and FBI officials. For some time, Justice Department Inspector General Michael Horowitz' was investigating the behaviors leading up to the Foreign Intelligence Surveillance Court (FISA) warrants. In early December, 2019, he published his report listing "17 significant errors and omissions" in the Carter Page federal surveillance application that enabled the investigation into Trump's presidential campaign in 2016.

In a rare public order on December 17, the chief judge of FISA strongly criticized the FBI over its surveillance-application process, giving the bureau until January 2020 to come up with solutions. A federal judge on March 2, 2020 signaled that he will order Hillary Clinton to testify about the decision to conduct official business on a private email server while she served as secretary of state.

About the same time Attorney General Barr appointed Horowitz, he assigned Connecticut prosecutor John Durham to investigate a wide range of misconduct within the FBI and DOJ. Durham, who had been with the DOJ since 1982, and had led numerous high-pro-file investigations of potential wrong doings by national security of-ficials, had the power to not only investigate, but indict. In May of 2020, Adam Schiff released a 2018 document showing some 50-some top-level officials interviewed by Schiff had no evidence of collusion. Former Director of National Intelligence James Clapper followed that release with a similar statement.

In an effort to protect themselves from the investigative storms, top officials like CIA Chief John Brennan, Mrs. Clinton, Assistant Director of FBI, Andrew McCabe, and FBI Director James Comey found themselves in the media trying desperately to defend their behaviors by *projecting the existence of their own unpleasant impulses to others*.

Within his rather comical, but bizarre state of tribal infighting, is where the rule of law gets warped and the public began seeing how powerful biased judges and bureaucrats who control key agencies and committees, can muddy the judicial water. With conservatives claim-ing existing laws were broken, the Gang of 5 rationalized the laws ar-chaic, or vindictive, or needed breaking given the horrors Trumps committed and would continue committing.

These emotionally charged projections and rambling linguistic logic—the empirical scientist Jared Diamond defines as neologistic jargon—were simply examples of "Experts" using "Intellectualized Linguistic Skills" to bamboozle the masses. The same logic George Lakoff used in his debate with Steven Pinker. The same logic Mrs. Clinton and her husband used and continue using in their many shady dealings and interviews.

Since Mrs. Clinton wrote her thesis in support of Marcuse's theory of dividing the nation via victimhood, the Clintons have been the masters of projection and intellectualized legalisms. James Comey is on the road to salvaging what's left of his reputation in the same manner as he nuzzles up to the media with his rendition of what the meaning of "is" is. It remains to be seen whether Deep State John

Brennan, James Clapper, Comey, Andrew McCabe, along with a host of minor conspirators like Bruce and Nellie Orr, Peter Strzok and Lisa Page lied and conspired in a variety of ways to get Trump? And if they did, what will be their rewards or punishments?

Rewards may seem out of the question, but we must remember these individuals were operating as professional guardians of a *principled culture they sanctioned* throughout their careers. Although many of the laws broken were established law unchanged by the Postmodern movement, the judicial system was extremely slow in resolving the many legal issues that were being challenged within the Postmodern context of their *prevailing culture*. By this time, the accepted US norms and truths had been stretched to their moral breaking point. Thus, the Gang, especially the media and Democrat Party, was forced to increase its hysterical attacks in hopes of gaining the upper hand in the court of public opinion via impeachment.

When challenged by Edward Wilson's book, *Sociobiology*, blank slate psychologists successful cleared the battle field of pesky empirical scientists using identity politics, political correctness, as well as a touch of violence. But those tactics didn't work with Trump. Nor, given his security, was a bucket of ice water poured on his head possible. Although various people and groups claimed President Trump had engaged in impeachable activities before and during his presidency, Mrs. Pelosi seemed reluctant to go there, but eventually sanctioned the process, hoping the Trump Hysteria had spread wide enough to support the idea. Luckily, the weapons used in internecine warfare are primarily rhetorical, centered around rationalizing behaviors, otherwise, given the level of poisonous French hatred for Trump, they might have guillotined him as the French rebels did to King Louis XVI.

Rationalizing behaviors like obfuscation, duplicity and mendacity are all extensions of the more acceptable term "rational" that leaders use in their fakery and hanky-panky attempts to destroy the enemy and muddy the political water.

Rationalized thinking is defined as any action attempting to explain a behavior or an attitude with logical reasoning even if the behavior or facts are illogical.

Rational reasoning is religious tribal reasoning: Irrational reasoning moralized as rational inside the tribal bubble. Rational reasoning like Christianity, Islam, communism, and democracy are wonderful examples of religious tribal reasoning. Christian-reasoning is rational logic if you're a Christian. You rationalize your Christian beliefs as rational to not only yourself, but to others around you. Same is true with Muslims, Democrats, Communists and all other ideologues. Looking in from outside these bubbles, the logic is irrational and the place where the destructive yin/yang, liberal/conservative forces come into play.

Rationalization became messy, frustrating and a serious problem for America when in-house rebels insisted their beliefs and standards be accepted by the conservative establishment or, as a last resort, they would impeach the president which they did. Two polarized tribes, spiritually rationalized to their cause, willingly and able to destroy the other when push comes to shove.

Any study of philology shows humans are exceptionally complex, rationalizing creatures who live in a *world full of irrational ideologies* and, therefore depend on a rationalized, irrational reasoned language for mental-health reasons. What they care about is simple, functional, short-term logic where questions of freedom, equity and self-interest rule the long day: Is the impeachment propaganda true or more fake news? How will it help put my kids through college? How much will it cost? For humans to survive, they must feel a behavior or assertion rational within the framework of what is practical for them in their bubble. It doesn't matter how much impeachment psychobabble they have to put up with, they want tribal harmony, even if they have to reach deep into the mysterious depths of the ridiculous and absurd Adam Schiff psychobabble to find it. Irrational thinking should create a problem for a rational mind, but it does not. Human minds don't like unpleasant feelings. It, and the rest of the body like feeling good. Emotional disharmony is a No, No. So, we rationalize.

Unless supported by codes and creeds, all the little white rationalized lies, constructive lies, Noble Lies, exaggerations, innuendoes and distorted linguistic jargon used to justify irrational behaviors makes political judgements difficult to achieve. Example: If a judge asks Mrs. Pelosi: "Is your impeachment constitutionally legal?" She might answer: "It depend on what the meaning of "is," is. The judge is left confused by such brilliant logic, lets her walk and all emotional disharmony is resolved. Such linguistic sophistry seems to work every time, especially if delivered by an "expert" Hollywood idol, religious or secular idol.

Even at night we rationalize in our dreams. When asleep, our brain is continuously stimulated by random impulses from its neural network and then tries to make sense out of them with material juxtaposed from real-life experiences. Dreams were, for our ancestors, a window into the spirit world and played a major role in our evolving sense of early reasoning. After all, no harm came if some buffalo spirit seen in a dream or drug-induced stupor explained the appearance of many buffalo and hunting improved. Given enough good hunting and drug-induced dreams, the buffalo spirit might be considered a reliable source of "knowledge" and eventually submerged into tribal lore as an idol of worship Here, reason impregnated with emotions, evolved a politic of the mind where answers to real or imagined problems need not be scientifically accurate or morally acute so long as they were practical and expressively adaptive—and made you feel good.

While lifting the human psyche above the reality of daily existence, such thinking permits believers to operate on a higher moral plane than nonbelievers; and, should the times require impeachment, the collective passion encased in the ideology bubble can be directed against nonbelievers with a clear conscience. Operating on this higher spiritualized, moral plain allows the God Module to energize the individual to more zealot levels of rationalization permitting *verbal vi-*

olence that might start with deceit and betrayal or some form of mendacity to intentionally destroy someone or group by way of character assassination. Where pure visceral hatred rules the day, and hanging is out of the question as with president Trump, impeachment became the most fitting last resort.

Traditional psychology defines such rationalization and its many hundred shades of duplicity, mendacity and obfuscation, as 'willful' acts that free-willed people carry out and, as such, are always discussed in a moral context. Indeed, many psychologists view these denials and self-deceptions as a subordinate category of defense mechanisms, encapsulating such behaviors under the general heading of cognitive dissonance, a state of tension that occurs whenever an individual holds two beliefs that are psychologically incompatible—rational yet irrational. Because the tension is unpleasant under such conditions, forms of self-deception are rendered to relieve anxiety, i.e., Freud's constructive lie.

Neurologists are just beginning to realize that much of human behavior—including cognitive dissonance and freewill—*are not under conscious control*. They also suggest rationalization, obfuscation, duplicity, mendacity, denial and self-deception play important sustaining roles in our lives. They consider these behaviors unconscious acts that evolved to protect our mind from emotional overload generated by anxiety and guilt.

Given that reality, a jury might claim the obvious mendacious behavior driving Mrs. Pelosi to approve impeachment, or committee chairmen Adam Schiff's, and Gerald Nadler's behavior in carrying out the obviously biased trial, were *unconscious tribal acts* to protect their minds from emotional over load, generated by years of anxiety, guilt and hatred for Trump? And what about the Whistle Blower and the many elite, expert witnesses that came forward to testify against Trump? Did they, by way of their academic or bureaucratic credentials, feel they had regulatory powers over President Trump? Or were these self-elevated elites, simply unable to recognize their behavior as *unconscious* biased, blind and tribal? Self-elevated elites claiming a freewill, yet unable to ignore their tribal baggage and provide objective examinations of charges free-willed people are expected to deliver.

As difficult as it is to understand and accept, such rational tribal reasoning—void of freewill—became the fundamental mind tool around which political intelligence evolved. An intelligence that only functions within a tribal context. This is why emotion-driven reasoning that may have little substance in reality, often trumps reasoning steeped in reality. Regardless, however such rationalized thinking evolved, the energetic and unflagging enthusiasm to rationalize irrational doctrine became a hallmark of the human condition, an extremely successful survival strategy. Without it, the tribal-self would be constantly faced with contradictions the social world is filled with.

Consequently, the question of why the human mind is unable to untangle the Gordian Knot the tribal virus has shown itself to be, is because the human mind was designed to think in a practical, selfish fashion that leaves itself open to contradictions and propaganda, starting at birth. The rights and responsibilities exhibited by the Taliban and American girls were examples of the normal, rationalized, indoctrination practices all tribes use to justify their brand of governing. Normal, rationalized, moral behavior for one girl inside her bubble, irrational, amoral behavior by the other girl looking into that bubble.

The common belief that humans have a freewill, and able to think beyond their own political tribal bubble, is an example of self-denial protecting humans from cognitive dissonance. Traditional psychology defines freewill as a mental process in which behavior is carried out willingly rather than compulsively. However, it's safe to say that the sticky tribal personalities exhibited by Pelosi, Schiff, Nadler, the dozens of committee members and elite witnesses to impeach the President, lacked the freewill to stop bothering the opposition with their pre-ordained impeachment failure.

A wonderful illustration of the range of influence sticky personalities, and their lack of freewill, can have for society to deal with, is

Jack Nicholson's marvelous portrayal of Melvin Udall in the 1997 movie *As Good As It Gets* that won him a Golden Globe Award. What made the film so illustrative and fun were the difficulties Melvin's young homosexual neighbor and one female friend had in dealing with him. A successful writer, Melvin doesn't see himself as eccentric and continues to meddle in their lives, driving them daffy with his peculiar habits.

Every family has a Melvin, a person that's somewhat out of the tribal norm, though not a serious threat to anyone, only annoying. Actually, the difference between Melvin and the rest of us is only one of degree. We are all a bit sticky in forming relationships, a bit neophobic in hating new ideas, and a bit neurotic in imposing our beliefs on others while seldom considering the consequences. Especially when those beliefs are hard-wired to a liberal or conservative belief in politics, the arts, religion or sciences.

To the surprise of everyone, the Republican Party also had a Melvin, President Trump, whose behavior is "somewhat" out of the tribal norm. A successful business man, Trump doesn't see himself as eccentric and continues to meddle in Democrat affairs, driving them insane with his peculiar habits: Using a pedestrian Twitter account to chastise and mock elite Gang members as Swamp Creatures; Routinely teasing the media with charges of practicing fake news; Monthly rally extravaganzas, with thousands of cheering fans listening to his ever-increasing list of marvelous accomplishments.

Trump's success was on the order of Jack Nicholson's marvelous portrayal of Melvin Udall where I'm sure all those leaving the movie theatre totally enjoyed Melvin for his nerdy behavior. The degree to which the Democrat Party was willing to go in matching Trump's nerdy behavior with frantic hate-driven behavior will be enjoyed and immortalized years from now in movies portraying the hatred for Trump in the facial expression of the 17 witnesses attempting to validate Trump's transgressions; the actress portraying Nancy Pelosi receiving a Golden Global Award primarily for her tearing Trump's

State of the Union Speech in half; as will the actors portraying Gerald Nadler and Adam Schiff's in corralling House Committee members for their flocking performances.

Given the many attempts to destroy Trump that failed was evidence of just how susceptible the human mind is to spiritualized propaganda overload. At the time, the range of duplicity and uncontrolled hatred was being recognized as pathological to the extent of questioning whether the US government would survive as a reality and, would an American jury be able to prosecute any of the swamp creatures for their failed attempt at a new world order?

One could argue making judgement so difficult was the possibility that all these dutiful Deep State individuals were reacting to *their* herding instinct they considered so fundamental to saving the nation. Tribal instincts we noted showing up as examples of 'unconscious synchrony' where humans are easily moved to dance, yawn, or laugh when they see associates dancing, yawning or laughing. Or …. when so ordered, soldiers tramp, stoically headlong, side by side, into deadly cross-fire from barricaded enemy a mere hundred yards away.

In the Woke World those were the complicated issues someone had to adjudicate either in the courts or in the voting booths; or be considered as just innocent expert assertions; or deep-seated, spiritual opinions to a religious cause and, therefore not open to judicial scrutiny; or a claims of "lack of intent" as was the excuse for the equipment and 33,000 emails Mrs. Clinton's destroyed; or invented mental disorders as defined by the APA.

Or …. was it possible Americans were accepting the whole Woke Movement and, everyone should simply forget all these "Ifs" and "Ors" and discharge any jury since the US had reached a point in our experimenting with free-ranging individualism where JUSTICE like art, music, poetry, globalism, objective news and science ceases to exist?

Chapter 34

ISLAMIC INROADS INTO WESTERN CULTURES

Individual Muslims may show splendid qualities, but the influence of the religion paralyses the social development of those who follow it. No stronger retrograde force exists in the world. Far from being moribund, Mohammedanism is a militant and proselytizing faith.

- Winston Churchill-1998

The progressives failed in their Postmodern efforts to destroy America's brand of nationalism because they ignored the power of our tribal inheritance. It's there, it's real, not to be denied and here to stay. The problems the US faces at this time centers around its inability to 1) fully recognize Postmodernism as a coup from the inside; 2) becoming tolerant and slavish to the woke movement; 3) opening the door to immigrant invasion; and 4) pushing our brand of free-ranging democracy on nation states around the world.

Along with our Western allies, we should come to respect other nations, and if war becomes a necessity, fight to win. As a nation we are no different in forcing our brand of nationalism on others than Postmoderns imposing theirs on our conservative population. The Muslim culture offers a good example of not only our slavish tolerance for the woke movement and its identity politics, but pushing our brand of free-ranging democracy on nation states around the world to no avail.

A hundred years after Mother Russia failed in its attempt to unify the hundreds of small ethnic tribes throughout vast expanses of central and northern Asia, resulting in ten-of-millions of deaths. A similar effort to impose a Western hegemony in the Middle East was underway with the Iraq War. And like the Bolsheviks, the effort to intimidate various Muslims sects to adopt Post-Modern democracy failed, with an extreme cost in money and American lives.

The reason the Iraq War failed and Islam survived throughout the whole Middle East is because Muslims don't stop to question the morality of their efforts as Postmoderns did with President George Bush during the Iraq War: Did the president lie about the war? Were we right to invade? Were we wrong? Is the war just? Is the war unjust? Etc., Etc., Etc. So, America backed-off and spent the next decades trying to manage Muslim infighting at another heavy cost in money, lives and our moralized principles.

According to modern standards, Muslims are a rare breed that use their religion to justify their takeover activities. For Muslims, morality does not exist with infidels. Only submission to their moral codes. Classic tribalism! There are thirty Muslim countries, mainly in Asia and Africa, with a total population of about 900 million, in which Muslims have an overall majority. Many more countries have sizable Muslim minorities. The total Muslim world population is close to 1.5 billion, one-quarter of the total world population and expanding rapidly.

Islam is uniquely successful because it's the *fastest*, most *regimented*, and largest *spiritually devoted tribe* in the world, outpacing the growth rate of the rest of the world. Muslims are the fastest growing population because of their focus on having large numbers of devoted Islam children, and the practice of polygamy to help produce those large families especially during times of war when men are lost in battle. After the Iranian Revolution in 1979 for example, the Iran government sponsored a breeding program. It lowered the marriage age to nine for girls, and fourteen for boys, legalized polygamy and raised the price of birth control. By 1986, the average family had six children.

They are the most regimented because they are spiritually de-voted to their Islamic ideology via demanding autocratic brainwash-ing: Early childhood indoctrination; Daily indoctrination with adult males required to pray, on their knees 5 times a day; Strict tribal codes and creeds enforced by Sharia laws and powerful Muslim clerics; And, highly structured, cultural and family lifestyles. The whole process is historic autocratic tribalism with a vengeful-God, codes and creeds imposed by aggressive, often angry elites. Unlike its youthful religious neighbor Christianity that imploded into thousands of quiet, tolerant subsects during the Enlightenment, Islam maintained its classic tribal conformity and belligerence.

While Western nations are critical of such restrictive regulations and aggressive behaviors, the Muslim culture has survived for some 12-hundred years using such strategies. And today, it's the only large, modern example of the hard-core spiritual excess *our paleolithic ancestors* practiced that catapulted them into the modern world as a means of surviving the competitive demands of classic tribalism. This adherence is most interesting because none of the other large cultures (except China) have maintained a spiritual devotion to the STM as has Islam. A process that puts community ideology first and individual interests lasts, and a process putting Islam first and all other nation last. Even large cultures like China and Russia that remain mainly autocratic, are less aggressive and more individually lenient than Islam.

Plus, with Muslims, terror and murder are accepted tactics, learned early. Nicolai Sennels, a Danish psychologist, has done ground-breaking work regarding difference between young Muslim and non-Muslim criminals. Sennels compared 150 criminal Muslim inmates with non-Muslim inmates and found fundamental and largely irreconcilable psychological differences in degrees of anger, aggres-sion, irresponsibility and insecurity.

According to Sennels, Islam has a very different view of anger and aggression. In the West, anger and threats are the quickest way to lose face and social status. Whereas, aggressive behaviors, especially threats, are generally seen to be accepted and even expected as a way of handling conflicts with Muslims. In politics, compromise, individual differences, and our casual diplomatic approach are seen by Muslim leaders as cowardice and a weakness to be exploited with some form of belligerence and, if necessary, violence. With a decrease in feelings and responsibility, he found there's a greater tendency to demand non-believers surrender and adapt to Muslim wishes and desires, quickly via terrorism or by playing the Long Game using identity politics and political correctness.

To add insult to injury, at the same time the Middle East democracy effort failed, the Muslims and China were making sustained inroads into the social, political, educational, and legal institutions of elite Western nations resulting in the gradual expansion of Islam globally. Clear evidence exists of a global, "Stealth Jihad" in which radical Islam hollows out the institutions, constitutions, and underpinnings of Western civilizations, and replaces them with Sharia, *from within*. Like the German professor Marcuse and his fellow academics who infiltrated our universities, and recommended revolution from within, Muslims play the same Long Game. They subdivide the host tribe like Postmoderns do, and expand their influence via mass immigration, extreme birth rates, overloading welfare systems, and insisting host cultures adopt Sharia law.

The Islam invasion started in the latter part of the 20th century, with immigration by two Muslim front groups, the Muslim Brotherhood and CAIR (Council on American-Islamic Relations). Since then, they were repeatedly in the news for their sympathetic portrayal of Islam and their activist drives against any speech that offends Muslims. The irony is American Postmoderns worked to justify their acting as the speech police in shutting down free speech by calling those who spoke against Islamic voices "Islamophobes." A practice that fell right in line with our Post-Political movement.

Combining Muslim identity politics with Postmodern identity politics during the same period, resulted in a death by a thousand cuts.

At taxpayer-funded universities and public schools, women-only classes were required along with separate swimming times at public pools. Christians, Jews, and Hindus were banned from serving on juries where Muslim defendants were being judged. Piggy banks and Porky Pig tissue dispensers banned from workplaces because they offend Islamist sensibilities, as was pork removed from school menus. Ice cream was discontinued at certain Burger King locations because the picture on the wrapper looks similar to the Arabic script for Allah. No Go Zones are demanded in cities where only Islamic rules and regulations permitted.

Regarding No Go Zones, Bernard Rougier, a professor at the University Sorbonne-Nouvelle in France, and director of the Centre for Arab and Oriental Studies, explains that Islamism "is an 'hegemonic project', splintering working-class neighbourhoods." He further states "these 'ecosystems' work on a 'logic of rupture' of the French society, its values and institutions, and are built in mosques, bookstores, sport clubs and halal restaurants."

Yves Thread, deputy director at the daily newspaper *Le Figaro*, writes: " Not a month goes by without a murderous attack with the cry of "Allahu Akbar" taking place on our French soil…In the name of diversity, non-discrimination and human rights, France has accepted a number of blows to its culture and history… Islamists are a hot-button issue. They continue the fight which, even without weapons, has all the allure of a war of civilizations." Noted French-Catholic historian Jacques Ellul cautioned: "Whether one likes it or not, Islam regards itself as having a universal vocation and proclaims itself to be the only true religion to which everyone must adhere. We should have no illusions about the matter: no part of the world will be excluded."

Nicolai Sennels claims "With such strong pressure and such strong emotions within such a large group of people — all pitched against us — we are facing the perfect storm, and I see no possibilities of turning it around. For people to change, they have to want it, to be allowed to change, and to be able to change, but only a tiny minority of Muslims have such lucky conditions. But based on my education and professional experience as a psychologist for Muslims, I estimate that we will not be able to deflect or avoid this many-sided, aggressive movement against our culture."

Far too many in America underestimate the power of God Module psychology embedded in Muslim cultures. Islam functions as a nation state driven by a unifying ideology that's lacking in the US and other Western nations. Once spiritually affixed in their neural makeup by God Modules, Islam followers represent a powerful *united force* that believes it need not change its world view because, that view reflects a reality the rest of the world *must adjust* to. So programmed, these devotees are convinced they and less devout Muslims will never assimilate into American, European, Chinese, Indian or any other culture not Islamic. Over the last 12-hundred years, it's difficult, if not impossible to find any established Muslim culture having been converted to any other ideology, including the religion of Postmodernism.

The truly amazing feature of this death by a thousand cuts, is that American elite fail to see the similarities between Islam and Postmodernism. Amazing! Talk about the power of God Modules providing early and late indoctrination to bias and blindness.

Consequently, *Islam*, is the modern embodiment of the STM on steroids. What Muslim devotional success proves is the existence of the God Module, its power to control a population of millions, and its marvelous ability to control a population of millions focusing its energy on the Community Mandate and not on the individual Freedom/Equity Mandate.

And .... China is not far behind.

Both, nationalistic to the core.

Both, set on world domination.

Of all animals, humans exhibit the greatest range of emotions designed specifically as moral and ethical bonding rules to hold the tribe together and destroy competing tribes, as with China and Islam, but lose their moral standings when used to destroy a tribe from within. The preface of this narrative ended with, "Until we learn to control tribalism, civil or international wars will be our children's future." A reality of that American future became obvious when the Gang of 5 was forced to destroy the opposition at all cost in the summer of 2020. Forced to flood the airwave with daily emotional doses of Black Lives Matter narratives designed to define scapegoats and elicit guilt; followed by protests, riots and mayhem ranging from killing, stabbing, looting, burning buildings and taking over large sections of a city; all done with no remorse or retribution. Like the Chinese and Muslims, it was democratic human nature in its rawest form: Survival of the fittest.

Chapter 35

A RETURN TO NATIONALISM
and Smart Science

The toxic mix of religion and tribalism has become so dangerous as to justify taking seriously the alternative view, that humanism based on science, is the affective antidote, the light and the way at last placed upon us.

- E. O. Wilson

Globalism as a driving cultural force has been a reoccurring process in which national borders were replaced by Roman, Byzantine, Russian, French and German globalists that failed, and throughout, nationalism remained as brooding, broken tribes left behind to once again flourish and grow into nations

The cult of Postmodernism and by extension the myth of a self-centered globalized state—the bond that held the liberal progressives together—began to dismantle around the world with the threats posed by struggling middle classes, mass immigration, and the moves back to nationalism. It's this drift back to nationalism that remains a real sore point with Postmoderns. Any survey of 21st century political science literature will show Postmoderns struggling to define and redefine nationalism to fit their changing philosophy, like the APA defining then redefining hysteria to fit their tribal needs.

Not surprising then, the first general consensus among political scientists was that the American and French Revolutions were regarded as the first, true manifestations of nationalism with the shift from autocratic rule to democratic rule. Their reasoning for this linkage was because the word *"nationalism" had a certain dynamic vitality and all-pervading character* that democratic rule gave to the governing process.

Given the devastating world wars since those revolutions, the political science community came to regard nationalism as evil. Why! Because nationalists acted as ignorant tribalists. They identified with their own nation, pledging support for its interests, especially to the exclusion or detriment of other nations. Therefore, all those righteous, democratic nations were responsible for the hundreds of millions persecuted and killed. So, now knee-deep in the 21st century, the political scientists, who defined such nations as having a certain dynamic vitality and all-pervading character, fell back on their only claim to fame, identity politics, and assert nations are composed of either racist, white supremist, and/or white nationalist.

Nationalism doesn't mean exclusion; it means assimilation and always has. Forgotten or ignored is a UNITED STATES made up primarily of migrants from all over the world. Forgotten or ignored, are the thousands of small tribes that came out of the Paleolithic Period sporting all the democratic beliefs and values, dynamic vitality and all-pervading character that came with their STM. Although lacking many democratic characteristics, the same objective-thinking communities prevailed under autocratic nations for some 30-thousand years before free-ranging individual democracy became a woke governing criteria.

Such failed assertions packaged and repackaged as Post-Truths, linguistically articulated with legalized identity sophistry, seem to always fail when balanced against the beliefs and values of nationalism. In December, 2019, the British Parliament passed a historic milestone towards leaving the European Union, by backing Boris Johnson's Brexit bill with a thumping majority of 124, a week after the Conservatives won a landslide victory in the general election. Italy is also thinking about a Brexit-like exclusion, as are numerous conservative counties in the states of Virginia, California, and Washington that are searching for some legal way to separate themselves from the liberal Postmodern establishment.

The impact of the coronavirus on the Europe Union's future has the potential to be even more significant than the migrant crisis of 2015, especially as it unfolds in almost biblical fashion atop a plague of other European maladies. They include the rise of populism and nationalism; a repeated migrant crises from Turkey; economic slow-down and possible recession; disagreements about how to handle trade talks with a departing United Kingdom; internecine fights over the Union budget; and ongoing German and French social upheavals and leadership strife. All made more difficult with the coronavirus.

At the same time India was passing assimilation legislation in-suring a more nationalistic state, as were Belgium, Hungry, Poland, China and Australia. Spain's trouble with Catalonia, the French trouble with Corsica along with Scotland, Croatia, Germany and Austria showing signs of nationalism. This upsurge in a failing global trend became especially urgent as many immigrants shock-ingly refused to assimilate while generating costly, and often violent resettlement issues.

Going back to nature with nationalism need not be survival of the fittest at all cost. That caretaker quality—developed with our pa-leolithic ancestor's STM that distinguished humans from other ani-mals by way of freedom, equity, trust, cooperation, community, dialogue and solidarity—is still with us today. Humans have the cog-nitive ability to see the system for what it is and work within the sys-tem as caretakers of the environment, including the social environment.

Along with numerous paleolithic-like tribes occupying remote places, there are hundreds of thousands of small towns and villages scattered all around the world that live off what the environment has to offer. There, villagers live a relatively comfortable lifestyle given the lack of crime and solidarity that close community bonding provides. While some residents leave for the glamour of big-city life, many go back for the quiet solitude.

Hardened God Modules seem never able to learn this simple concept. The Postmodern cult was a revolution where rights over responsibilities produced enormous cultural disruptions. It's the same old tribal canard, the viral-paradox humanity has had to contend with since the Enlightenment: If everyone has unlimited rights, then no one has rights. It's a paradox the empirical sciences should be able to solve.

After millions of years of genetic evolution, a few thousand really smart hominids came up with advanced social software and conquered the planet in the last 1-2% of our history. Progressives, in the short span of 50 years, are in the process of destroying one of the world's most advanced culture in history. For some 50 years we have ignored these facts and worked diligently to break apart the chains that unite us, to shred those concentrated bodies of beliefs that made us a great nation, those unifying threads knitting us together under the umbrella of a benevolent God. As a result, we find ourselves in a difficult situation. From out of our remote past we are stuck with cruel genetic hardware demanding allegiance to a tribal virus by Western modernity forces demanding equal rights for all, everywhere.

Here is where the empirical sciences have left humanity down, and raises the question: "What's their function if not to help humanity survive?" Is it more important for those sciences to use trillions of American dollars on policies that build rockets, bombs, pesticides, opiates and the like, or use part of those trillions, working collectively teaching leaders how classic tribalism can work if done intelligently, and how internecine tribalism is supposed to work?

While its true human success is due to survival of the fittest tribe, we must first accept that reality and, then seek to work within those cognitive parameters. Our ancestors did not have the scientific understanding behind human behavior and how it works. They were forced to internalized a variety of myths as comfortable survival forces for themselves and the clan, a legacy we are left with today. Without sound science to moderate myth, myth narratives were reinforced by divinity modules and deeply embedded into the collective subconscious that came to dominate political discourse.

Since then, science has bridged most of the myth gaps, yet the potential for devotional excess remains. If, as enlightened beings, we cannot grasp that fact and go beyond its limitations, then we are no better off than all the countless illiterate organisms that have gone extinct. To a degree they were all intelligent organisms, but their intelligence was insufficient to override their intolerance and reasoning mandates.

Lacking high-level analytical options, survival for such lower life forms depended, and depends today, on the least intellectual aspects of biology: randomness, chance, coincidence and callousness. For example, a basic principle of natural selection is that nature does not provide for animals by giving them protection. Mother Nature offers no birthrights, has no goals, no preset purposes, no coded prescriptions for the future. Protective coloration is not given to grouse to enable them to avoid the hawk. Whitetail deer are not given thick, hollow hair to protect them from the cold. What grouse and deer receive is genetic diversity across their populations. In a diverse grouse population, birds with genes for protective coloration and deer with thick, hollow hair live, those that don't, die. If the environment changes, those genetically adapted to the new habitat will live while others perish. The fact that some variations benefit some and not others is a coincidence. If there is a plan, it is for randomness, which for 21st century humans is no plan at all.

With humans, chance, coincidence, randomness and callousness need not drive the system. As enlightened beings, humans can replace chance with choice, coincidence with thoughtful planning, randomness with predictability and callousness with compassion. We can allow for empathy over greed to drive our collective intelligence. It might be comforting if Mother Nature gave man the gift of innate integrity, an inbred necessity to forever eradicate social injustice.

But…She didn't. Like grouse and deer, we are not given traits to override amoral ideologies; we are given diverse groups of individuals with different reality models who by chance and coincidence find themselves in alliance with others of like mind or in conflict with those of unlike minds.

People make choices all the time but, regrettably, always done within classic tribal rules. Americans, like Germans in the thirties, might have come to appreciate fascism if different men of different minds had not chosen free-market, representative government. Mexico, Guatemala, Peru and the rest of South and Central America drift toward strangled brands of socialism because different people with different political ambitions came to govern and indoctrinate generation after generation in their form of tribalism. But classic tribalism cannot reign in the 21st century. Tribes must accept the fact cooperation between and within tribes is essential in global markets with atomic weapons.

Looking back at Ms. Lee's book, *The Dangerous Case of Donald Trump,* and the controversy over the APA's approach to human behavior, one might ask the question: "Do the social sciences have any right to claim scientific credentials given the degree of unscientific rancor so evident from within and throughout their long history? As a rule, we turn to the empirical scientists for answers to problems surrounding human issues, but the empirical sciences—in stark deference to Enlightenment intellectuals predicting their moral authority—seem unable to solve a single ethical issue.

The research evidence is there showing an approach plausible, yet noted scientists are reluctant to get involved with those in the metaphysical, political debate business. The few hardy souls who tried to attack the concepts of god and religion, such as "The Four Horsemen of the New Atheism"—Richard Dawkins, Sam Harris, Daniel Dennett, Christopher Hitchens and later, Hirsi Ali—failed to make any headway due to trashing by the religious and social science elite.

Hirsi Ali deserves a special note. She was born in Mogadishu, Somalia, from where she fled in 1992 to the Netherlands in order to escape an arranged marriage. There she became heavily involved in Dutch politics, rejected her faith and opposed Islamic ideology in a very vocal way. After writing the *Infidel* and the *Caged Virgin* in which she details the medieval treatment of women in her home country, she got involved in the production of the film, *Submission*, for which her friend was murdered with a death threat to Hirsi Ali pinned to his chest. That sent Ali into hiding in the US where she now lives and continues criticizing.

The problem the Four Horsemen and Ali had was attacking religion as metaphysical nonsense. God is not dead. He exists and is doing very well. He survives as God Modules for both secular and religious ideologies. An appetite, a hunger in the mind to satisfy inherent tribal needs. Not an obligation like oxygen to fuel cells, but rather a deep, neural demand to fuel spiritual and political needs. So, until the empirical folks find a substitute, we have to work with the old reliable, God Module. As an organism, humans require few essentials to live. Food, water, and shelter are the basics, but just as essential are those God Module passions to see our idols and their ideology prosper. Is our devotion to Muhammad, Jesus, Obama or Trump any less or more devotional than that expressed for Apollo and Caesar or the thousands of other civilizations for their gods and leaders?

One must assume empirical scientists fully understand how destructive the ugly tribalism occurring every day is to America and, either 1) have no idea of what to do; 2) realize the futility of engaging in a debate with powerful tribal zealots who can cut public funding for their institutions; or 3) or choose not to debate a topic that includes the power of God Module neurology given the prevailing anti-God thinking among academic elites. God-related debates would be troublesome because, they'd have to acknowledge the existence of the God Module and its importance to humanities' success. Perhaps, substituting another name for God Modules would help.

Simply recognizing the dynamics of tribalism is largely useless for solving problems unless we learn to appreciate how individual similarities and differences function within the group at which the empirical sciences should be good at. Tribalism is real. The many elements making it real are easy to observe. This is not rocket science. Tribalism has quantifiable variables that worked for over a million years: clearly definable conservative cultures with a focus on community solidarity, spiritualized ideologies and limited individual rights; leaders and followers clearly exhibiting biased and blind behaviors; and neurological behaviors clearly supported by cultural evidence, like the God Module's long, unbroken evolutionary history. If you apply these evolutionary traits to 10 or 20 of the major isms—take your pick—you will find the same correlations and conclude tribalism a reality and not some social science concoction to play around with.

What we need is a Teddy Roosevelt-like leader with the political, intellectual capacity of an Einstein who will focus these talents at forging a collective example of aggressive tribes working with and not against each other. A god-like idol who can redirect all the enormous ugly, bizarre hatred that was the Trump Hysteria into symbiotic forces bonding tribes together. Something on the order of the countless thousands of Amish and Mennonite-like tribes living within the borders of larger tribes today.

The reason we need reliable, creative science is, reliable knowledge consists of contrasting variables and observations about patterns of similarities and differences between individuals, sexes, families and ethnic groups. Differences of opinion will always exist, and they should, but they must not become the Order of the Day. The natural order is not a process in which diversity is dumbed down so that all are equal in their quest for status and recognition. Natural order is a disorderly process where diversity exists for its own sake, for the creativity it offers in meeting daily challenges in a complex society where tribal solidarity should reign. After all, those hundreds of thousands—

past and present—small communities composed of diverse individuals have shown living in harmony is possible.

Johann Wolfgang von Goethe was considered one of the most important thinkers in Western cultures in the 18th century who understood the importance of small communities and, in his 1795 book *Wilhelm Meister's Apprenticeship* wrote:

> Man is born to fit into a limited situation; he can understand simple, close and definite purposes, and he gets used to enjoying the means which are close at hand; but as soon as he goes any distance, he knows neither what he will nor what he should be doing.

As an enlightened species we must, somehow, recognize the tribal virus for what it is, Community Mandates and Freedom/Equity Mandates for what they are, and work to smooth out the amoral bumps they create. Though our eternal quest for equality is a universal enigma, it doesn't mean a viable solution cannot prevail. If we agree that equity is a necessary illusion driven by tribal Freedom/Equity Mandates, what prevents us from digging ourselves out of this enigmatic muck? These mandates are known to be controllable through God and fear. Be it love of God or love of fellow man or fear of God or fear of fellow man, are there not within these behavior dominions generous standards to keep us in relatively straight line? Must we always be bamboozled by slick elites and their media who believe their evolved intellect is beyond the rule of natural law.

No democratic society can survive without unifying standards that science can provide to balance rights with responsibilities. Without core principles there can be no standards on which to underwrite sustainable creeds or codes, there can be no comfort, no security; there is only different, distorted reality models searching for critical mass. It might be nice to see the lion lie down with the lamb, and every child an honor student, all prisoners rehabilitated, companies and unions working toward a common cause, or Nancy Pelosi embracing Rush Limbaugh, but that's not in the evolutionary cards. Could be possible though, since we're not lions and lambs, but highly cognitive animals with the ability to work together, if we only admit we are social animals, with mass hysteria tendencies.

EPILOGUE

From a purely philosophical point of view, the idea of a single governing entity like globalism defies the whole biological concept of tribalism that has ruled the world since modern man came to dominate. The tribal virus has shown us time and time again, that individualism and human biology don't mix very well. Add to that, goals of equity and generational sustainability for all life forms raises a host of other serious questions.

First, can global harmony exist where inequity and disharmony rule? Can anyone really balance the wants and needs of millions of distorted-reality models beating out a steady tattoo for equity? Even if harmony could prevail, should it prevail? Who would ever consider everyone having the same values and beliefs? Does this not speak of a world full of androgynous nerds right out of North Korea or the Twilight Zone? Should we not stick with the null hypothesis that all people are different and the dialectic, that tension existing between two conflicting forces, a valued commodity?

Second, science is a long way from rearranging brain cells much less rearranging the social intellect of tribes at opposite ends of religious or secular spectrums. To get so many disparate groups working toward a common cause will take the talents of Dr. Doolittle's two-headed creature, Push me-Pull you, capable of going forward both ways. Or the Roman two-faced God, Janus, capable of looking both ways at the same time. And what about those nasty behaviors that keep percolating throughout society like self-interest, greed, envy, humiliation and hate that Freedom/Equity Mandates bring to the table? The real nutcracker will be in eliminating or controlling the God Module effects of belief bonds that result in addictive behaviors like nepotism, cronyism, groupthink and idol worship.

The fact that all great minds today and throughout history fail to see the tribal virus for what it is illuminates the role self-deception plays in confirmation bias by hiding reality from belligerents struggling to control a narrative. Looking back over this million-year struggle it is obvious man was not designed for self-reflection. He was designed first for survival by way of tribalism, everything else, secondary or not worth thinking about.

There is even a rising tide of political academics who feel the present state of democratic drift an unhealthy trend and wrangle for international consensus on new models to handle the discrepancies. They talk and write about ideology narratives defined and aligned with long-term social and economic interests able to handle the increasing connectivity of the tech age. Some talk and write about a model in which neutral goals and objectives are aligned with quality and equity data being deliberated by thoughtful, experienced, unbiased individuals, a process similar to Kant's categorical-imperative philosophy that doesn't seem to be working very well. Others wish to redesign the one-person-one-vote electoral process of its many flaws, and pass legislation to ensure deliberative institutions remain non-polarized. Many have become so frustrated, they elaborate on the value of meritocracy, like in China. None surveyed had a STM perspective.

Plus, those devoted to capitalism/nationalism must recognize the influence that repressive secular and theocratic governments have on the majority of humans around the world. These are cultures with settled hierarchies, reflecting independent economic values that work because they offer the essential security and comfort that comes with national unity. Until humanity is capable of providing such unity in a truly equitable fashion, let us not be too superior in thinking the US and the rest of the world is ready for their broad-band democracy.

In addition, let's not be too superior in thinking humanity is ready for a world without God. As a first step in solving our nature-over-man dilemma, we must appreciate how addictive our belief tendencies are and the depth to which myth addiction is individually and culturally internalized. Those extolling Nietzsche's view that God is dead simply deny the latest research that divinity modules exist in the human brain.

Nevertheless, those who trod the daily path must realize this divine force is as malevolent as it is benevolent and its intelligence as misguided as guided. Therefore, we can no longer afford addictive minds trumping physical realities by placing humanity on the brink of annihilation with overpopulation and weapons of mass destruction. There must be a measured balance. Therefore, we should be suspicious of leaders choosing to indoctrinate susceptible minds with their devotional addictions. Whether God is the artful creator of such addictive minds or they evolved through natural selection without divine intervention is a reasonable debate, but the fact remains that addictive minds remain as much a constant in our search for comfort and security on Earth and in the hereafter, as they are constant promoters of discomfort and insecurity.

With the explosive power of cell phones, computers, the Internet and social networking, people around the world now have access to ideas and ideals their freedom and equity modules will emotionally identify as personal, categorical rights beyond those defined by their respective cultures. Today, social media can generate mob-mentality scenarios quicker than authorities can deflect the ensuing violence.

Nor can we depend on the social scientists who are too hard-wired to their ideology of 'whatever works' to be honest environmental caretakers. Therefore, if humanity is to survive, there must be a sustained effort by the empirical sciences to forewarn the public of how devastating the existing political scene has become. Human can work within the confines of tribal restraints in a humane fashion. The examples are there. We need only look.

****

The intent on writing this book was not a conservative or liberal intent. The intent was to show tribalism for what it is, the ability of the God Module to control both the bias and blindness that liberalism and conservativism can engender; the hazards of inflated idealism; and the fatalness of the status quo as it exists in 2020. As Emerson so beautifully affirms: "We are reformers in spring and summer; in autumn and winter, we stand by the old; reformers in the morning, conservers at night."

The End

Important Concepts

Confirmation Bias: a type of cognitive thinking where a person remembers information selectively, interprets it personally, and acts on it in a bias "manner.

Cognitive Blindness: an unwitting type of thinking in which people are incapable of recognizing and accepting a political ideology that is contrary to their political ideology.

Cultural Capture: a practice in which a small number of elites, recognized for their ideology intellect, 'capture' believers and set policy by defining, implementing and enforcing their ideas and values.

Cognitive Fluidity: a neural module that manifest itself with a variety of altruistic, aggressive and denial behaviors that evolved to express, protect or reveal one's values, talents, beliefs or worldview.

Community Mandate: An inherent social mandate demanding the individual set aside his/her desire for freedom and equity *(the Freedom/Equity Mandate)* and focus God Module energy on community interests to ensure the community functions as a single organism to maximize survival in a competitive world.

Cultural Cognition: A biased way people use to reinforce their predispositions by using 'experts' with similar political beliefs. Or, when society unwitting allows the intellectually powerful to dissembles conventional social standards for their convenience.

Fractal Biology: Fractals are complex patterns made up entirely of copies of successful genes from past generations. Example: the eye, group think.

Freedom/Equity Mandate: a neural module that manifest itself as intolerance to environmental pressures seeking to change one's values and beliefs that make up one's worldview.

God Module: A cluster of nerves that spiritualize the human brain to a secular or religious ideology to ensure tribal solidarity that, in turn, promotes survival for the tribe.

Gotcha Game: (1) Identifies or manufactures a problem, (2) Transfers the guilt, and (3) Reaps the benefits.

Lateral Mind Behavior: a form of collective intelligence where many minds work as one with party wishes not explicitly stated.

Neural modules: clusters of neurons in the brain that function as pre-adaptive learning templates for specific cultural patterns of behaviors like music, language and ideologies.

Obfuscation: an enforcement strategy to intentionally obscure the meaning of words or phrases in communications by making messages confusing, intentionally ambiguous, or difficult to understand with intellectualized jargon, perplexing wordiness, or un-named sources

Objective relativism: the view that the beliefs of a person or group of persons are "true" for them, but not necessarily for others. Sometime referred to as moral objectivism, where truths, morals, ethic and gods are tribal truths are true.

Phronetic Theory: a creative, subjective, reflective form of linguistics and thought used in many areas of human interaction to justify cause.

PMP: any social construct exhibiting *mental, social* or *linguistic abnormalities* contrary to established mental, social and linguistic norms.

Post- Science: A science that attempts to intellectualize, textualize, and validate highly questionable philosophical theories into acceptable public policy.

Post-Normal: Postmodern claim that the belief of tribal normalcy standards does not exist and all biological diversity is normal.

Posts-Truth: Postmodern claim that tribal truths are replaced by Postmodern truths.

Projecting: an advanced rendition **of** Freud's constructive lie where humans defend themselves against their own unpleasant impulses by denying their existence and attributing them to others.

Rationalization: is defined as any action attempting to explain a behavior or attitude with logical reasoning even if the attitude or behavior is not logical or reasoned thinking.

Reasoning Mandate: a neural module that manifest itself with a variety of altruistic, aggressive and denial behaviors that evolved to protect or display one's values, wants, beliefs or worldview.

Socially Smart: the ability to measures the degrees of happiness, empathy or reciprocity needed to actualize one's goals by manipulating social relationships with whatever means available.

Subjective relativism: the view that an action is morally right if one approves of it. A person's approval makes the action right. This doctrine (as well as cultural relativism) is in stark contrast to the view that some moral principles are valid for everyone.

10/20 Percent Rule: a population rate of devoted and aggressive political activists that govern the majority of a population and, in the process, make the views and values of the majority often irrelevant.

Tribal ideology: a political tribal narrative that binds tribal members to their view of how the world should work while blinding them to contrary worldviews.

Tribal virus: a type of cognitive dissonance, a state of tension that occurs in a tribe whenever liberal and conservative forces exhibit contradictory creeds severe enough to result in tribal infighting and possible destruction.

Bibliography

Asbridge, Thomas. (204). The First Crusade. New York: Oxford University Press.

Bagehot, Walter: Physics and Politics, Cosimo Press.

Bentley, Author. F. The Process of Government. Ed. P.H. Cambridge, MA. Odegard, Belnap, Harvard University Press.

Bloom, Howard. (1995) The Lucifer Principle. New York: Atlantic Monthly Press.

Campbell, Jeremy. The Liar's tale: a history of falsehoods. New York: Norton & Company

Chomsky, Norm. Who Rules the World. Metropolitan Books, Henry Holt & Co., New York.

Conlon, Paula. www.Worldliterature-today.org/2013/ march/world-music-contemporary-inuit-music).

Dawkins, Richard. (1976). The selfish gene. New York: Oxford University Press.

Damasio, Antonio, R. (1994). Descartes' error: Emotion, reason, and the human brain. New York: Avon Books.

Diamond, Jared M. (1997). Guns, germs, and steel: The fates of human societies. New York: Norton.

Donald, Merlin. (1991). Origins of the modern mind. Cambridge: Harvard University Press.

Dueant, Will. Caesar and Christ: A history of Roman civilization and Christianity from their beginnings to A.D. 325. New York: Simon and Schuster.

Dunne, Daisy. For mail.online. Are Religious Experiences all in your head. March 2017 10

El-Hai, Jack. 2013. The Nazis and the Psychiatrist: Hermann Goring, Dr. Douglas M. Kelly and a Fatal Meeting of the Minds at the End of World War I. Public Affairs, Perseus Books.

Flyvbjerg, Bent. Making Social Science Matter: Why Social Inquiry Fails and How It Can Succeed Again, ,: Making Social Science Matter: Why Social Inquiry Fails and How It Can Succeed Again, Cambridge University Press

Fukuyama, Yoshihiro Francis F. (1992). The end of history and the last man. New York: The Free Press.

Giovannoli, Joseph. (2002). The biology of beliefs: How our biology biases our beliefs and perceptions. New York: Rosetta Press, Inc.

Grohman, W. A. and Gorham, B. ed. (1909) Edward of Norwick: The Master of Game. New York: Duffield & Co.

Johnson, Eric A. and Reuband, Karl-Heinz. (2005). What we knew: terror, mass murder and everyday life in Nazi Germany. Cambridge, Mass: Basic.

Kahan, Dan: Fixing the Communication Failure. Nature 463,296-297 (20102.

Hall, Manly Palmer. (1973). The Secret Teachings of all Ages. 19th edition. Los Angeles: The Philosophical Research Society, Inc.

Hanson, Victor. D. (2003, September). The august of our discontent. National Review.

Hitler, Adolf. Mein Kampf, translated by Ralph Manheim, Boston: Houghton Mifflin Company.

Klein, Naomi. This Changes Everything: Capitalism vs the Climate. Simon & Schuster, NY.

Magee, Bryann. Confession of a Philosopher, A journey through Western philosophy. New York: Random House.

Mettrie, Julien Offray de La. (1996). The Man Machine. France: Universite de Caen.

Newberg, Andrew & D'Aquili, Eugene. (2001). Why god won't go away: Brain science and the biology of belief. New York: Ballantine Books.

Nietzsche, Friedrich. (1954). The portable Nietzsche. Ed. Kaufmann, W. New York: Viking Press.

Pinker, Steven, A. (2002). The Blank Slate. New York: Viking Penguin, Inc.

Rahe, Paul. 2012. Soft Despotism, Democracy's Drift, Yale University Press.

Rawls, John. A Theory of Social Justice. Cambridge: Harvard University Press

Ridley, Matt. (2003). Nature via Nurture: Genes, experience and what makes us human. New York: Harper Collins.

Toby, John & Cosmides, Leda. (1992). Psychological foundations of culture. The Adapted Mind: Evolutionary psychology and the generation of culture. New York: Oxford University Press.

Tuchman, Barbara, W. Guns of August. Macmillan, New York.

Wilson, Edward. Consilence. Knoph, New York.

Wilson, Edward. Biophilia. Cambridge, MA: Harvard University Press.

Wolfgang von Goethe, Johann. Wilhelm Meister's Apprenticeship. Anyesite Press, An Amazon Company.

Von Hagen, V.W. (1960). World of the Maya. New York: The New American library.